For the Glory of the Union

Advance of the Twenty-sixth Regiment across the Rappahannock River, June 5, 1863 *(Photo courtesy of Irvington Historical Society).*

For the Glory of the Union

Myth, Reality, and the Media
in Civil War New Jersey

Alan A. Siegel

Rutherford ● Madison ● Teaneck
Fairleigh Dickinson University Press
London and Toronto: Associated University Presses

Associated University Presses
440 Forsgate Drive
Cranbury, NJ 08512

Associated University Presses
25 Sicilian Avenue
London WC1A 2QH, England

Associated University Presses
2133 Royal Windsor Drive
Unit 1
Mississauga, Ontario
Canada L5J 1K5

Library of Congress Cataloging in Publication Data

Siegel, Alan A., 1939–
  For the glory of the Union.

  Bibliography: p.
  Includes index.
  1. United States—History—Civil War, 1861–1865—
Regimental histories. 2. United States. Army.
New Jersey Infantry Regiment, 26th (1862–1863)—
History. 3. New Jersey—History—Civil War, 1861–
1865. 4. New Jersey—History—Civil War, 1861–1865—
Journalists. 5. American newspapers—New Jersey—
Newark—History—19th century. 6. Newark (N.J.)—
History. I. Title.
E521.5 26th.S54 1983   973.7′.449   82-48576
ISBN 0-8386-3172-X

Printed in the United States of America

Contents

Preface

They sed the press was the Arkymedian Leaver
which moved the world.
—Artemus Ward, 1862

Historians of American journalism speak of the "partisanship" of the Civil War newspaper and the "prejudice" that ruled its columns. There is general agreement that publishers and editors for the most part lacked any genuine concern for the truth so long as what they printed sold newspapers and served their own political ends at the same time. But these conclusions (which sound a trifle smug in light of the latest journalistic peccadilloes) are based on the files of the great metropolitan dailies, the major papers of New York City, Philadelphia, Boston, and Chicago. This book narrows the focus of study to the newspapers of Newark, New Jersey's largest city, and to a single news story that occupied the attention of Newark's editors for nearly a year. On one level this work is the story of the Twenty-sixth New Jersey Volunteer Infantry; on another, it is the story of that story, that is, how Newark's journalists reported the news of the regiment, given the political imperatives of the age. In short, it is a history of myth, reality, and the media in Civil War New Jersey.

Some time ago a Pulitzer Prize-winning Washington *Post* account of an eight-year-old child addicted to heroin turned out to be a fabrication, prompting *Harper's* editor Lewis H. Lapham to observe that "people need to be reminded that the media tell stories." Today's journalists, Lapham remarked, "play the part of the courier, reassuring their patrons that the world conforms to the wish of the presiding majority." By telling their readers what they assume they already know, added Lapham, a former newsman himself, "the media reflect what society wants to think of itself. The images in the mirror compose the advertisement for reality." Matters of politics are as prone to media imagery as any other and perhaps more so; it is, said Lapham, "permissable in a daily newspaper to sustain those myths that its audience wishes to believe." During the 1976 presidential campaign, as an example, "the media wanted to believe that Jimmy Carter was a romantic figure embodying the rural virtues of the imaginary South," conveniently ignoring "those aspects of Mr. Carter's character that might have confused the image." According to Lapham, the "distinction between the degrees of fabrication have less to do with the chicanery of editors than with the desires of an audience that pays for what it wants to hear."

Whether the media has "become a theater" during the last quarter of a century may be open to debate not so much because the claim is exaggerated but because it implies there was a time when journalism was not theater. In fact, "Gilding the News," the title of Lapham's thoughtful essay, has been a hallmark of American journalism throughout much of our history. It should come as no surprise that the tradition endures. Perhaps the most "theatrical" were the newsmen of the Civil War. The papers called Lincoln a "hyena," accused him of drawing his salary in gold bars, of drunkenness and even treason. The editors who generaled the war from their office armchairs, crying, "On to Richmond" when few in the North as yet comprehended the meaning of total war, would have dismissed their modern-day counterparts as nerveless imposters. So intense were the emotions roused by the Civil War, so partisan were the newspapers, that journalists of the day bent every oar to the cause they supported. The newspaper we read may be somewhat more subtle but, to use Lapham's word, the media is as "artful" as ever. Then as now, a newspaper could "lend its voice to the pieties of the age"—or at least those "pieties" currently in favor with the editor and publisher.

The late-twentieth-century press loftily proclaims that the fabricated quote, the fictitious source, and the slanted story have been safely banished from its pages. Prejudice and passion are relics of the past, so they say, and the old partisan ways abandoned. Not so during the Civil War. Newspapers in the Northern states were expected to wear their opinions on their sleeves; few readers would have bothered subscribing to a paper that did not come down squarely on the issues of the day. Whether War Democrat or Copperhead, Abolitionist or Republican, the Civil War newspaper reader demanded a paper with a definite viewpoint forcefully expressed. An "unbiased press" simply did not exist.

Not everyone, of course, approved the way Civil War newspapers manipulated the news, especially after they had seen firsthand what reality was like. The Reverend David T. Morrill, chaplain of the Twenty-sixth New Jersey Volunteers, a nine-month infantry unit from Essex County, was one who objected. In early January 1863, while the Army of the Potomac was still reeling from the pounding it suffered at Fredericksburg, the chaplain penned an indignant letter to his hometown paper, the Newark *Daily Advertiser*. He had joined the army, he wrote, "fully persuaded" that the men were "eager for the fray and confident of success." Surprised to find that the soldiers were "weary of the war," he concluded that the "true feeling of the army has not been fairly represented in the press." Said the chaplain:

> The most of our military movements in this department of the army have been influenced if not controlled by the pressure of public opinion uttered by

and through the press. To this there is no objection, so long as the press gives a true . . . sound. That it does not in many instances, I appeal to the experience of thousands, who will bear me witness to-day that their ideas of the army, and of the war, heretofore gathered from the usual channels have been erroneous. . . . This war in part originated in a partisan press, it has been fed and fanned by public misrepresentation, and shall it be continued and concluded thus? I should be sorry to discourage anybody's patriotism, but I see an evil and a wrong greater than even that. I see the true feeling of the army concealed or misrepresented, and the army made the suffering slaughtered victim of such misrepresentation.

Far too little has been written about New Jersey's Civil War experience. It is a fascinating subject. Deeply split on the issues, the state had immense difficulty making up its mind whether the war was worth fighting at all. A surprisingly vigorous antiadministration, antiwar movement tested the resolve of Jersey Unionists at every turn. Not unexpectedly, the state's eighty weekly and daily newspapers covered a wide spectrum of opinion, from Copperhead to Abolitionist. In Newark, where pro- and antiwar forces battled furiously for the loyalty (and the votes) of the people, the press was at its most diverse. The *Daily Advertiser*, a solid conservative journal and the state's largest daily newspaper, normally supported Lincoln but questioned many of his policies. To one side of the *Advertiser* stood the ultra-Republican *Daily Mercury*, to the other, the Copperhead *Daily Journal*. Fiercely competitive, the *Mercury* and the *Journal* (and even on occasion the *Advertiser*, when it descended from its lofty perch) gloried in the parry and thrust of public debate. Truth was a major casualty of Newark's newspaper wars: even a casual reading of the major stories reported by the three papers reveals a surprising variance not merely of opinion, which is to be expected, but of fact as well. The news often underwent an amazing transformation, assuming the cast and color of the editor's political point of view.

Into this theater of the media was thrown the Twenty-sixth New Jersey, a volunteer outfit recruited from the farms and factories of Newark and its suburbs to avoid the draft threatened by Lincoln in the summer of 1862. Despite the glib promises of the *Mercury* and the *Advertiser* that nothing more dangerous than garrison duty would be expected of it, the regiment was attached to the Army of the Potomac, where it served during the darkest days of the Union war effort in the East. Equipped at first only with smooth-bore muskets of antidiluvian vintage, the regiment was held in reserve at Fredericksburg, saved from the carnage of Burnside's futile assault by its antique arms and lack of training. After five weary months in camp, the Twenty-sixth took the field at Chancellorsville, enjoying a brief moment of triumph before it broke and ran in the face of a Rebel counterattack. A bold daylight reconnaissance across the Rappahannock River at Franklin's Crossing restored the unit's confidence two weeks before it marched home (minus some forty men courtmartialed for refusing to cross the river) to a hero's welcome, ignoring the government's call for troops to

meet Lee's sudden thrust into Maryland and Pennsylvania. "The calling out of
the nine-months' men at the end of last summer was one of the most absurd
things the wiseheads at Washington could have done," complained Colonel
Charles S. Wainwright in 1863. "Any fool could have told them that the regiments would not be fit for service until last year's campaign was over and that
their time would be out just as this year's commenced." Wainwright could have
cited the Twenty-sixth as an example of Washington's foolishness; its career
was far too short for it to be of any real contribution to the Union war effort.
Notwithstanding its modest accomplishments, the regiment was a major news
story from the day the first call went out for volunteers until the last picnic in
honor of the returned veterans eleven months later. All of this attention had less
to do with the military importance of the regiment—units that fought better and
far longer received less coverage—than with New Jersey politics, which had
reached a critical stage during the months the Twenty-sixth wore the Union
blue. Newark's partisan press had vital work to do throughout those crucial
months, and news of the regiment served their purposes exceptionally well.

The American Civil War may well have been the most exhaustively reported
news event of the nineteenth century. Some 300 war correspondents, known as
"specials," followed the Union armies into the field. News of campfire and
battlefield, of politicians and generals was in such heavy demand at home that
for nearly four years the Northern press printed little that was not related
directly or indirectly to the conflict. New York City's papers surpassed the
journals of any other city in their quest for war news. James Gordon Bennett's
Herald, with forty specials during the final, climactic year of the rebellion, spent
more than a half-million dollars covering the war. The *Tribune*, the *Times*, and
the *World* were only slightly behind the *Herald* in reporting the greatest circula-
tion-building story of the era. Although none could approach the New York
papers in lavish expenditure of money and manpower, newspapers in Chicago,
St. Louis, Boston, Baltimore, Cincinnati, and Philadelphia fielded their own
war correspondents as well. The newly formed Associated Press and such
popular journals as *Harper's Weekly* and *Frank Leslie's Illustrated Newspaper* added
to the horde of specials that hung on every Union army of importance.

New Jersey's newspapers were at a competitive disadvantage with the popular New York and Philadelphia dailies that circulated widely in the state. Unable to afford special correspondents, they relied chiefly upon clippings from
the major papers, the A P wire service if they subscribed to it, and on letters
written by front-line visitors or the soldiers themselves. Andrew D. Fowler,
who covered the Peninsula campaign for the *Daily Advertiser* in the spring and
summer of 1862, was one of the few specials who worked for a New Jersey
paper. News of the Twenty-sixth Regiment reached Newark in letters written
by three of its members: Chaplain Morrill, a Baptist minister who helped
recruit the unit but was later cashiered for disloyal correspondence; Sergeant
Major Amos J. Cummings, a War Democrat who gained postwar fame as a
New York newspaper editor; and Private Charles S. Woodruff, a proadminis-

tration Republican. Their letters, together with news stories and editorials relating to the chief issues of the 1862–63 period, comprise by far the largest part of this book. To insure coherence, occasional gaps in the regimental story as reported by the press have been filled by official reports, soldiers' letters published after the war, and the warmly personal memoirs of Ira S. Dodd, a sergeant in Company F.

The reader will find that Newark's three dailies have been extensively quoted. The images that filled the pages of the *Advertiser*, the *Mercury*, and the *Journal* cannot be understood if they are filtered through an intermediary, no matter how faithful. If we seek a glimpse at reality as our Civil War ancestors saw it, what better means than to turn to the words their newspapers printed? Nearly twenty years ago John T. Cunningham, a former newsman turned historian, ventured the opinion that newspapers were "an historical document" as important as "an old diary, an old document, or an old stack of letters." They were, he added with pardonable pride, "the richest and brightest source of history." Citing the New Jersey Historical Society's thirty-volume collection of New Jersey newspapers published during the Civil War, he called them the society's "most valuable possession." To read those papers, Cunningham said, is to understand "the spirit, the sadness, the despair, the divided opinions of a state." The society's priceless newspaper collection is the chief source of this work. Hopefully, some of the "spirit" of Civil War New Jersey entombed in those brittle, yellowed pages has now been set free.

A brief comment is in order regarding my treatment of the newspaper articles used in this book. Typographical errors have been corrected. Punctuation has been added or amended where required and an occasional paragraph rearranged or tense altered to smooth the narrative flow. Names of places and persons have been regularized. Finally, while obvious errors of spelling have been eliminated, the idiosyncratic orthography of the period has been left generally unmolested in the belief that to modernize it would destroy something of the flavor it conveys.

I am deeply indebted to the many people without whose kind assistance this work could not have been completed. James Burster, a Civil War buff whose great-grandfather served in the Twenty-sixth New Jersey, and Arthur T. Vanderbilt II, author of several recent books on New Jersey history, read early versions of the manuscript, offering many valuable comments. George Sobin Jr., the Reverend William A. Tieck, and staff members of public libraries in Monmouth County, Orange, Bloomfield, Irvington, and Montclair (all in New Jersey), Troy, Watervliet, Richmond Memorial—Batavia, and New York City (in New York) responded promptly to requests for information. The staffs of the Minneapolis Public Library, Iowa Historical Library, American Baptist Historical Society, the Department of History of the United Presbyterian Church of the U.S., and the New Jersey Archives and History Bureau, New Jersey State Library, were likewise especially helpful. Donald Sinclair, curator of Special Collections of the Alexander Library, Rutgers University, pointed the way to source material I would have otherwise neglected, while Charles F. Cummings, supervising librarian, New Jersey Reference Division, Newark Public Library, and his staff met my every request. At the New Jersey Historical Society, where the bulk of my research was accomplished, Barbara S. Irwin, library director, Kathleen Stavec, librarian, and Dr. Carl A. Lane, keeper of manuscripts, were of immense help. Never have so few carried so many dusty newspapers in and out of a library vault in the name of history. In addition, I am grateful to the society for permission to quote extensively from the Horace N. Congar and Thomas T. Kinney papers. Portions of the manuscript have been typed by Mildred Dawson, Donna Mutch, Grace Church, and Susan Van Ness. I owe a special note of appreciation to Professor Kalman Goldstein of Fairleigh Dickinson University, who perceived my theme and made valuable suggestions on ways to focus this study better. Finally, my greatest debt is to my wife, B. J., who suffered through three long years with the Twenty-sixth New Jersey. Her patience and constant encouragement made this book possible.

—Alan A. Siegel

For the Glory of the Union

Colonel Andrew Jackson Morrison, Twenty-sixth Regiment (*Photo courtesy of Irvington Historical Society*).

1

The Northernmost of the Border States

New Jersey was the only Free State to reject Abraham Lincoln in both the 1860 and 1864 presidential elections. Lincoln lost the state in 1860 by a margin of 62,800 to 58,000. Four years later George B. McClellan, twice-dismissed commander of the Army of the Potomac, defeated the president by 8,000 votes. New Jersey's political inconstancy was both a source of anguish to Unionists and an inspiration to opponents of the administration throughout the nation. An Illinois politician speaking before a Lincoln-Johnson rally in Newark in 1864 confided to his audience that he had come to New Jersey despite warnings that "there were no Lincoln men there and it was a Godforsaken place."[1] Horace Greeley's New York *Tribune* once declared, in a fit of exasperation: "In no other Free State are disloyal utterances so frequent and so bold as in New Jersey."[2] Antiwar Democrats viewed the state as "a city on a hill to the Democratic party in other States."[3] New Jersey's Copperhead press, led by the Trenton *Daily True American* and the Newark *Daily Journal*, was vociferous, sometimes near-treasonous, in its denunciation of the Republicans, the president, and the war. Concludes the author of one recent state history, with pardonable hyperbole: "In heart and mind, in politics and economics, New Jersey was . . . separated only by an accident of geography from the rebellious South."[4]

Many and varied are the factors that explain New Jersey's curious role in the Civil War. The state's prewar economy had been based largely upon Southern markets: Newark manufacturers and Trenton merchants carried on an active trade with the slaveholding states; Jersey cereals and cider found a ready market below the Mason-Dixon line. Social as well as economic ties bound many Jerseyans to the South: half the student body of Princeton College in 1860 called the South their home; hundreds of wealthy planters from Virginia, Maryland, and the Carolinas vacationed regularly at Jersey seacoast resorts. New Jersey's large (and to some, threatening) Black population had long been a source of friction. Alone among the Northern states, New Jersey permitted the capture of runaway slaves within her borders. New Jersey's proximity to New York City, a hotbed of Copperheadism, and the sense of insecurity that had made tiny New Jersey a conservative champion of state's rights as early as the American Revolution were among the many elements that produced what one modern historian has rightly termed "the northernmost of the Border States."[5]

The state was a Democratic citadel throughout the war. Although Republican Charles S. Olden had been narrowly elected governor in 1859, both houses of the State Legislature remained overwhelmingly Democratic until the 1865 elections. In 1863 Joel Parker, whose halfhearted measures in support of the war infuriated Unionists, succeeded Olden in the governor's chair, defeating Republican Marcus L. Ward, the "soldiers' friend," by some 15,000 votes, to that time the largest majority won by any state candidate. While a large body of opinion opposed secession and supported Lincoln, New Jersey's Unionists were disorganized and largely ineffective throughout the war years. In perhaps no other Northern state was the conflict between supporters and opponents of the administration so bitter as in New Jersey.

The fateful presidential election of 1860, hotly contested from one end of the state to the other, was the opening gambit in a five-year struggle for the heart and soul and mind of one of the most important states of the North. Painfully aware of their weakness, especially in the central and northern counties, the Republicans ran Lincoln under the banner of the Opposition party. Democrats, united only in their hatred of the "Abolitionist" Republicans, could not agree on a single candidate, placing three presidential nominees before the public, Stephen A. Douglas, John Bell, and John Breckinridge, known for his Southern sympathies. Republican "Wide Awakes" and Democratic "Hickory Men" paraded through hamlet, town, and city in one of the most acrimonious campaigns ever waged in the state. Leading Democrats in Newark, the state's largest city, fearful that Douglas could not defeat Lincoln, threw their support to Kentucky's Breckinridge. The Newark *Daily Journal* warned the city's workingmen, thousands of whom were employed in factories wholly dependent upon Southern buyers, of the dire results of a Republican victory:

> Every man in Newark is interested . . . in her continued prosperity. That prosperity must cease if the Republican party succeed in carrying out their feelings of hostility to the South. Even now we feel the effect of a partial withdrawal of the Southern trade. No manufacturing house in Newark is working more than about half the usual force. Should Lincoln be elected, many of our largest factories will be compelled in self-defence to make still less work, and many mechanics and journeymen will be compelled to face the rigors of winter, and meet the terrible answer everywhere—no work! no work!!
> Workingmen of Newark. . . . Are you prepared to vote for that party which will be the instrument of taking the bread from the mouths of your wives and children?[6]

The staunchly pro-Republican Newark *Daily Mercury* labeled the *Journal's* appeal "ridiculous" and "laughable." Lincoln and his running mate, Maine's Hannibal Hamlin, said the paper,

> represent the only . . . principles which can give peace to a country distracted by the wild and reckless policy of the present Administration. Abraham Lincoln was born in a Southern State, and holds strictly to that Constitution which guarantees the rights of every section of the Union. His election will still the sectional warfare which the South has waged, and over all the land will be felt the beneficence of his firm, but just administration.[7]

Republicans tried without much success to pass Lincoln off as a Southern-born conservative. A city that shipped much of its industrial output to the Southern states was not of a mind to vote for a "Black Republican," casting fully fifty-five percent of its ballots in November for the Fusion ticket. So poorly did the Republicans do that much-respected Newark Congressman William Pennington, elected speaker of the U.S. House of Representatives in February 1860, lost his seat in the tide of anti-Lincoln votes. Pennington's defeat, lamented the *Daily Mercury*, was the product of a "band of mercenary and unprincipled men engaged in the Southern trade. If they had been slaves themselves, and every morning had been lashed into humility, they could not have worked more heartily to carry out the wishes of their Southern masters."[8] Lincoln's failure in Newark was typical of his performance throughout the more densely populated areas of the state. The president-elect carried only ten counties, Cape May, Ocean, Atlantic, Mercer, Morris, Passaic, Burlington, Salem, Gloucester, and Cumberland.

Lincoln's election was a bitter pill for New Jersey Democrats to swallow. The *Journal*, which had supported Breckinridge, nevertheless claimed that the state's repudiation of Lincoln was "a political triumph."

> Of all the Northern States on the Atlantic side, she alone has proved her conservatism by the voice of her people through the ballot-box. . . . New Jersey alone breasts the storm of fanaticism, and amid the din of triumphant rejoicing by the Northern abolitionists, and the gloomy forebodings which like a dark cloud pall the Southern skies, her clarion voice rings out to her sister States in a cheer of glad triumph.[9]

On December 20 South Carolina seceded from the Union, thrusting the nation to the verge of war. New Jersey's leading Democrats lent early support to what they perceived to be the Southern cause. Commodore Robert F. Stockton, a naval hero of the Merican war, told a peace meeting in Trenton that New Jersey "must suplicate to the North to yield." Edward N. Fuller, editor of the *Daily Journal*, praised South Carolina for saving the nation from "a worse calamity than disunion—abolitionism."[10] The Democratic press enthused over reports of a plan for "a great middle confederacy, to be called the 'Central United States,' or the 'Federal Republic of Washington,'" that would include New

Jersey, Pennsylvania and the border Slave states.[11] New Jersey's natural place was with the South, said the *Journal*:

[A] junction with the Southern Confederacy would place us in a position of unexampled prosperity. Our climate, favorable to the welfare of white labor, would enable us to manufacture largely for the Southern trade.

We have one port . . . where ships of any size may enter, lay in safety and discharge their cargoes, and which would, from our position be the main *entrepot* for all the border Southern States. Being a portion of the Southern Confederacy, without holding slaves herself, New Jersey would be a barrier to the system of negro stealing, now carried on by Northern States, and her cereal productions could find a ready market. Released from her inferior position by reason of her proximity to the cities of New York and Philadelphia, the State, small as she is, would soon become a leading one in the Southern Confederacy, and Perth Amboy . . . would be the rival of Philadelphia.[12]

The Somerset *Messenger*, another paper that had endorsed Breckinridge, blamed the nation's troubles on the Republicans:

The Republican papers and the Republican leaders are determined to prevent if possible any reconciliation of the difficulties now existing in the country, and all sorts of false reports are given currency to embitter the Northern people and by exciting their prejudices thus turn aside their minds from the contemplation of the great main cause of all the troubles—Republican sectionalism[13]

In February 1861 President-elect Lincoln spent twelve days journeying by rail from Springfield, Illinois, to his inauguration at Washington, crossing eight states and delivering more than twenty speeches in the process. New Jersey, then as close as she ever came to outright secession, was wisely included on the president-elect's itinerary. Despite the state's alarming pro-Southern tendencies, Lincoln's reception at Jersey City, Newark, Elizabeth, Rahway, New Brunswick, and Trenton was wildly enthusiastic. At Elizabeth 15,000 turned out to cheer him, at Rahway, 3,000, and another 5,000 at New Brunswick. Near Princeton, wrote a reporter on the president-elect's train, "the people from every house on the [rail]road came out. At one place handkerchiefs failed the large hearts of the ladies and sheets were substituted." All along the route, continued the newsman, "Every farm house which could boast a gun or large pistol, had them out, and gave us a salute."[14]

Newark's reception, by far the warmest along his route across New Jersey, must have both amazed and deeply satisfied the president-elect. "There was no music, no military display, scarcely any organized arrangements," wrote the Newark *Sentinal of Freedom*, "but the people turned out in numbers that were astonishing, and evinced a hearty cordiality exceedingly gratifying."[15] A reporter described Lincoln's passage through the city:

A large police force cleared the way. The President, in a fine open barouche, escorted by a large body of citizens, mounted, started off. Our route through the city was about a mile long, and upon emerging from the depot, a scene was before us that, for wild, crazy excitement, had not been equalled since we left Springfield [Illinois]. On both sides of the streets was one dense mass of people.

Ladies waved their handkerchiefs, and men uncovered their heads. Stalwart mechanics cheered as though their lungs were made of bell metal. Small boys were all happy, and one, as he ran along by our carriage, "wished he had his mother here."

Thousands rushed wildly after the cortege, and, one man falling down, there was soon a pile of men about five feet high, accumulated. From every window and housetop the fairest of the fair bid us welcome and adieu. . . .

Hanging by the neck to a lamp-post was an effigy, with a placard attached, inscribed "The Traitor's Doom." At the Public School about one thousand small children were assembled in front of the building, and as we passed, sang the well known Hutchinson melody of "We are a Band of Brothers." Mr. Lincoln's carriage halted a moment; he bowed to them, and we passed on.[16]

In Trenton the State Legislature, convened in joint session, gave Lincoln a surprisingly friendly reception, cheering when he finished his brief address. The Trenton *State Gazette and Republican* viewed the president-elect's visit in a hopeful light:

The visit of the President elect to this city . . . gave great satisfaction to our citizens, and tended to dispel many prejudices which had existed in the minds of Democrats against him. We heard several prominent Democrats say on Thursday that, though they had come here with strong prejudices against Mr. Lincoln, they would return to their homes fully satisfied that he was "the right man for the right place." What he said, and the manner of his saying it, had made this change in their estimate of the man.

No man could look upon Mr. Lincoln's face, and hear his voice, without becoming thoroughly satisfied that he was an honest man, and that he had no thought but what was in consonance with the good of his whole country. With such innate honesty of purpose, and with a will that knows no such word as "fail" in pursuing what he believes to be a right course, the whole country may rest satisfied that he will speedily bring the country out of its present difficulties, and again place it on the high-road to prosperity.[17]

The cheers of the Jerseyans who lined the president-elect's route from Jersey City to Trenton muffled only for a moment the voices of disunion. Typical of the Democratic press, the *Somerset Messenger* was far from impressed by the Illinois Republican:

At every stopping place he addressed the crowd that rushed to see him. None of his speeches evince either ability or statesmanship. On the contrary they are very common place and indifferent, and in some cases leaving the impress of "slang phrases," and evince generally ignorance of the events now taking place in our country. In one place he refers to our "bond of union" as a sort of "free love affair" held together by "passional attraction"—in another he congratulates the people that "nobody is hurt"—"nothing is suffering." The whole progress of the "President elect and his suite" is more like the moving of a crowned prince than the "is-to-be ruler" of a Republican country—and is in fact a sort of "raree-show" got up for the satisfaction of the gazers.[18]

If Lincoln's visit heartened the state's Unionists, it failed to persuade those who argued that New Jersey's proper place was with the South. As late as the first week of April 1861, former New Jersey Governor Rodman C. Price virtually urged secession. "I say emphatically," he wrote, "[that New Jersey] should go with the South, from every wise, prudential and patriotic reason." Price believed that within six months a new government would be formed by the union of New Jersey and other "conservative" Northern states with the South under the Confederate Constitution. Added Price:

> I will say and advise the thousands who contemplate a removal to the South to seek employment, quietly to remain. Do not suffer the loss and sacrifice of property necessary to make so great a change; patiently endure the loss and suffering from the want of employment for a time longer; for, in my judgment, coming events have foreshadowed New Jersey in union with the Southern States in six months, and our people fully restored to their various occupations and pursuits, labor abundant and well rewarded, and all again happy and prosperous, with the old flag waving over all the States again.[19]

The ex-governor's advice made good sense to many Jerseyans in the turbulent spring of 1861. With the South gradually loosening its economic and political ties with the Union, New Jersey's factory production slowed, leaving thousands unemployed. The *Journal's* preelection warning of "No Work! No Work!!" had seemingly been fulfilled. Those who disagreed with Governor Price were outraged by his gloomy forecast. "I am pained to hear that some of the politicians of New Jersey are advancing and urging the treasonable idea that our State will join the Southern Confederacy," wrote on *Daily Advertiser* reader:

> Is New Jersey to follow the course laid out for her by politicians, to benefit her trade, when it is proverbial that politicians know but little about any trade . . . and care for it less if they can only fill their pockets from the Public Crib?
> Are New Jersey Freemen so lost to love of country, the Union, Constitution and the Laws, that she will throw herself into the arms of treason, hoping thereby to benefit her trade? I trust and believe that a large majority of her sons have that noble patriotism which will cause them to scorn such a treasonable proposition.[20]

The Princeton *Standard*, which had supported Lincoln in the November election, called Price's remarks "weak, treasonable [and] adventurous." One of the paper's correspondents, styling himself "A Mechanic," ridiculed the former governor's proposal:

> As a Jerseyman, I want to know what authority Mr. Price has for saying that in six months we'll be under the Southern Confederacy. In that time, it is certain the people of New Jersey will not have time to transfer themselves to that model Government, and I wish to know who is to transfer us. Is it to be done by Rodman M. Price, Fernando Wood & Co.? or is it by Wigfall and his 25,000 of the chivalry, who are to subjugate the North, and proclaim from the top of Bunker Hill Monument that Beelzebub shall be the God of the North as he is the God of Cottondom. . . ? I want to know the means by which it is supposed we will be thus speedily transferred, so that I may judge for myself whether to fly immediately to some land where liberty is still respected, or stay, hoping the plans of transfer to our Southern despotism may fail to be carried out. I have lived all my days in New Jersey, under a Government where life, liberty and property are sacred, and now to be transferred to one where neither life, liberty nor property are respected, but are at the mercy of every drunken mob—where stealing, perjury and murder are not crimes; where lying and treason are not even venial sins in the eyes of D.D.'s of the secession stripe, and the people are to have no voice in the Government—is entirely too much of a change for me.
>
> Come now, Ex-Governor, do explain, that we may judge for ourselves the chances of escape from this worse than Vandal government of the South.[21]

As first one and then another Southern state followed South Carolina's example, Republicans along with a growing number of Democrats rallied to the Union cause. In early February 1861, while delegates from seven states met to adopt a constitution for the newly formed Confederate States of America, Trenton Republicans filled every seat and standing place in Temperance Hall, cheering "several eminent speakers" with "great enthusiasm." Resolutions denouncing "the pro-slavery party of the South" were adopted unanimously. Trenton Republicans minced no words in condemning the rebellious South:

> The open seizure of the National forts, arsenals and navy-yards, the firing upon the National flag, and the robbery of the national mints and Sub-Treasuries by the Secessionists of the South, are acts of treason and should be punished as such: . . . it is the bounden duty of the National Government forthwith to despatch a sufficient naval and military force to recover and protect all the national property, to enforce the laws in all parts of the Union, and summarily to arrest and punish all who violate them.[22]

Later the same week "An Honest Democrat" aired his views in the columns of the Princeton *Standard*:

We have approached a period in our history, when the great question should not be, will our party be weakened by taking measures in favor of the government, or be strengthened by opposition? but, will it be for the good of this nation, to meet the enemy and put down anything that may tend to a dissolution of these United States. . . ?

The men of the South . . . have taken measures to withdraw from this Union, which measures cannot be looked upon in any other light than acts of treason. . . .

In view of all this, what course shall the government pursue? Make compromises with them? they have been made and as often broken; give them the reigns of government in their own hands? they have had this for a long period in a great measure, and even now they have the majority in both houses. Shall it let them go and set up for themselves? in doing so, they break the compact, which is the foundation of the reputation of this Republic with other nations.

The union of these States must be preserved; the stars and stripes, which have so proudly waved over us, must be unfurled to the breeze and continue to float over succeeding generations, not one star or stripe being erased, or clouded by the hand of vile men.[23]

On April 12 Confederate batteries opened their long-expected bombardment of Fort Sumter, stilling New Jersey's voices of disunion in a noisy outpouring of patriotism. Crowds gathered outside newspaper offices in every part of the state, awaiting the latest news from South Carolina.

Thousands of people gathered in the streets, mournfully discussing the imperfect items and conjecturing as to the result. Suddenly there flashed over the wires "The Flag is down and the Fort is in flames!"

Then burst forth the long-pent patriotic enthusiasm! The cities suddenly became resplendent with flags! The women and children vied in displaying the National Colors, in badges, rosettes, and in every possible manner. Crowds paraded in the streets, with drums and shouts, visiting the residences of supposed disloyalists and demanding that they show their colors.[24]

The excitement in Newark was palpable as news of "the long dreaded calamity" clicked off the telegraph repeater.

We have never witnessed such intense excitement as was manifested in this city on Saturday evening and Sunday. Up to 5 o'clock the despatches announced nothing but misfortunes at Charleston, the conflagration in Fort Sumter, etc. At that hour the rumor spread that the Fort had capitulated, and was confirmed by some private despatches. Our regular despatch announcing the fact did not arrive till about 6½ o'clock, and the information spread with electric rapidity, causing a most painful sensation. Throughout the evening the streets and public places were thronged by agitated groups, and almost everybody discredited the intelligence. On Sunday it was corroborated by the papers, which were sold in the city by thousands. The various despatches were analyzed, and their announcements generally rejected as contradictory and improbable. Many actually believed that no conflict had taken place, and that the secessionists were telegraphing the various accounts only to alarm the North. The final confirmation this morning produced feelings of acutest grief, and at the same time the sternest determination to sustain and reestablish the honor of the country. These feelings are almost unanimous. Whatever may have been the former political divisions, there are but few sympathizers here with the rebels in this community, and a deep seated indignation is felt against them.[25]

The Confederate attack on Fort Sumter solidified political opinion in New Jersey behind the president, at least for a time. The *Somerset Messenger* spoke for many Democrats:

To admit that secession is right is to admit that this Union is a failure and Government by the "people" a farce. This we cannot admit. It is then the duty of every good citizen to oppose secession and support the Government and the Constitution; to stand by the Union and preserve the institutions of this Confederacy. We see no cause now for party wranglings. The house is on fire, let us put it out, and then there will be time enough left to seek out the incendiaries. The Democratic party has always stood by the Country—the motto of that party always has been "OUR COUNTRY—RIGHT OR WRONG!" Let that be the motto still. That is our motto. We are for the Union, now and forever! come from whatever quarter the foes may, and this we believe to be the position of every democrat in the land.[26]

Elizabeth's leading newspaper, *The New-Jersey Journal*, neutral in the 1860 election, had assured its readers only in December that disunion was impossible. Now it called for "a stern determination to stand behind the banner":

It is infinitely better to sustain great hardships rather than to have the flag . . . trampled beneath the feet of those who have ceased to cherish its multiplied glories. War, in its sternest reality, is far less to be dreaded than dishonor. . . .
    The volumes which contain the glorious achievements of revolutionary worthies, will not, thank God, be sullied by records of their sons' degeneracy. The friends of the Union are unwilling that the blood and treasure poured out to cement its bonds shall have been vainly devoted. The fires of patriotism, though for a season they may have emitted but feeble light and heat, burn with a ferver that attests the care with which they are watched and trimmed. The events of the last few days have called forth a spontaneous outburst of enthusiasm highly gratifying to every lover of his country. On every side strong-handed, brave-hearted men are responding to the appeal of the nation's Chief Magistrate. The spirit of loyalty is thoroughly aroused, and woe to the madmen who rush against their serried ranks.[27]

The Newark *Daily Advertiser*, the most respected journalistic voice in the state, struck a somber note when it called on Jerseyans "to abandon partisan prejudice and take their stand either for the government or against it." The Union, said the paper, would never be destroyed:

> [D]oes the conceited Davis imagine for a moment, that this great drama, which has its opening in the port of Charleston is to have its consummation and end there also? Never, never. The gallant little garrison may be starved out, they may see the walls of Sumter reduced to dust by the iron balls and shells of infernal machines, and be obliged to surrender to a beleaguring foe comprised of the better part of the population of Carolina; but this will be but the first scene of the first act of a drama which bids fair to become immortal. The Union and Constitution, which were the work of Washington and Jefferson, of Adams and Hamilton, shall never be crushed like the ramparts of Sumter.
>
> Before the work of these apostles of liberty and constitutional government shall be reduced to ruin, thousands of the stalwart forms of the freemen of the North will be laid low. And then the republic of the North will not be overthrown. If the fathers shall perish, their sons will fly with alacrity to the field of fight, where liberty and law are the prizes.[28]

News of Sumter's fall and Lincoln's call for 75,000 volunteers three days later stirred the spirit of the Northern states. In New Jersey, "[e]very town and city from Sussex to Cape May rang with the sounds of a state deliriously at war."[29] Elizabeth's reaction, according to the *New-Jersey Journal*, was typical:

> War is upon us. . . . Our citizens have, in common with those of every other place, been thoroughly waked up to these facts during the past week, and have endeavored to testify their devotion to the Union by hoisting flags of every size and kind; from the large banner floating gracefully from the tapering flag-staff, to the miniature stars and stripes decorating the harness of the horses on our streets. And on Friday the feeling was fanned into a perfect blaze of enthusiasm by the passage through our ward of the Providence [Rhode Island] Marine Corps of Artillery, on its way to the seat of war. This old corps . . . came from New York by the Steamer Kill Von Kull, with all the necessary accoutrements; horses, baggage wagons, supplies, etc., and a battery of six brass pieces, and with them were transferred to the cars and despatched to Easton, to await further orders. In number about 150, they are composed of the elite of Providence. . . . Great was the excitement here among all our citizens, and many were the souveniers left by the gallant soldiers behind, in the way of handkerchiefs and rings and buttons cut from their uniforms, and given to our fair damsels who were watching the transfer at the depot.[30]

Within a week of Lincoln's call 10,000 men had volunteered for the militia, three times New Jersey's quota. On May 6 four regiments of Jerseyans were marching through Washington, the first fully organized brigade of any state to reach the capital. Governor Olden borrowed $450,000 from private banks to support the state's war effort. A special emergency session of the State Legislature voted a $2 million war chest. Enthusiasm for the war was matched only by confidence that it would be over quickly. "This rebellion," said a New Jersey Congressman a few weeks after Fort Sumter, "could easily be put down by a few women with broomsticks!"[31]

The dream of a short, swift, and only slightly uncomfortable war was abruptly shattered when news of the Federal rout at Bull Run on July 21–22 reached New Jersey. "[E]nough is known," wrote the *State Gazette and Republican* as it sorted out conflicting accounts of the battle, "to warrant the statement that we have suffered in a degree which has cast gloom over the remnant of the army and excited the deepest melancholy throughout Washington. The carnage has been tremendously heavy on both sides, and ours is represented as frightful."[32] The ignominious retreat of the Federal army emboldened New Jersey Copperheads, as the antiwar Democrats came to be known, to demand an immediate truce. Otherwise, predicted the *Daily Journal*, the nation was in store for a long war that would surely end in Northern defeat.

> No intelligent man now harbors the delusion that the South can be crushed or starved out, conquered or subjugated in months or years to come. . . . With our own time for preparation, with the choice of the battle-field, and the available military talent of the North at our command, we have offered the enemy battle in force, and in a fair and well contested fight, where our soldiers nobly vindicated the bravery of the country, we have been disasterously defeated, and our capital placed at the mercy of our enemies.
>
> But does this defeat prove that the North may not again rise in her strength, and, gathering fresh armies to the field, meet and perhaps emerge successfully from the next campaign? By no means. We have still abundant resources, great credit, a determined will and the force of State organizations and overpowering numbers in our favor. We may raise a half million of soldiers and equip and appoint them as [an] army was never equipped and appointed. We may rectify the blunders of the past and retrieve its defeats by great victories. Success may perchance perch upon our banners for years; and yet, in the end, the North is destined to sure defeat.[33]

The *State Gazette and Republican*, while conceding that it would be "useless to even attempt to disguise our mortification" at the outcome of Bull Run, denounced any notion of a truce. Bull Run, claimed the paper, meant nothing more than a six- to twelve-month delay before the Rebels were subdued:

> Because defeated once, however, it is no reason for permanent despondency. Like, at the defeat of Fort Sumter the first impulse of the nation was to mourn and the second to avenge, so now, when the smoke of the battle shall have all cleared away; and the honored dead shall have been laid in their narrow tombs; and the first gush of anguish of those whose loved-ones have thus been hastily summoned away, shall have subsided, the whole North will again arouse itself to the great and glorious work of subduing this most

unrighteous and causeless rebellion. Again upon the wings of the lightning will fly the order "To arms!" "To arms!" and from every town and hamlet—from every hill and valley, will come the response, "We are ready!"

We are no less confident of success now than before; and though the final triumph will doubtless be put off somewhat longer by the recent reverse, yet come it must and will, sooner or later.[34]

Bull Run sobered the nation to the realities of war. In New Jersey the antiwar politicians and editors grew bolder again, and more vocal, convinced now of the righteousness of their cause. The battle for the conscience of the state began in earnest.

2

True Patriotism

On Christmas Eve, 1861, Lieutenant Colonel Robert McAllister of the First New Jersey Infantry wrote to his wife from camp near Alexandria, Virginia, complaining bitterly of those "at home sympathizing with Rebellion." What was needed most now, wrote McAllister, a Republican, was "True Patriotism." The man who failed to give "hearty support to our bleeding country in this day of our country's trial," he added, "is not worthy to be a descendant of our forefathers, and he ought to be denied the protection of our laws and shipped at once to South America, where they will have a government that suits them."[1]

McAllister's words would be echoed again and again during the war years by New Jersey Unionists, in uniform and out. Public sentiment had shifted considerably since the opening days of the war when, according to John Y. Foster, "party lines were obliterated, party restraints uncared for, and the claims of the country . . . recognized as sacredly paramount and supreme."[2] Three weeks into the war, on May 10, 1861, the Democratic-controlled State Legislature had eagerly approved a loan of two million, provided taxes for its payment, and declared that "the most certain and speedy mode of restoring peace is by the most vigorous prosecution of the present war."[3] But in the aftermath of Bull Run, when it became clear the Confederacy could not be subdued in a matter of weeks, criticism of the Republican administration in Washington reared its head once more. Antiwar elements began a steady drumbeat of opposition that waxed in effectiveness as success on the battlefield eluded first one and then another Union army. When news of the Union disaster at Bull Run reached the state, "crowds openly rejoiced," celebrating the Southern victory by "disporting upon the pavement and exchanging congratulations."[4] Lee's invasion of Pennsylvania in the summer of 1863 was, wrote one highly placed Republican politician, "the occasion of undisguised joy among disloyalists, and they would gladly have welcomed him to our city and state."[5]

The contest for New Jersey's allegiance was to continue until the end of the fighting, and beyond. In April 1865, when word came that Richmond had fallen to the Union army, the State Legislature debated resolutions expressing New Jersey's thanks to Lincoln, certain generals, and the soldiers. The Democratic-controlled Assembly adopted the resolutions only after deleting any mention of Lincoln as commander in chief. When on April 5 the Senate took up a similar resolution, it could not bring itself to express its appreciation to the victorious army, sending the measure back to committee.[6] Not until November of 1865 was New Jersey "redeemed," at least in the eyes of Unionists. Hoisting the double banner of reunion and the martyred president, the Republicans campaigned with an enthusiasm and confidence they had never shown before. On election day they were victorious, carrying both houses of the legislature and electing the governor. "God be praised," wrote one jubilant Republican to Governor-elect Ward after the ballots had been counted, "not so much, that Marcus L. Ward is elected Governor, as that the people of New Jersey, have at the 'eleventh hour,' returned from all manner of wickedness and declared themselves *Loyal* and true to the *Union*."[7]

The political tides that ebbed and flowed across New Jersey during the Civil War reflected the state's ambivalent attitude toward the rebellion. Both the Democratic and Republican, or more precisely, Union, parties were split into opposing and at times contending factions. The Union or Union Republican party, forced to defend both an unpopular war and administration, was consigned to the role of the opposition throughout the war period.[8] There had been no formal Republican party organization in the state before the war. During the 1860 campaign, little effort had been made to perfect the party organization, so confident were its leaders of success. Once secession was a reality, Republicans sought to enlist all Union-loving men under a single flag, supporting War Democrats as well as Republicans in the 1861 and 1862 elections. Unfocused and poorly organized, New Jersey's Union movement was by and large a failure. Although federal patronage was at the disposal of Jersey Republicans, the state's political apparatus was firmly in Democratic hands from 1863. Moreover, a constitutional provision against soldier's voting in the field deprived the party of valuable support at the polls.[9] In June of 1862 Horace Greeley diagnosed New Jersey's Union Republican ills as a case of "timidity":

The Republicans of New Jersey are too generally timid, bolting, shameful in the proclamation of their principles. They have tried to beat the Democrats by being as like them as they could, and are under foot of course. . . . The Republicans of New Jersey—we speak of their leading politicians and presses—have pursued a mistaken policy from the start. . . . Fearing to attack slavery they have surrendered their State into the hands of slavery's tools and parasites.[10]

Greeley's harsh but accurate criticism of the Union Republicans echoed that of the Radical Republicans, a small but noisy faction within the party. The state's Union Republican leadership, while supporting Lincoln's war effort, shied from advocating a more vigorous antislavery policy. Not so a determined minority of Republicans who urged ever stronger measures to suppress the rebellion. The Radicals enjoyed a large following among New Jersey's German-Americans. Early in February 1864, a state convention of radical Germans held in Newark demanded the abolition of slavery in the entire Union, confiscation of the landed property of the rebels, and its distribution among Union soldiers.[11] Chief spokesman for the Radical Republicans was the Newark *Daily Mercury*, whose longtime editor, Horace N. Congar, had served as a Seward delegate to the 1860 Republican national convention. Unqualified support for the president, a refusal to deal with the War Democrats, as the Union Republicans were prone to do, support of abolition, and full political and civil rights for Blacks were the chief programs advocated by the Radicals.

The Democrats were similarly divided. Small in number, War Democrats supported administration measures to defeat the Confederacy, cooperating with Union Republicans to elect mutually acceptable candidates. State Senator Joseph T. Crowell of Union County was typical. Elected in 1860 on the Democratic Fusion ticket, he came out strongly in support of the war, later joined the Union Republicans and was a delegate to the 1864 Republican national convention.[12] The largest group within the party were the regular Democrats. Opposed to secession and willing to support the war effort generally, they were unfailingly critical of what they regarded as the administration's shortcomings and eager to condemn its "unconstitutional" acts, including emancipation. One such Democrat expressed the views of many in his party when he wrote, in 1862:

> Whilst I am a Democrat as warmly attached to its time honored principles, whilst I am opposed as ever to Republicanism in every shape, I feel it is my duty to oppose Secession and all its aiders, abettors, sympathizers and apologists with as much energy, and sincerity as I ever have and ever will oppose Abolitionism and its kindred heresies.[13]

Joel Parker, a Monmouth County lawyer elected governor in 1862, represented the mainstream of his party. Brigadier general of the New Jersey Militia at the beginning of the war, he supported the Union and opposed secession. Lincoln's conduct of the war, however, met with his disapproval. In his inaugural address, Parker criticized the administration's disrespect for "Constitutional privileges" and expressed his strong opposition to freeing the slaves. "Abolition and Secession," he said, "are the authors of our calamity, and Abolition is the parent of Secession." Conciliation with the South was possible, added Parker.

> We should not be afraid of peace—an honorable and permanent peace— whether it come to us by the exercise of power, or by the exercise of conciliation. It should be a peace on the basis of "the Union as it was," not a Union of states where parts are held in subjugation as conquered provinces. . . . It should be a peace founded on the submission of all to the rightful authority of

the Government, and the guarantee of all their constitutional rights by the Government. It should be a peace bringing with it such unity as will have the Constitution for its foundation, and obedience to law for its corner-stone.[14]

Regular Democrats such as Parker were opposed as often by the Union Republicans as by a third faction within the Democratic party, the Copperheads. The so-called Peace Democrats held extreme views: they were against the war, bemoaned every step taken in Washington to prosecute the war effort, savored each Confederate success, and would have agreed to Southern independence on almost any terms, believing it impossible for the Union armies to conquer the South. Their strength lay in Essex and among the conservative Dutch farmers of Bergen County.

Two months before Lincoln's inauguration, William C. Alexander of Princeton, unsuccessful Democratic candidate for governor in 1856 and the choice of Jersey Democrats for the vice-presidency in 1860, expressed the sentiments of many who would later become Copperheads when he wrote to the editor of the Fredericksburg, Virginia, *News*:

> The South has been wronged and outraged. The mercies of black republicanism are cruel, and the tone of its leaders uncompromising, insolent and defiant. If you cannot find protection for your rights and your property within the Union, I admit, *ex animo*, that it is your right and your duty to seek it beyond its pale. Your rights are older than the Union or the constitution, and if not inalienable, they have certainly never been surrendered.[15]

Copperhead leaders, who had before Sumter bid the Southern states depart in peace, became more strident as the war continued. Former Governor Rodman Price, who had once envisioned New Jersey as part of a Southern Confederacy, charged in 1863 that "the Republican Party have all been disunionists and traitors, they have broken the Constitution and dissolved the Union. . . . I regret that New Jersey ever permitted her troops to invade the soil of any State.[16] The Newark *Daily Journal*, in a statement of principles published on New Year's Day, 1864, denounced the war as "sectional and unjust." An "immediate and honorable peace," it claimed, was the "only means of restoring constitutional liberty and preserving the blessing of free government.[17] In June 1864, shortly after the notorious Copperhead leader, former Ohio Congressman Clement L. Vallandigham, returned to the United States from Canada, Bergen County Democrats met "in large numbers" at Schraalenburgh to excoriate Lincoln, "this corrupt tyrant" and "wicked usurper," calling upon the people "to unmask the reeking crimes of an infamous administration." Bergen Copperheads resolved:

> That the kidnapping and abduction of Mr. Vallandigham was an act of unexampled and unmitigated villainy, and has covered its author and all

abettors with undying infamy, and now that the wicked motive which prompted it is understood, the people heartily rejoice in the triumph of the gallant exile over the cowardly tyrant.

. . . The past lawless conduct of Abraham Lincoln and his present position as a candidate, thrusting himself forward for a new lease of power, makes it incumbent upon the American people to guard their liberties with the most jealous care, and demand with a united voice that neither Mr. Vallandigham nor any other citizen shall again be made the victim of arbitrary power for a single moment.[18]

The Copperheads were a strong force within New Jersey, reaching the zenith of their influence in the spring of 1863 with the passage of the Peace Resolutions, a Negro exclusion bill, and the election of a United States senator.

New Jersey understandably soon came to be known as a "Copperhead State." The weakness of the Union Republicans and disunity within regular Democratic ranks gave the vociferous Peace Democrats the advantage, at least until the tide of battle began to turn decisively in favor of the North. Jerseyans were of so many different minds about the war that the most radical opinions easily appeared ascendant. New Jersey's political "apostasy," as one scholar has called it, became a byword of reproach among Union men everywhere.[19] "As a native born Jerseyman," wrote an Illinois Republican, "I love her reputation, and when I am so often compelled to hear the anathemas hurled against her . . . I get to be fighting mad at those who have brought this shame upon us."[20] New Jersey, concludes one recent student of the period, was "a northeastern state with a semi-border mentality" whose people clung to "a conservative view toward the Civil War, race, and the removal of certain constitutional guarantees." The state's larger cities in particular were centers of Copperhead strength, a movement born of lost Southern markets, wartime inflation, and the workingman's inordinate fear of Black job competition.[21]

The struggle for New Jersey's loyalty was fought with great intensity in the pages of the state's weekly and daily newspapers, the nineteenth century's most important forum for the expression of political opinion. By 1860 there were some 370 dailies in the United States with a combined circulation in the millions. Most were political papers in the sense that they were either controlled or subsidized by the parties, or their editors or owners important figures in party councils. So partisan had the daily and weekly press become that one Philadelphia journal expressed the fear that the entire profession had become "nothing more than a vehicle of party intemperance."[22] Wrote another observer: "Every shade of political persuasion has its organ. . . . The leading presses of the country, even with the best intentions, are in continual danger of becoming mere tools of public men, to whom they act as sycophants."[23] The partisan political press dominated American journalism throughout the war years. One Democratic paper complained bitterly in February 1862 that in the eyes of the Republican press, "an abolition General" could "do no wrong, commit no blun-

Thomas Kinney, editor of the *Daily Advertiser* *(Author collection)*.

ders, make no mistakes, moral, social or political." He lost battles, said the paper, only by the "treachery, cowardice or ignorance of . . . subordinates."[24] By the same token Copperhead editors gloried in the superior courage and generalship of the rebel troops who, they claimed, were invincible. Management of the news to suit the politics of the owner or editor was commonplace, whether the paper was Republican or Democrat. Upon hearing news of the Union debacle at Fredericksburg in December 1862, the owner of the Philadelphia *Press* wired his managing editor: "Don't treat the affair at Fredericksburg as a disaster." So well did the editor obscure the magnitude of Burnside's blundering that a week later the owner expressed his thanks: "It is a splendid tribute and I know will be appreciated by the administration."[25]

New Jersey's newspapers were no better or worse than their contemporaries elsewhere in the North. Each political faction had its press, and there were few truly independent or neutral publications to be found. All but a handful of New Jersey's fifteen daily and sixty-five weekly papers were dependent upon official patronage and partisan support. In turn, their prejudices colored not only their editorial columns, as expected, but their political and military news as well. Armchair generalship was in the natural order of things: editors had not only favorite politicans to puff but pet generals to magnify. Newspaper strategies for winning the war grew to epidemic proportion.[26] In short, the Civil War press "saw itself as dedicated to the pursuit of whatever principles its publisher might espouse." Impartial reporting of the news more often as not took a distant second place to "electing candidates, and ousting those in power," ends served with whatever means were available.[27]

None of New Jersey's papers was in the same league as the great metropolitan journals of the day. "Newspapers have not made their mark in New Jersey as in many of the old states," wrote Frederic Hudson, managing editor of the New York *Herald* during the war. "Situated between New York and Philadelphia it has been placed in a position to enjoy the news facilities of those two cities." Only the Newark *Daily Advertiser*, which Hudson called "the most enterprising sheet in the state," and its sister paper, the *Sentinel of Freedom*, a weekly, could hold a candle to the New York dailies.[28]

With few exceptions, New Jersey papers were as blatantly partisan as any in the North. The Copperhead press in particular gained an early reputation for partiality that bordered on outright treason. On September 25, 1861, a federal grand jury sitting in Trenton brought in a presentment against the Newark *Daily Journal*, Warren *Journal*, Hunterdon County *Democrat*, New Brunswick *Weekly Times*, Plainfield *Gazette*, and Hackettstown *Gazette*, charging that the newspapers "have been acting, either wilfully or ignorantly, as enemies of the country, more dangerous than open foes."[29] Three years later the editors of the Newark *Daily Journal*, *Somerset Messenger*, and Bergen County *Democrat* were arrested on charges of inciting insurrection against the United States.[30] The list of Copperhead newspapers was a long one, including, in addition to those mentioned, the Paterson *Daily Register*, Trenton *Daily True American*, Mount Holly *Herald*, and *New Jersey Herald* of Newton.[31] *The Old Guard*, an extreme antiwar magazine published in New York City, was a significant influence within New Jersey because of the prominence of its editor, C. Chauncey Burr, one of four or five acknowledged leaders of New Jersey's Peace Democracy.

Editor of the weekly Bergen County *Democrat* until May 1862, and later a frequent contributor to the columns of the Newark *Daily Journal*, Burr, whom one writer has called a "specialist in extremism," was founder and editor of *The Old Guard*.[32] A leader of the Bergen County Clique, as it was known, Burr was arguably the most influential Copperhead outside of the State Legislature.[33] In speeches made throughout the state in 1862 and 1863, Burr maintained that the federal government had no power to make war upon a state for any reason. "Every Jersey man in favor of this war is a foe to his state," said Burr in late November 1863, "and to the very principles of the government on which the Union of the states was founded."[34] Lincoln's call for a draft in March of 1863 prompted *The Old Guard* to label the president a "deluded and almost delerious fanatic."[35] A month earlier Burr had written: "We have great confidence in Mr. Lincoln as a great storyteller, an excellent joker, and a first class buffoon; but no confidence in him whatever as a military strategist." Emancipation Burr considered a total failure, slavery a glorious chapter in American history. The Southern people, he claimed in June 1863, had been at "the pinnacle of their glory at that precise period when the institution [of slavery] was most extended."[36] While intimating that Lincoln had some Negro blood in his family, Burr insisted that Vice-President Hannibal Hamlin was of African descent. Secretary of War Stanton received a lighter sentence: Burr called him a "Nero."[37] The war against the rebellion would fail because of the South's military might, said Burr. Meanwhile, discontent within the federal armies was rampant on account of Lincoln's "tender concern for negroes, and . . . unnatural indifference to the rights and dignity of white soldiers."[38] In short, *The Old Guard* was an opinionated, anti-Black, antiwar journal that represented the most extreme views of the Copperhead movement.

Less outrageous in its sentiments but just as capable of enraging New Jersey Unionists was the Trenton *Daily True American*, owned and edited by David Naar, a Sephardic Jew from the West Indies. Naar bought the *True American* in 1853, turning what had been a moribund paper into one of New Jersey's most influential Democratic organs. During the war years Naar's paper was the unofficial South Jersey spokesman for New Jersey Copperheads.[39] The *True American* was against the war, the administration, and the Blacks: Naar considered Negroes greatly inferior to whites, emancipation a "most stupendous act of folly," and abolitionists insane troublemakers.[40] Conscription so confounded Naar in March 1863 that, at a mass meeting held in Trenton, he cried out: "We are cutting our throats for the sake of a few worthless Negroes."[41] In a statement of policy printed shortly after the outbreak of the war, the *True American* laid down principles entirely consistent with the major Copperhead themes:

All true patriots, of either Section, must desire peace; but, to be effective, it must be an honorable one, the terms of which are not to be dictated, but mutually agreeable. . . .

Meanwhile, in the midst of war, bankruptcy, and general distress, we have a great duty to perform for ourselves, our country, and our posterity. We must prevent the spread of pernicious doctrine—we must exercise vigilence to save the Constitution from being overridden by "Higher Law" abstractions, and our institutions from being supplanted by irremediable evils. By tongue and pen and ballot, we must protest against the subversion of the civil by the military authorities. We must insist upon the enjoyment of the sacred privilege of writ of Habeas Corpus—the only safeguard of popular freedom. We must oppose the creation of a large standing army, and an unnecessary public debt. We must rebuke the substitution of paper for specie currency. We must object to an unconstitutional centralization of power in the hands of the Federal Government as dangerous to our liberties—and we must resist by all constitutional means the freeing of four millions of southern slaves, as inimical to the welfare of northern white labor, and ominous to the whole country.[42]

Although the *True American* softened its rhetoric as the North's armies penetrated deeper into the Confederacy, Judge Naar's paper remained a wartime favorite of the Copperheads (and many Democrats as well) and a frequent target of the Unionist press. Typical was the reaction of the staunchly Republican *Sussex Register* to reports that Naar had filed a libel suit against the *Gazette* and the *True Democrat*:

Old David Naar . . . makes oath that the editors of said papers have falsely accused him of being a traitor, etc., for the purpose of bringing him "into public contempt." This is the best joke of the season. The time when old David was not more or less an object of contempt, is not remembered by the oldest citizen. Indeed we have at times felt great contempt for him ourself, but we doubt whether he could mulct us into the payment of damages for indulging so natural and unavoidable an emotion.[43]

Moderate Democratic journals reserved the right to question the administration's abilities and motives, but they opposed secession and urged a vigorous prosecution of the war. At least in the early years they spoke unfavorably of emancipation. Such papers had little use for the Copperheads: in August 1862 the Morristown *True Democratic Banner* dismissed the *Daily Journal* as unpatriotic and its course as ultimately disastrous for the Democratic party. Said the *Banner*:

The Newark *Daily Journal*, ever since the battles on the Chickahominy, has been crying for immediate peace. Its mode of getting immediate peace is for the Government to immediately discontinue the prosecution of the war. That is the same as advising and urging an immediate surrender to the rebels. . . .

That all that is bare-faced disunion—that it is lawlessness and anarchy of the worst and most destructive kind, is too plain to need, or even permit of elucidation. That such conduct on the part of a public journal is adhering to and giving "aid and comfort" to the armed and war waging enemies of the United States, is too obvious to be denied. Such "aid and comfort," in the language of the Constitution, is "treason against the United States". . . .

The *Journal* professes to be pursuing its unpatriotic and unlawful course in the name of Democracy. Against that pretension we enter our solemn protest. Its course aids and abets the most arrogant, domineering aristocracy the world has ever seen. It is supporting the most inveterate foes of Democracy. . . . For the Democracy to adopt its course would render the party odious and execrable for all time to come. Such a course would not only be wrong in itself, but it would damn the party forever.[44]

The Sussex *True Democrat* and the Jersey City *Standard* also raised the banner of the regular Democrats throughout the war.

Republican papers of moderate stripe included the Newark *Daily Advertiser*, Jersey City *Courier and Advertiser*, Sussex *Register*, New Jersey *Freie Zeitung*, New Brunswick *Fredonian*, Paterson *Daily Guardian*, West Jersey *Press*, published in Camden and Trenton *Daily State Gazette and Republican*, the official spokesman for the Union Republican movement. The *State Gazette*, founded in 1840, supported the Whigs, the Opposition party, the Union Republicans, and, after the war, the Republican party. A favorite of South Jersey Unionists, it was locked in vituperative struggle with its neighbor, the *True American*.[45] Early in the war the *State Gazette* published a "prescription . . . for the treatment of traitors wherever found." Merchants and professional men were to be boycotted, all others avoided "as you would a walking pestilence." Special medicine was reserved for traitorous newspaper editors.

If he be the publisher of a paper, treat his paper as you do him—LET IT SEVERELY ALONE—Neither buy it, read it, nor support it in any way. If your name is in it to an advertisement, or in any other way, get it out as speedily as possible, lest you, too, be suspected of sympathising in his traitorous sentiments. If you see that paper in any man's hand, or in any office, store, or work-shop, mark the man or the place as you would a viper, or a viper's nest—let it, and all who have anything to do with it, SEVERELY ALONE.[46]

The Radical Republican press of the state, chief among it the Newark *Daily Mercury*, urged the most stringent measures to subdue the South, including immediate emancipation of all slaves. In their approach to the news the Radical Republican papers were not unlike their archenemies, the Copperheads: Union defeats were minimized, victories, exaggerated. Cooperation with the War Democrats, or indeed any act that might be construed as not supportive of the administration, was condemned. At midwar the *Mercury* self-righteously proclaimed itself "the unflinching champion of the right, and the uncompromising opponent of the wrong." It would, it said in February 1863, "continue to give the national administration a hearty and unwavering support in its efforts to preserve the Union, and to subdue the present atrocious rebellion."[47]

New Jersey's press fought the war in its columns more vigorously at times than did the contending armies on the battlefield. Truth, so elusive under even the best of circumstances, was the chief casualty of the newspaper wars. Jersey's papers were clearly not unique in this regard nor any better or worse that their contemporaries across the North. The Civil War "was a struggle in which political biases permeated every consideration," wrote Joseph J. Mathews in his history of Civil War newspapermen. "The Copperhead and disloyal press in the Union deemphasized victories and warped military intelligence, but the supposedly loyal press often allowed its prejudices to affect not only its editorials but military news as well."[48] In May of 1863 William Cullen Bryant's New York *Evening Post*, one of the best-written, least partisan papers of the era, proposed a set of tongue-in-cheek "rules" by which a "sound, conservative Union paper" should be edited.

It is a mystery to many readers how certain "democratic" journals, which profess the warmest devotion to the Union, nevertheless manage to play into the hands of the secessionists. But the thing is easy enough—quite as easy as lying—if you will only consider it for a moment. The editors of such journals are of course compelled to parade their Unionism, because of the overwhelming sentiment of the North; at the same time, however, by observing any or all of the following rules, they are able to do very effective work for the other side. The rules we give, by the way, are without charge to the parties concerned.

Bryant's "rules" were simple enough. While "[a]ll the military successes of the rebel armies should be magnified" and "those of the North . . . deprecated," the "war reports of the Southern papers should be paraded at great length, especially those which swell the number of their army, or which extol the exploits of their generals." The North's best generals "should be calumniated in every possible way." On the other hand, officers "who have distinguished themselves for donothingism" were to be hailed as "the master Generals of the age." The North's economy should be spoken of "sneeringly," wrote Bryant's paper, Union army victories should be ignored, Lincoln and his cabinet abused without regard to "the consistency of your charges," and the use of Black troops and employment of conscription protested "vehemently."[49]

New Jersey's Copperhead journals followed Bryant's rules to the letter, the regular Democratic press adhered to some of them. Ironically, the Republican and Unionist press, including those newspapers which approvingly reprinted the *Evening Post* column, merely inverted its formula. The state's eighty or so newspapers bore witness to what historian John Cunningham has called the "[b]itter political currents [that] seethed within the state."[50]

3

Daily Doses of the Nauseous Drug

Nowhere in New Jersey was the clash of political opinion sharper than in Newark, the state's largest city. There, Republicans, Unionists, Abolitionists, Democrats, and Copperheads contended fiercely for supremacy. Not surprisingly, Newark was home not only to New Jersey's most influential paper, the *Daily Advertiser*, but to two of its most radical as well, the *Journal* and the *Mercury*.

Founded on the grassy banks of the Passaic River by Connecticut Puritans in 1666, Newark was one of America's great industrial centers in 1860. Her factories, manned by Irish and German immigrants, employed 21,600 workers earning an average annual wage of $305. Representing a capital investment of $13,820,000, some 765 establishments produced goods worth nearly $28,000,000, ranking Newark seventh in the nation in the value of its manufactures. The city's five leading industries—men's clothing, hats, harnesses, shoes, and patent and enameled leather—employed 9,531 workers or 44 percent of the total workforce.[1] During much of the nineteenth century the Southern coastal states were Newark's most lucrative market. The South bought an estimated sixty-five to seventy-five percent of the city's annual output, a large part of it made expressly for customers in Virginia, the Carolinas, and Georgia.[2] When war broke out the city was, according to a contemporary, "essentially a Southern workshop. For about two-thirds of a century the shoemakers of Newark shod the South, its planters and its plantation hands. . . . For generations the bulk of the carriages, saddlery, harnesses and clothing manufactured in Newark found a ready and profitable market south of Mason and Dixon's line. And so it was to a greater or lesser extent with all our industries."[3]

The year 1860 was a good one for Newark, its economy almost fully recovered from the depression that began three years earlier. Factories, some of which had closed their doors following the Panic of 1857, scrambled to fill orders. While a number of workers still received city welfare, and the public charities that dispensed clothing and groceries had not yet disbanded, there was

38

an encouraging air of prosperity about the city of 71,941 people. As the presidential election drew near, the chance that Abraham Lincoln might be elected struck fear into many a Newark heart. The *Daily Journal* was not alone when it warned: "The evidence is overwhelming, that if the Republicans succeed, such a season of dullness and depression of business will be witnessed as has not been seen for years."[4] Newarkers voted their pocketbooks on November 7 when they cast fifty-five percent of their ballots for the Democratic Fusion ticket; the *Daily Mercury* placed the blame for Republican defeat squarely on Newark's businessmen. "The Southern trade in Newark is safe," croaked the paper, adding that the election of Newark clothier Nehemiah Perry to Congress amounted to "a pledge to the secessionists that we stand prepared to do their bidding at every call upon us. That of course secures the sale of our hats and harnesses and clothing."[5]

If New Jersey was a state with conservative views regarding race, rebellion, and the war, the chief exemplar of her conservatism was Newark. Economic factors were largely responsible for the city's "Southern" cast. Even before the first cannon fire at Fort Sumter, Newark's traditional markets began to wither. When the Southern States actually seceded from the Union, severing commercial as well as political ties with the North, Newark's economy staggered from the blow. Lost sales conspired with uncollected accounts to "cramp and strain" many of the city's largest concerns, forcing some out of business entirely, leading others to curtail production sharply.[6] Newark businessmen and their employees suffered alike. Lincoln's election brought hard times to Newark, blackening the name of the Republican party and making fertile the soil in which Newark's Peace Democracy would later flourish.[7]

Newark's opinion of the South's "peculiar institution" had much to do with its attitude toward the Civil War. Newarkers generally agreed that slavery was the South's own business, its eradication no cause for war.[8] Many in Newark had seen slavery firsthand, or had some passing acquaintance with the Northern version of the system, and they found it unremarkable. New Jersey was one of the last of the Northern states to come to grips with the evil in its midst. Antislavery forces won a major battle in 1804 when the state legislature approved an "Act for the Gradual Abolition of Slavery," a feeble measure that freed females born of slaves after 1804 when they reached age twenty-one, males upon reaching twenty-five. The legislature finally abolished slavery in 1846, in a fashion: all slaves were made apprentices; their children were free but were bound out to the local overseer of the poor when reaching the age of six. Vestiges of slavery lingered on through the 1850s. Farms in rural Clinton township, Newark's neighbor to the southwest, employed slave labor until 1846, apprentices for another decade or more.[9] Although all of Newark's Blacks had gained their freedom by 1860, none could vote nor was any considered the equal of whites. They were tolerated or ignored as long as they "kept their place."

In such an atmosphere Newark's Abolitionists made slow headway. On July

31, 1834, the Reverend Dr. W. R. Weeks, pastor of the Fourth Presbyterian Church, delivered his usual Friday evening sermon on the topic, "Slavery as a Sin." Possibly forewarned, a menacing crowd of a thousand quickly gathered outside the church, then rushed inside, breaking windows, mutilating the altar, and smashing furniture. A lone Black in the congregation escaped the mob's fury only when younger members of the audience surrounded him.[10] The First Congregational Church, where the principles of Abolition had been preached by the Grimke sisters as early as 1836, was scorned as the "nigger church." In 1851, when the congregation printed the Reverend Charles Beecher's sermon against the Fugitive Slave Law, a young boy selling copies in a railway car "was obliged to desist for his safety." Reverend Beecher, who preached the sins of slavery at First Congregational from 1850 to 1853, found himself ostracized from Newark's ministerial community: contrary to well-established custom, he was never invited to exchange pulpits with any other pastor in the city.[11] Beecher's congregation, some of whom did service as conductors on the underground railway, was a tiny billow on a sea of indifference. By and large Newarkers found no moral objection to what the *Daily Journal* blandly called the South's "social institution."

When it gradually became clear that the war was being fought as much to free the slaves as to reunite the Union, many in the city were not pleased. A war to save the Union might be worth fighting, but sacrificing money and lives to free the slaves was quite another matter. Newark's racial attitudes during the Civil War have never been adequately explored, although students of the period agree that Lincoln's Emancipation Proclamation, announced in preliminary form in September 1862, triggered the stinging Union Republican defeat in that year's fall elections. What a historian has called "the spectre of four million freed Negroes inundating the North in pursuit of freedom and employment" does much to explain the larger than normal Democratic margins in 1862. Even though he was a native Newarker, the Republican gubernatorial candidate, Marcus L. Ward, carried but two of the city's thirteen wards. Only two Republican assemblymen were elected.[12] On March 18, 1863, the New Jersey General Assembly took up for consideration a bill to deport to Liberia "or some island in the West Indies" any Black who "shall hereafter come in this state and remain therein for ten days or more." All five of Newark's Democratic assemblymen present for the vote supported the Negro exclusion bill, which its sponsor claimed would prevent "the negro 'influx.' "[13] Black competition for the white man's job was a favorite theme of the *Daily Journal*. Insisting that "[a]bolition fanaticism and its kindred heresies must be crushed out," the *Journal* warned its readers in January 1864 that the "abolitionists would continue the war to abolish slavery and let loose upon the country over three millions of happy and useful laborers."[14] The fact of Black competition for Newark jobs was farfetched, but the threat was quite real to many.[15]

The hard times that followed close on the heels of Lincoln's election faded as the federal war machine groaned into action. Government orders soon filled much of the void left by the lost Southern markets. "Every factory was run to its utmost capacity," wrote a nineteenth-century historian, "and there is no doubt that manufacturers made money faster than during any previous period in the history of Newark."[16] Swords, pistols, rifles, knapsacks, tents, blankets, and uniforms flowed from Newark factories in unprecedented volume. The demand for manpower, though enormous, was quickly met by new waves of German and Irish immigrants. Despite the absence of several thousand soldiers, Newark's population stood at 87,413 in 1865, a jump of 16,000 in five years. Whether Newark's working men and women fully shared the prosperity the city's businessmen enjoyed is at best problematical. The scant evidence available would indicate that many did not. Wartime inflation drove prices up. Competition from immigrants eager for work tended to hold wages down.[17] In the summer of 1861 the wife of one Newark soldier complained to Marcus L. Ward, head of the city's relief committee, that she was subsisting on an income of two dollars a month: "Some days we would have $.05 worth and some days nothing and it has not only been so lately but it has been so ever since last spring, and it was nothing but that that drove my husband to enlist in the Army. He only went for the sake of having some way to keep his family from starvation."[18] That at least some workers suffered during the war is evident from the *Daily Journal's* continual reference to the "invidious" effects of the administration's soft-money policies. "The laboringman, who Mr. Chase's greenbacks is crushing to the earth by their fictitious character," wrote the *Journal* in January 1864, "should come to the rescue of the country and cry for peace and the return of the hard money era."[19]

It comes as no surprise that Newark voted consistently Democratic during the war years. In 1860 Lincoln gained only forty-five percent of the city's vote, four years later, forty-eight percent. On the state level, the Democratic candidate for senator lost Newark narrowly in 1860 but won handily three years later, while a majority of Newark assemblymen elected annually from 1860 to 1863 were Democrats. Newark voted heavily Democratic in the mayoralty contest of 1861 when incumbent Moses Bigelow received fifty-eight percent. In 1863 Democrat Theodore Runyon received fifty-five percent. The Democratic hold on the city was broken only in November 1865 when Mayor Runyon, then running for governor, lost to his fellow Newarker, Marcus L. Ward, by nearly 1600 votes.[20]

Newark forgot its silent factories and smokeless chimneys in the giddy rush to the colors that followed the Confederate bombardment of Fort Sumter. For a brief time political considerations were abandoned. Six days after Sumter fell, Newark's Common Council, two-thirds Democratic, unanimously resolved "[t]hat it is the high duty of every citizen to ignore all past political issues and promptly and heartily to rally under the banner of the Stars and Stripes." Less than a week later the council again acting unanimously appropriated $100,000 "for the support of the families of our citizens who shall enter the military service" and $5,000 "toward the purchase of suitable clothing for the volunteers."[21] An emotional open-air mass meeting that drew "all classes, professions, sexes and conditions" to the county court house on April 22 heard one speaker after another extoll the Union and decry the Southern insurrectionists. "Party spirit," intoned Joseph P. Bradley, a leading Republican, "is buried deep in the ground. There are no Republicans, no Democrats; we are to-day American citizens, and nothing else." Theodore Runyon, who had cast one of New Jersey's electoral votes for Stephen A. Douglas, spoke for the Democrats. They had gathered as citizens of the Republic, ignoring all party politics, he said, "to counsel upon the great question of upholding the banner of our country." Runyon admitted what everyone in the audience knew: he had opposed Lincoln, and done all he could to keep him from the "Presidential chair." But the election was over, said Runyon, and "he had but one duty now to do, and that was to recognize [Lincoln] as the legal president of the United States, and to support his Government." Before disbanding, the crowd roared its approval of a resolution declaring "that it is the firm, unanimous and unalterable determination of the citizens of Newark, . . . laying aside all party distinctions and associations, to sustain the Government." Within a matter of days after Lincoln's call for three-month volunteers, the city's quota was heavily oversubscribed. Newark's volunteers left for Washington on April 30 under the command of Brigadier General Runyon. "The streets, house-tops and windows along the route were filled with people," reported a local newspaper, "and the troops were constantly cheered." Passing the high school, the regiment halted briefly while the schoolgirls presented the men with a hand-stitched flag.[22] "And thus," wrote a Newark Republican with immense satisfaction, "the people of Newark had grandly answered the slanderous charge . . . that they included 'mercenary and unprincipled men' who cared more for 'Southern trade' and 'the wishes of their Southern masters' than for the . . . indivisibility of the American Union!"[23]

Newark's dalliance with political harmony was as brief as it was ardent, ending abruptly three months later when the chilling news of Bull Run reached the city. On July 21, 1861, an inexperienced Union army under the command of General Irvin McDowell marched toward the railway junction at Manassas, Virginia. Its advance across Bull Run was initially successful, then checked and thrown back by Confederate reinforcements. A withdrawal ordered in late afternoon suddenly turned into a rout as the green troops panicked, threw down their arms, abandoned their supplies, and ran pell-mell for the defenses of Washington. The exhausted and equally inexperienced Confederates could not pursue. An estimated 30,000 Union troops engaged at Bull Run suffered 2,600 casualties. Confederate strength was 33,000, with 2,000 killed, wounded, and missing.

The way Newark's three major dailies treated the Bull Run story speaks volumes about the workings of the city's partisan press. Preliminary telegraphic reports of the battle reaching the *Advertiser*, *Journal*, and *Mercury* on July 22 were confusing at best. Dispatches at first spoke excitedly of Union victory, then told of panic and retreat. The *Advertiser* handled the contradictory accounts as best it could, reporting both the good and the bad news in its July 22 edition. The Confederates, trumpeted its lead story, "after a most desperate and deadly battle," had "finally been compelled to yield to the prowess of our army and fall back in confusion, leaving the field strewn with their dead and dying." A brief paragraph hastily inserted above the lead reported that Confederate reinforcements "opened upon our troops so unexpectedly that they were surprised, and fled panic stricken toward Washington, leaving their batteries, and everything to be captured by the enemy." In succeeding issues the *Advertiser* sorted out the facts more accurately, conceding that Bull Run had been a "calamity" but assuring its readers that accounts of the retreat had been "fearfully exaggerated." Union losses of 600 killed and wounded were to be expected, said the paper, when a force of 20,000 men was "projected against formidable batteries, guarded by 80,000." According to the *Daily Journal*, which had 50,000 Union troops on the field of battle, the Confederate army had "completely routed" Union forces and "driven them with great loss toward the Capital." The carnage on both sides, it said, was "fearful," Union generalship "incompetent," Secession scouts already two miles from Georgetown. Confederate reports of the Bull Run victory taken from the Charleston papers were reprinted without comment.

The *Daily Mercury*, whose news columns pitted 20,000 Union soldiers against 90,000 Rebels, agreed that Bull Run had been a "disaster." Enough is known, said the *Mercury* on July 23, "to warrant the statement that we have suffered in a degree which has cast gloom over the remnants of the army and excited the deepest melancholy throughout Washington. The carnage is tremendously heavy on both sides, and on ours it is represented as frightful." Between 2,500 and 3,000 Union soldiers had been lost, added the paper. The *Mercury* attributed the "original cause of the retreat" to the "misunderstanding" of a telegram ordering Union troops to "retreat a little"; what it persisted in calling the "retrograde movement" of the army was due, it said, to "overwhelming odds" and poor "management."

Newark's papers were quick to draw the lessons of Bull Run. The *Daily Journal* called for peace.

The armies upon either side of this terrible civil war have been successful and have met with repulse. Both have shown a terrible front; yet neither has proved to be invincible. It is hardly possible to exaggerate the ability of either to cripple and injure its antagonist. If the contest should be continued for years the only effect of it would be utter ruin—perhaps anarchy and bloodshed over the whole country. More likely foreign governments will step in and insist that we shall keep the peace, or they may assume a protectorate over the nation.

In view of these contingencies, the people of the North should rest satisfied with their laurels of war, and demand of their rulers an armistice to open

proposals for peace. There is no immediate prospect of carrying out the
programme of Southern subjugation—why not try another tack?

The *Daily Mercury* was by turns intransigent, bellicose, and exultant. A
"great and sudden reverse" had dimmed the glory of the Union, it conceded,
"and our colors . . . to-day hang dishonored." But valuable lessons learned from
defeat would insure tomorrow's victories. "Treason will yet swing at the yard
arm," promised the *Mercury*, and "all rebels compelled to submit or bite the dust
in inglorious death." Bull Run's great "advantage" was "that everywhere the
purpose of the people will be quickened, their estimate of duty enlarged, their
hatred of treason . . . intensified." The North, added the *Mercury*, still did not
fully understand the "wickedness and enormity" of the rebellion:

> We have not measured the full breadth of its causelessness and inhumanity,
> nor sounded the lower depths of its atrocious purpose. We have not . . .
> remembered that piracy, robbery and murder are the chosen weapons, the
> distinguishing outgrowths of this traitorous enterprise against Constitutional
> Government. Now, in the light of later events, we see the truth as it is—we
> realize the more than infernal character of the rebellion. We see the army it
> has rallied butchering our people—firing upon the wounded and defenceless,
> plundering and mutilating the dead—chopping to pieces the exhausted falling
> by the way—in a word committing atrocities which shock the age, and sur-
> pass in enormity even Attila's murderous inhumanity. We shall be the better
> and stronger for thus comprehending more completely the character of the
> foe.

As befitted its reputation, the *Advertiser* expressed a measured view of Bull
Run. While the disaster would prompt "increased energy and preparation on
the part of the Government," said the paper, it should not be cause for doubt
"about the future."

> On the contrary, and we utter the sentiments of the great community on all
> sides of us, as well as our own profound convictions, that never before this
> day, since this rebellion showed its ugly head, have they and we felt so entire
> a confidence in the wonderful daring, fortitude and firmness of our noble
> army, regulars, militia, volunteers and all without exception, as at this very
> moment after a full and deliberate survey of their achievements of the 21st—
> including their panic and flight, and all. The taking and occupation by Bull's
> Run, considering the masked batteries, and how much they were outnum-
> bered by the enemy, was of itself worthy of the veterans of England and
> France.[24]

Newspaper coverage of the First Battle of Bull Run set a pattern that was to
continue throughout the Civil War. The *Advertiser*, the *Journal*, and the *Mercury*
(until its demise) rarely agreed on anything touching the war or politics. It is no

exaggeration to say that each paper reported, and sometimes within its columns fought, a different war.

Newark journalists had been an unruly tribe from the day in May of 1791 when John Wood published the first issue of his Newark *Gazette*. Strictly Federalist in viewpoint, the *Gazette* declined steadily after 1800 when the Republicans became the dominant force in Essex County. The *Gazette* and the Republican *Centinel of Freedom* were vigorous rivals: on one occasion the *Gazette* called the *Centinel* publishers "poltroons" whom it held in "sovereign contempt." Much to the unrestrained joy of its adversaries, the *Gazette* succumbed on December 31, 1804. "This illegitimate child of Federalism," the *Centinel* called it, ". . . was generated by corruption, it progressed in infamy and finally died in disgrace." Newark's second paper, the *Centinel of Freedom* was founded in 1796. As intensely Republican as the *Gazette* was Federalist, the *Centinel* prospered on a diet of anti-Federalist diatribe. Three-quarters of a century later a descendant of Aaron Pennington, owner and editor of the *Centinel* from 1797 to 1799, recalled that the "animosities of party strife did not always expend themselves in mere newspaper squibs, but personal brawls and even street fights were not of infrequent occurrence. In one instance, an editor enfeebled by pulmonary disease [Pennington] was assailed by a robust antagonist [John Wallis, editor of the *Gazette*], and only rescued from violence by a more vigorous brother, who seized the threatening lash and laid it effectually about the shoulders of the assailant." The Newark *Telescope*, a Federalist organ published in 1809 and 1810, the *Tariff Advocate* (1844), a Whig paper, and the *Morning Post* (1843), a Democratic journal, all were short-lived, fiercely partisan newspapers. During the heated presidential campaign of 1828, the *Anti-Jacksonian* (1828) traded heavy blows with the Newark *Intelligencer* (1827–30), a breathless champion of Jackson and Calhoun. The *Intelligencer* in one of its milder moments flayed its rival as a "perfectly irresponsible" paper printed solely for the purpose of "swelling the tide of defamation and slander against the bravest of our citizens, and the truest of patriots." In short, said the *Intelligencer*, "The Anti-Jacksonian will engage to prove . . . that Gen. Jackson can neither read nor write, that he was born in Ireland, of Hottentot parents, and that, since his residence in this country, he has done little else than fight cocks, race horses, and cut off men's ears." No less passionate though somewhat longer-lived was the Newark *Daily Eagle* (1820–57), an ardent defender of the Democratic faith that grew weak and died when its editor espoused the Know-Nothing party. Still another of Newark's political papers was the *Daily Jacksonian*, founded in 1856 by John C. Thornton, a Northerner by birth who had made his fortune in the South. Politically ambitious, Thornton was a Democratic state assemblyman in 1856 and 1857. His staunchly Democratic journal failed a little more than a year after it appeared, and Thornton left the city soon afterward.[25]

Newark's Civil War newspaper readers had a choice of five dailies, two of published in the German language. The New-Jersey *Volksman* (1856–75), by Conrad Hollinger, embraced the Democratic party. Founded by

Benedict Prieth in 1858, the more successful New-Jersey *Freie Zeitung* was an influential voice in Newark Republican circles for three generations. Patriarch of New Jersey journalism was the *Daily Advertiser*, the state's first daily newspaper, founded on March 1, 1832. A "champion of the Whig party," the *Daily* was a "bright quarto-sheet, almost wholly given to the discussion of party politics" when it was first issued by two young Newark politicos. William B. Kinney acquired the paper in 1833, toned down the *Daily*'s partisan rhetoric, and expanded coverage to include state and national news. Kinney also purchased the *Centinel* the same year, making it the *Advertiser*'s weekly edition. A man of literary ambition with nearly a decade of editorial experience in both New York and New Jersey, Kinney made the *Daily* New Jersey's most influential paper. For many years the *Daily* was New Jersey's only newspaper outside of Trenton to assign a correspondent to state-house affairs. Joseph P. Bradley, later an associate justice of the United States Supreme Court, began his career as Kinney's man in Trenton. Kinney occasionally dabbled in Whig politics, although characteristically he preferred the role of observer. In 1840 he was elected a delegate to the Whig national convention, but refused to attend. Four years later he was chosen delegate at large, condescended to attend, and was credited with the choice of his close friend, Theodore Frelinghuysen, as Clay's running mate. Kinney was nominated as the Whig candidate for Congress from the Fifth District in 1843. After a bruising campaign, the Democrat, William Wright, was elected by a coalition of Democrats, Whigs, and Independents. Kinney's party loyalty had its reward in 1851 when President Zachary Taylor appointed him United States minister to the Kingdom of Sardinia. [26]

Kinney's son and successor at the *Daily*, Thomas T. Kinney, was inclined to concentrate on the business of running the family paper. Acknowledged by his contemporaries as a pioneer of journalism, Kinney was the first publisher in the state to introduce high-speed steam-powered presses. He helped found the New York Associated Press, to which the *Daily* subscribed, and in 1852 installed New Jersey's first telegraphic news service. Publisher of the *Daily* until 1893, Kinney was a powerful figure in Newark business circles. A member of the Board of Trade, he was director of the National State Bank and one of the founders of the Newark Electric Light and Power Company. Unlike so many of his fellow editors and publishers, Kinney held himself aloof from public and party office. With one exception, he refused all offers, including the post of minister to Italy proffered by Secretary of State James G. Blaine in 1881. Kinney's solitary trip to the political altar came in 1860, when he was a delegate to the Republican national convention. In Chicago Kinney spared none of his considerable influence within the New Jersey delegation to advance the nomination of Abraham Lincoln. Although himself a thoroughgoing Whig and later a Republican, Kinney refused to publish a "political paper." His editors, among them Samuel K. Gardner, Charles D. Deshler, and Dr. Sanford B. Hunt, w chosen more for their newspaper skills than their political views. Durin war the paper supported the Union Republican cause, reserving the ri differ from the administration or the party when conscience dictated. The *Daily*'s circulation in the 1860s was over 4,000, making it the largest paper in New Jersey at that time. Read throughout the state, moderate in its tone, and carefully edited, the *Daily* "spoke with the voice of one having authority— almost with the effect of a lawgiver."[27]

Newark's other two dailies never pretended to be anything but partisan. The Daily *Mercury* was founded on January 12, 1849, by William H. Winans, a wealthy Newark printer and Free-Soiler. His first editor was William E. Robinson, a native of Ireland and a well-known political writer for the New York *Tribune*. No sooner had it established itself than the *Mercury* pitched into battle with the Democratic *Eagle*. Robinson and the editor of the *Eagle*, Charles K. Bishop, a South Carolina native, matched words and wits in what was until then Newark's greatest newspaper rivalry. "Bishop and Robinson," wrote Joseph Atkinson, himself a Newark newspaperman, "handled each other without much regard for the amenities of journalism or of common politeness." At one point the *Mercury* likened the *Eagle* to a cornered animal that in desperation throws its own droppings at its enemy. Understandably outraged, the *Eagle* fumed that its adversary "has got itself into such bad odor, for it renders its position toward the *Eagle* shockingly offensive, in more sense than one!" Added Bishop: "Wouldn't a little Cologne be acceptable to you, neighbor?"[28]

Robinson's successor at the *Mercury* was Horace N. Congar, a native-born Newarker who had studied law and gained admission to the bar in 1847. Early in 1848 Congar closed the doors to his law office forever, joining a handful of staunch antislavery men to organize New Jersey's Free-Soil party. Attending the Buffalo Free-Soil convention, Congar cheered the nomination of Martin Van Buren for president on a platform that advocated "the rights of free labor against the aggressions of the slave power" Congar returned to Newark to edit the *Free Soil Standard*, a campaign paper issued from September to November, 1848.[29] In 1850 he joined the *Mercury*. Under his leadership the paper fought vigorously against the spread of slavery, embracing the Republican party in the mid-1850s. According to Joseph Atkinson, Congar was "a political writer of great pungency, who exercised for many years a powerful influence in shaping the public policy of New Jersey."[30] Congar's Abolitionist views led him to throw his vigorous support behind the candidacy of William H. Seward in 1860. Seward, he wrote, was a man of "positive, outspoken stamp." Congar labeled Seward's opponents, presumably including Lincoln, "those negatives and imbeciles, whose political status needs to be determined by special bulletins from irresponsible admirers."[31] As a delegate to the Chicago Republican convention, Congar fought as tirelessly for Seward as Kinney did for Lincoln When the New Jersey delegation swung to the Illinoisan on the third ballot, Congar stubbornly refused to change his vote.

Swallowing his immense disappointment, Congar placed the *Mercury* squarely behind Lincoln's candidacy. Congar himself labored tirelessly for Lincoln's victory as a member of the "Opposition" party state executive committee.

After the president's inauguration, Congar met in Washington with the new secretary of state, none other than William H. Seward, to resolve the patronage claims of the state's Republicans. Congar's appointment as United States consul at Hong Kong, a post in which he served until the end of the war, was widely viewed as a reward for his determined support of Seward.

Throughout its fifteen-year history the *Mercury* was kept afloat with loans and contributions from Newark Abolitionists and Republican business and professional men. Sheer determination substituted for profit: The *Mercury*'s circulation of some 1,500 copies barely met expenses, and when Congar's vigorous editorials drove advertisers away, as they all too frequently did, the paper had to limp along on a day-to-day basis. Moreover, county and municipal legal advertising, then an important source of newspaper revenue, went largely to the *Advertiser* and the *Journal* even when the Republicans were in power. Congar's salary during his decade as editor was meager. After he accepted the $3,000-a-year Hong Kong post, he had to turn to his friend, Marcus L. Ward, for money to make the voyage to China.[32] When Congar sold his interest in the *Mercury* to his partner, Daniel Porter, in the spring of 1861, the paper was $16,000 in debt, nearly half that amount owed to Theodore P. Howell, a wealthy Newark patent-leather manufacturer. Former three-term Newark mayor and incumbent Republican state senator, James M. Quinby, owner of the city's largest carriage factory, was another major creditor.[33]

The *Mercury*'s new editor was thirty-year-old John Y. Foster, a staff member since 1853. Foster was a forceful writer, an effective public speaker, and a Republican from the day the party was organized in Newark. Although he enjoyed none of Congar's reputation or his ability to wheedle loans from wealthy businessmen, Foster was a sound newspaperman and as strongly partisan as his predecessor.[34] On September 21, 1861, Daniel Porter wrote at length to his former partner in Hong Kong:

> I was somewhat apprehensive that when the great centre of attraction had left we should at once lose the reputation we had previously enjoyed both as a party organ and as the place where schemes were concocted and carried through, as well as plans divulged and frustrated, but our nightly visitors are even more numerous than ever while John [Foster] peppers away with all the impetuosity which has ever characterized him. Our friends say the paper is better than ever before.[35]

The *Mercury* had always been suspicious of the *Advertiser*'s Republicanism. Indeed, a Democrat critical of both papers claimed that the *Mercury* had been established to counter the "lukewarm course" of its rival.[36] In the summer of 1860, when the *Advertiser* supported Lincoln and the *Mercury*, Seward, editors Kinney and Congar clashed regularly. The Mercury Clique, as Congar's friends and associates were known, waxed livid in early December 1860 when the *Advertiser* editorially endorsed the idea that the South be allowed to depart the

Union in peace.[37] The *Mercury*'s suspicions were confirmed in mid-1861 when Charles D. Deshler, who had worked for the Constitutional Union ticket of Bell and Everett in the presidential campaign, was named editor of the *Advertiser*. Wrote Porter to Congar:

Tom [Kinney], as I expected, is endeavoring to assume the political importance so long enjoyed by you, but as he hasn't brains enough to last till sundown, he is likely to fail. His very position, however, as editor of the Daily gives him some importance. He is more jealous of the Mercury than ever, and in all his movements, appears to have but one object, that of striking at some of the "Clique."[38]

Why Kinney, the owner of New Jersey's largest paper, would be "jealous" of an ailing competitor Porter fails to explain. A letter signed by "A Conservative" published in the *Daily Journal* nearly three years later tends to confirm, however, the intensity of the rivalry.

The effect of the establishment of the *Mercury* . . . created a feeling of bitter rivalry and intense jealousy; after degenerating into positive hostilities between the two papers. The *Mercury* became a perpetual torment to the *Advertiser*, and was a perpetual club held over its head to force it to pursue a prescribed course or to admit certain articles into its columns. This rivalry extended to every department of their business; they never asked or granted favors to one another; and they looked with disfavor upon their respective patrons and adherents. The "*Mercury* clique" was a perpetual nightmare to the *Advertiser;* and although it was often forced to yield to their dictation, it ever did so sullenly and with an ill grace. . . . [F]or a time the strife for preeminence was very active and bitter—the *Mercury* frequently casting slurs upon the *Advertiser*, and the *Advertiser* repaying it with increased aversion, privately expressed, for the *Mercury* clique, which was so troublesome a "thorn in its flesh."[39]

The Porter-Congar letters offer an insider's view of the ways of journalism in Civil War New Jersey. Porter and Foster kept the *Mercury* on its feet through most of 1861 but when a Democratic mayor and sheriff were elected in November, they realized they could continue the paper no longer. "The result of the election," wrote Porter to Congar, "of course crushed what remaining hopes I had entertained of being able to keep the Mercury going because the loss of the City patronage and the Sheriff's included, rendered it worse than hopeless." Soon after the election, Porter conferred with Newark attorney Daniel Dodd, Jr., the unsuccessful Opposition candidate for mayor two years before, on ways to keep the *Mercury* alive. As a result of their meeting, a circular letter signed by Anthony Q. Keasbey, United States Attorney for New Jersey, Ira M. Harrison, a well-off patent-leather manufacturer and former Republican assemblyman, and John C. Beardsley, another former assemblyman, was sent to fifty leading Republicans and Unionists. Some forty of them met, agreed that the

Mercury must be continued, and appointed Dodd, Essex County Prosecutor Cortlandt Parker, and Marcus L. Ward a committee of three to develop new financing. Among the chief supporters of the *Mercury* at this crucial period, besides those already mentioned, were Judge Charles R. Waugh, Luther S. Goble, an attorney and state agent for the Mutual Life Insurance Company of New York, George W. Richards, a doctor from Orange, and Lewis C. Grover, a former assemblyman and vice-president of Mutual Benefit Life Insurance Company. So little progress was made by Dodd's committee, however, that Porter threatened to suspend publication on December 31, 1861. On New Year's Eve Porter agreed to continue the paper after the general committee, meeting in emergency session, voted to raise $1000 immediately. Essex County Sheriff Elias N. Miller's proposal that he assume the paper's management on a six-month trial basis was accepted with gratitude and relief. Although Porter's indebtedness had by now risen to $17,000, what he called "the new management" gave him hope the *Mercury* could be continued. "The Advertiser folks are terribly worried," he told Congar on January 12, 1862, "as they for the first time in their lives feel that we are after them."[40]

Porter's new confidence lasted little more than two months. On March 19, 1862, he complained to Congar that

> the Mercury in the hands of E. N. Miller is not what it used to be. He is a capital businessman, but he is no more fit to be editor of the Mercury than Tom Kinney. And in this he has made a grand mistake. He has attempted too much. Instead of giving his readers the strong pointed paragraphs to which they have become accustomed, he touches matters gingerly, and compels John to write gingerly, to multiply words without saying anything, for fear of offending somebody or losing a subscriber.

The *Mercury*, according to Porter, was no longer the conscience of the Radical Republican movement.

> Since you left, the party in the State as well as in this city, have been entirely at sea, tossed about without either compass or rudder. The press of the State who used to take their texts from the Mercury, who regarded that paper as indicating the policies to the pursued, now look in vain for a line, a word or even a hint as to what to advocate or what to denounce. It is true there hasn't been much to say on political subjects, save an earnest support of the measures of the Government, but our old party friends . . . [know] that the time will soon arrive when an important election will be upon us, and when it will be necessary that a given line of policy shall be pursued.[41]

Ex-Sheriff Miller bought the *Mercury* for $1,000 in March 1862 despite Porter's "faint hope" that Howell, its largest creditor, might agree to take it over. Needless to say, Porter was left with enormous debts and no apparent means of paying them. "I never felt so sick of human nature in my life, as I did when t bargain was closed," Porter wrote in June 1862. "However, it has gone, past redemption, and we are both left to see another reap the fruit of our toil and suffering."[42]

Although a complete stranger to journalism, the paper's new owner was a well-known and popular politician and shrewd businessman. An auctioneer before the war, Miller had served three successive terms as Essex County sheriff before declining to run again in November 1861. Miller, whose victory margin of nearly 2,000 votes in 1860 was one of the best Republican showings to that time in Essex County, was commissioner of the draft for the county in 1862–1863 and served on the county executive committee of the Loyal Union League in 1863.[43] His Republican credentials were impeccable, he was affluent, and he had the good sense to retain Porter as the paper's manager and Foster as its editor. New presses and larger quarters to replace what Porter called the paper's "tumble-down" office on Market Street gave the *Mercury* a semblance of prosperity. Porter's lament that Miller drew back from controversy out of fear of losing subscribers is not borne out by a review of the *Mercury*'s final two years. Copperheads in general and the *Daily Journal* in particular were its favorite targets of opportunity. The *Mercury* lashed out almost daily at the *Journal*, scorning it on one occasion as "that organ of secession sentiment by which this community is outraged and humiliated."[44] The *Mercury*'s reputation as New Jersey's leading Radical Republican journal was untarnished during Foster's editorship. Before the war many Newarkers had found the paper's editorials both politically offensive and potentially damaging to the city's Southern trade. The paper was no less unpopular during the war among those who laid the blame for secession at the feet of the Radicals. At the height of Newark's draft riots in July 1863 an ugly mob turned its fury on the *Mercury*, breaking windows and tearing off the office door. One lone Newark policeman who managed to find a flag and fly it from a window saved the building from destruction. Later the mob surged through the streets to Miller's home, and amid shouts of "Hang him!," hurled a heavy barrage of stones at its windows and doors.[45]

Financial problems continued to plague the *Mercury* even under Miller's ownership. On December 31, 1863, the paper breathed its last. The *Advertiser* observed its passing only briefly, noting with some envy that the *Mercury* had lasted as long as it had "by the extraordinary and combined efforts of many sagacious managers, aided by a diversity of interests, with contributions of capital from time to time, such as has rarely fallen to the lot of any similar enterprise."[46] Sarcasm fairly oozed from the *Daily Journal*'s obituary of its erstwhile rival:

> Newark has taken its last dose of Mercury. For many years past a few of our citizens have deemed the city in a physical condition requiring a daily dose of this renovating and searching medicament, and they have cheerfully paid the expenses and forced the nauseous drug down the corporate throat, which has been sometimes swallowed with a wry face, but oftener evacuated

without any perceptible influence upon the body politic. Not a few of our citizens recollect how Mr. Congar, while he occupied the post of physician-in-ordinary, by the grace of the Abolition party, employed all his genial facilities to sugar-coat the bitter pill which it was his business daily . . . to issue. . . . But even under his admirable system of practice, the medicine failed to work the required cure, and Mr. Congar was transported to Hong Kong, China, where he now enjoys a more profitable practice, viz.: that of pocketing greenbacks. . . . After he left his post . . . the business finally fell into the hands of E. N. Miller, Esq., who has daily administered his pills without the sugarcoating in which Congar used to disguise his doses. This change in the practice was too much for the long-suffering patients, who had been dosed time out of mind, and with one accord they threw the Provost Marshal's physic to the dogs.[47]

The Newark *Daily Journal* sprang from the ruins of the *Daily Eagle* and the *Jacksonian* on November 2, 1857. William Wright, the paper's principal owner until late 1861, had made an "immense fortune" in the saddlery and harness business in Newark. A Whig originally, he was mayor of Newark from 1841 to 1843, a congressman from 1843 to 1847, and a candidate for governor in 1847, losing to the Democrat, Daniel Haines. A delegate to the 1848 Whig national convention and an admirer of Henry Clay, he gradually lost faith in his party when it equivocated on the slavery issue, becoming a Democrat after the Compromise of 1850. Wright's political fortunes were unaffected by his about-face. In 1853 the Democrats in the state legislature elected him to the United States Senate, where he served one term. When the Democrats were back in power in 1863, he was again elected, serving in the Senate until his death in November 1866. Seriously ill from heart disease during his latter years, Wright sold the *Journal* in the fall of 1861 to a stock company headed by John C. Denman, a Newark carriage dealer and former one-term state assemblyman. Wright continued to underwrite the *Journal* with liberal infusions of cash even after Denman's company took control.[48] The paper was apparently no more a financial success than the *Mercury*, however. "For more than a decade the *Journal* had a hard battle for existence," wrote Joseph Atkinson, himself editor of the paper in the postwar period. "It was constantly cramped financially. Once or twice it came to the brink of the fate of its forerunners . . . and once was forced to suspend temporarily."[49] The *Journal*'s one advantage was Wright's fortune and, after 1861, the deep pockets of Newark's Democratic business community.

Editor of the *Journal* from 1857 to 1865 and again from 1866 to 1871 was Edward N. Fuller, a New Hampshire native "of the strongest Democratic proclivities" who began his journalistic career as a printer's apprentice two decades before the Civil War. C. Chauncey Burr, editor of *The Old Guard*, and Colonel James T. Wall, a fiery Peace Democrat, were both regular contributors to the paper's wartime columns.[50] Under Fuller the *Daily Journal* was an object of pure hatred to New Jersey Republicans. The *Mercury* in a moment of kindness called it "venomous."[51] An angry crowd stormed the paper's offices in

1862, threatening mayhem unless the national colors were flown from its flag-pole. Many Democrats were equally repelled by its imprudence, and some found it "obnoxious."[52] But Fuller was a man of fearless conviction and strong words. Lincoln, in one of Fuller's favorite phrases, was a "smutty joker." The war, he wrote, was a bloody failure that would end with the conquest of the North by the South.[53] "Abolition fanaticism and its kindred heresies must be crushed out," wrote Fuller in early 1864 even as thousands of newly freed Blacks donned the Union blue, "and practical common sense views of our social and civil institutions [must] take the place of the destructive and revolutionary theories of the present day."[54]

After Lincoln, the Republicans, and the war, Fuller's favorite adversary was the *Daily Mercury*, for which he reserved his sharpest barbs. Typical was an exchange of editorial broadsides in August 1862. The *Mercury* opened the battle when it lambasted "the treasonable course of that organ of secession sentiment." Fuller replied with a heavy cannonade. The *Mercury*, he wrote, was "sad, doleful, and evidently miserable."

> Its waking moments are troubled with secessionists and its dreams are haunted with visions of "spectres and chimeras dire." It sees Stonewall Jackson lurking in a harmless cup—treason upon every street and in every pleasure excursion. . . .
>
> The poor *Mercury* is in a very bad way. Under the regime of Mr. Congar, there was a genial tone visible through all its political heresies, which some-what relieved its unpalatable and unpopular features. But now it is one dull, weary waste of blackness and darkness. It has outlived its patronage, its brains and even its party, with the exception of a handful of abolitionists and government officers, and being envious of the popularity and success of the *Journal*, seeks to get up a clamor against us in order that our property may be confiscated to support its failing fortunes. . . .
>
> What a delightful picture of these times is exhibited by the howling dervish of the *Mercury*. Everything is going wrong with himself and his party, and he would drag down the whole world with him to the infernal regions, and reading the hand-writing on the wall, it will waste the few days still alloted to it in cursing the Democracy and the Constitution, until it has finished its Tory work and lies buried in popular oblivion, never more to trouble the people.

Two days later the paper derided *Mercury* editor John Y. Foster as a "great war orator." Foster, sniggered the *Journal*, had told a Union rally that the Copperhead paper ought to be suspended and its editor jailed.

> We thank Mr. Foster for his kind wishes in our behalf; but has he yet enlisted? He never loses an opportunity to ventilate his eloquence before the ladies in behalf of the war, but continues to dodge the responsibilities of the service, while urging the entire community to fall into the ranks and buckle on their arms. What keeps this valiant Boaneges at home. . . ? If Foster is as

anxious to get us in Fort Lafayette as we are for him to stop blowing and
threatening, and back up his windy editorials and speeches in favor of the
war, for the credit of the editorial craft we might consent for that watering
place, provided Foster would shoulder his gun and knapsack and march to
Dixie, keeping step with his favorite tune, "Old John Brown." But if fear
deters him from rushing to defend his "sacred cause" at the cannon's mouth,
the ladies should raise a subscription to get up the young man a petticoat, in
which to appear at all war meetings in future.[55]

From time to time the *Journal* lobbed an explosive at the *Advertiser* as well. In
July 1862, after an *Advertiser* editorial scorned Copperhead peace pleas as "absurd" and "senseless," the *Journal* gleefully reminded its readers that Kinney's
paper had itself once urged a peaceful separation of the states if that were the
only means of avoiding bloodshed.[56] When the *Advertiser* published what it
called "disloyal" Copperhead letters in June of 1864, the *Journal* again cited
Kinney's earlier "secession proclivities." Kinney's refusal to rise to the bait irked
Fuller no end. Other Republican journals, he complained, "do not think it
inconsistent with their dignity to break the lance with an opponent" or engage
in "discussions, and attacks, and rejoinders." But Kinney, whom Fuller could
never drag into battle, did "not consider it dignified to respond to attacks."

> The plea of dignity, by which [the *Advertiser*] preserves a safe silence when
> pushed into a corner, is merely a convenient cover and cloak to hide its own
> timidity, lack of manly spirit and want of ability, or to conceal the badness of
> the cause it advocates. . . . An adversary may tweak its nose with perfect
> impunity, or lay on the lash or apply the retributive kick, and yet the *Adver-
> tiser* . . . makes no sign. To defend itself would be to endanger its brittle and
> fragile dignity. It prefers, like a windy poltroon of old, to maintain its charac-
> ter for "deportment" by yielding. . . . And it is a very safe, very convenient
> and very easy, but we must be excused for saying, very pusillanimous pol-
> icy.[57]

Fuller's passion for "attacks and rejoinders" finally led to his arrest on July 21,
1864, on charges of inciting insurrection. Lincoln's call for 500,000 draftees
infuriated Fuller. His editorial of July 19, published in the same issue with the
president's proclamation, called for resistance.

> It will be seen that Mr. Lincoln has called for another half million men.
> Those who desire to be butchered will please step forward at once. All others
> will stay at home and defy Old Abc and his minions to drag them from their
> families. We hope that the people of New Jersey will at once put their feet
> down and insist that not a man shall be forced out of the State to engage in
> this abolition butchery and swear to die at their own doors rather than march
> one step to fulfill the dictates of that mad revolutionary fanaticism. . . . This
> has gone far enough and must be stopped. Let the people rise as one man and
> demand that this wholesale murder shall cease.[58]

The following day the *Journal* spoke encouragingly of a national antidraft movement soon to be formed. On July 21, as rumors flew that Fuller was about to be arrested, he challenged the government "to suppress the *Journal* and place its editor in one of the convenient bastiles at the command of Old Abe."

We court the fullest investigation of our record as the conductor of a popular newspaper during the war, and if an opportunity is allowed us, shall not fail to ventilate to some extent the history of the super-loyal men of this city, who have never ceased to charge us with being a traitor of the deepest dye, who have incessantly abused us in the vilest terms and sought in every possible way to secure the destruction of a press which has boldly spoken the truth in regard to the tyrants and revolutionists in power. . . .

As to the threats of Fort Lafayette, they do not materially disturb our equanimity or peace of mind. . . . We have no honeyed words for such a ruler as Abraham Lincoln who . . . is a perjured traitor, who has betrayed his country and caused the butchery of hundreds of thousands of the people of the United States, in order to accomplish his own selfish purposes, or to put in force a fanatical, impractical idea.

We shall continue to advance by all legitimate means . . . a union of the people against this accursed Administration. We shall never seem to favor a measure which we regard as utterly wrong, however others may see fit to trim their speech to the demands of the usurpers in power. We shall never sing paens to this wretched abolition war . . . nor advocate the raising of money to allow the butchers at Washington to spill more blood. We shall not eulogize the draft as a merciful institution for the benefit of patriotic poor men, or insult their intelligence and manhood by urging them to submit tamely to be dragged from their families. And we say to the Administration at Washington, and to its minions, civil and military: "If this be treason, make the most of it."[59]

Federal authorities were careful to deny Fuller the imprisonment and consequent martyrdom he so obviously courted. After he was indicted, arrested, and released on $7,000 bail, his case was delayed for months. Finally he appeared before the United States District Court on February 15, 1865, pleaded guilty on the advice of his attorneys and was fined $100. Fuller's arrest was an issue in the 1864 presidential campaign in the state, but not a major one. His guilty plea, entered as Confederate armies were everywhere in retreat, attracted little attention.[60] The *Journal* kept up its opposition to the war, in somewhat muted tones, through the end of 1864.

Fuller resigned as editor of the *Journal* on April 15, 1865, ironically the very day the *Advertiser* and the *Journal* printed the news of Lincoln's assassination. His farewell editorial insinuated that his publishers had forced him out, not an unreasonable conclusion in light of the collapse of Southern resistance. They were now claiming, he wrote, the right to dictate editorial policy "while refusing to specify any cause of complaint as to our conduct." A "series of annoying incidents," added Fuller, did little to "enhance our opinion of the present management of the affairs of the *Journal*." Fuller left his post wih no excuses for his conduct during the war.

> What we have written and published has been dictated in an independent spirit by an honest and patriotic desire for the welfare of our beloved country. . . . What ever faults may have occurred in the execution and promulgation of these ideas will not, we are assured, be charged to mercenary motives . . . ; nor have we at any time waived the presentation of those great constitutional principles which have always been regarded by our wisest statesmen as essential to the maintenance of a free republican government. On the contrary, it has sometimes during the past four years been our fate to contend with the objection originating, we regret to say, in leading Democratic circles, that we have carried the old standard of the Democracy too high at the mast head; that our policy has been too unflinchingly straightforward and unbending to secure the highest temporary success and the largest degree of popular favor.[61]

The *Journal* survived as Newark's only Democratic daily for another generation, finally expiring from a lack of patronage on December 5, 1894.

One of the more intriguing chapters in the history of New Jersey journalism, one that sheds considerable light on the Civil War party press, has been long forgotten. While the *Mercury* yet lived, it "unhesitatingly" claimed for itself "the position of being the only daily journal published in this section of New Jersey not under Democratic influences."[62] Considered by modern historians a Union Republican paper, the *Advertiser* was repeatedly accused by Radical Republicans and even some Unionists of harboring secession sympathies. Both William and Thomas Kinney labored to make the *Advertiser* distinctively less partisan than its competitors, and thus more acceptable to a wider body of readers. They believed, correctly as it turned out, that there was a large market for a "dignified" paper that, while inclined toward one party, was not blatantly political. On that premise they built the state's most respected and probably its only consistently profitable newspaper.

So far as many Republicans were concerned, however, the Kinneys succeeded only too well. During the critical war years Radical Republicans especially were disappointed that the *Advertiser* withheld its unqualified support of the administration. A Democrat writing in the *Daily Journal* in mid-1864 described matters this way:

> It is well known that for many years past the political course of the *Advertiser* has not been satisfactory to the party with which it was ostensibly acting in concert. It was too cold . . . ; it refused to do the dirty work of the party, and elected, as a matter of business policy . . . to enact a conservative role, and while lending a feeble support to its own pary, not to offend the Democratic party. Thus it hoped to secure patronage and favor from both sides, and it succeeded. It was also a part of the policy of the *Advertiser* . . . to avoid those excitements and wranglings which are expected from a positive party organ.[63]

When Kinney named Charles D. Deshler editor of the *Advertiser* in 1861, New Jersey Republicans were livid, for Deshler was a Democrat and an active one to boot. A New Brunswick druggist, Deshler had served as corresponding secretary of the National Council of the American or Know-Nothing party in 1854–56. In 1859 he moved to Jersey City to become editor of the *Standard*, a moderate Democratic paper that endorsed Bell and Everett for president in 1860. Deshler was anathema to Newark Republicans in particular after he supported Nehemiah Perry over William Pennington in the race for Congress from the Fifth District, which comprised Hudson, Essex, and Union counties. Perry's victory in Hudson, large enough to offset Pennington's slim margin in Essex, was laid at Deshler's feet.[64] Five weeks after the presidential election, as the gravity of the national crisis became more apparent, leaders of the Democratic party convened at the State House in Trenton to approve resolutions blaming "Northern agitators," that is, Republicans and Abolitionists, for "the present portentious crisis." Deshler not only signed the call for the convention but served on the committee with Judge Naar, former Governor Price, and four others that prepared the resolutions.[65] Deshler's appointment to the *Advertiser* seriously undermined the paper's Republican credentials in the eyes of party stalwarts.

Hardly had the *Mercury* expired on December 31, 1863, than rumors began circulating that it was to be revived. "There were reports of fabulous amounts pledged to this end," wrote the *Journal's* correspondent, "and it was known that influential men of the [Republican] party had made pilgrimages to Washington to secure public patronage."[66] The rumors remained just that until the spring of 1864 when the old "Mercury Clique," in concert with the Union League Council of Essex County, began canvassing for subscribers and advertisers for a new paper. According to the *Journal's* correspondent, whose account is confirmed by independent evidence, "[T]hey gave out that they had fabulous sums upon it, varying from $30,000 to $100,000, that it was to be a thorough-going, 'root and branch,' 'hip and thigh' concern; and that it would be quickly put into operation. This maneuver was at once reported to the *Advertiser* folk and they were mortally scared."[67] The impending Republican convention in Baltimore on June 7 and 8 spurred the project's organizers as much as did the *Advertiser's* ominous silence on the subject of Lincoln's renomination. "The *Advertiser* had made no sign," wrote the *Journal's* contributor. "It talked of everything in heaven above, the earth beneath, and the waters under the earth, but said nothing about 'Uncle Abe.' He was as completely ignored as if he belonged to the antidiluvian period."[68]

Whether Kinney was "mortally scared" by the prospect of renewed competition will probably never be known. He was sufficiently moved, however, to write twice to Daniel Dodd, Jr., one of the principle organizers, suggesting that the *Advertiser* might serve the purposes of the organizing committee better than a new paper. On June 8 Dodd's committee replied to Kinney, asserting that their "new political paper" would be operated upon "the general and well recognized principle that in a city like this every political party, in order to exert its due influence must have an organ which shall advocate its views and aid its purposes." The committee was quite candid about its "political views" and the "means by which we propose to accomplish our objects," so candid in fact that Kinney must have winced as he read Dodd's prospectus:

1. Our paper shall earnestly support the administration in its measures and efforts to suppress the rebellion . . .

2. It shall zealously sustain such candidates for official positions in the city, county and state as may be nominated by the recognized authorities of the party. It shall . . . maintain the views of the party in all municipal affairs.

3. No person holding opposite political sentiments from ours shall, directly or indirectly, have any connection with or control over the editorial column or department of the paper. The working and all other members of the party shall at all times feel at liberty to visit our office for purposes of consultation, acquiring or imparting information. . . .

4. In matters of . . . principle and policy, such views as may be fairly said to be those of the party, shall have their just influence on the tone of the paper, while the paper shall be entitled to the cordial support of the party.

Kinney's "intimation" that the *Advertiser* "may be made to answer the purposes we have in view," said the committee, might just persuade it to drop its project provided "the same objects can in that way be attained." Assuring Kinney that it meant "to suggest or propose nothing inconsistent with the high position and character" of the *Advertiser*, the committee concluded on an incongruous note: "We should deplore as much as you could," it wrote, "that [the *Advertiser*] should ever sink from that position, or, degenerate into an instrument of partizan [*sic*] bitterness or individual advancement." Besides Dodd, the letter was signed by Anthony Q. Keasby and Ira M. Harrison, both associated with Dodd in the ill-fated effort to keep the *Mercury* afloat, and by Joseph P. Bradley, a prominent Newark attorney, Emil Schuiffner, another attorney and ardent German-American Abolitionist, Cornelius Walsh, a carpetbag manufacturer, Henry J. Mills, provost marshal of the Fifth Congressional District, Dr. James A. Cross, E. B. Whitehead, an active member of the Union League, Monroe Porter, formerly with the *Mercury*, and Samuel P. Smith, the owner of a Newark varnish factory.[69]

Kinney's reply was penned the day after the *Advertiser* put to rest Republican concerns by endorsing Lincoln's bid for renomination. Noting that he found "no difference between us as to the principles involved in the approaching campaign," Kinney cited his endorsement of Lincoln as evidence that he had "fully committed myself, and dedicated the paper to a vigorous and unreserved support of the candidates and platform" of the Baltimore convention. Wrote Kinney:

As incidental to the bigger object I of course recognize the claims of those engaged in promoting the same cause, and whoever may become their standard bearers in this or more local contests will have my unreserved and hearty support as I shall expect to receive theirs and yours to strengthen me for the common good—for we should all remember that in the appalling crisis which now threatens our liberties, our property and all our dearest rights, our national salvation depends in a great measure upon the zeal and fidelity which the friends of Republican institutions sustain each other. We can no longer afford divisions nor lukewarmness—especially in this community.

It therefore remains for me only to say that our general objects being the same, I cannot believe that any serious difference can occur between us as to details. . . . Meanwhile, let me ask you and all who are interested in the same cause to favor me with your counsel and aid, assuring you that you shall have mine as freely and unreservedly whenever it may be needed.[70]

We have only the partisan comments of the *Journal's* correspondent to tell what happened next.

Negotiations were at once opened, and the *Advertiser* was given to understand that if it would come out flat-footed as a party organ, accept an editor who should be dictated to them by the "*Mercury* clique," and discharge Mr. Deshler. . . . the opposition paper should not be started. . . . The *Advertiser* hesitated. It was willing to go the whole figure for the party; but the terms dictated to it . . . were most galling and offensive. It was true that Mr. Deshler was a Democrat, but he had nothing to do with the political opinions of the *Advertiser*. . . . But it was urged by the "*Mercury* clique" that he was a Democrat . . . and that he wrote political articles for the Jersey City *Standard* and other Democratic journals. Therefore he must be proscribed. His removal was demanded as a *sine qua non;* and again the club of the new paper was raised over the devoted and shrinking head of the *Advertiser*.[71]

Deshler's subsequent resignation and Kinney's appointment of John Y. Foster to the editor's chair led to the abandonment of the newspaper scheme. Whatever accommodations were reached between Kinney and the committee can only be conjectured, although Kinney's acceptance of the former *Mercury* editor was a major concession in itself. An assistant editor at the New York *Evening Post* and *Harper's Weekly* after the *Mercury* folded, Foster's newspaper credentials were supurb; it was his uncompromising partisanship that surely must have made Kinney swallow hard.[72]

The *Journal's* correspondent called Foster's appointment "a grand victory for the *Mercury clique*."

The *Advertiser* will henceforth be controlled by that influence—which it has always hitherto hated and feared. . . . Whether the title "*Mercury*" will be added to that of the *Advertiser*, I am unable to say; but there can be no doubt that, in any event, the "*Mercury*" will rise again—phoenix-like—from its ashes, and will enter upon the political arena with renewed vigor, on a capital ready furnished to its hand, without the necessity of its friends administering to it the periodical pecuniary "bleeding" which was the principal feature of its old existence.[73]

Printed on June 18, the *Journal's* embarrassing revelations provoked an immediate denial of sorts from Kinney himself. On the 20th, the following notice appeared directly beneath the *Advertiser* masthead:

> In order to correct recent misrepresentations and prevent future misunderstandings, we deem it proper to state that no change has been made or contemplated in the management of the *Daily Advertiser*. It will continue to be conducted, as it has been for years past, by the undersigned as its sole editor, and manager of every department, subject to no control, and influenced only by such considerations as the best interests of the nation, and this community especially, may from time to time require.
>
> Thomas T. Kinney[74]

Kinney's disclaimer aside, a deal had in fact been made. On October 1, 1864, Monroe Porter, a member of the organizing committee, wrote to his old friend in Hong Kong, Horace Congar.

> The arrangement with the "Advertiser" was the best that could have been made under the circumstances but it has not as yet proven to be what was confidently expected by the parties to the arrangement, and it is far from being satisfactory to the working Boys of the Party. Foster is not fitted for a Politician, at least the kind of Politician which we so much need in New Jersey. He does very well to be subordinated to a more better, sagacious, prudent and far seeing politician than himself. . . . Besides the antecedents and associations and surroundings of the Advertiser are not all satisfactory or congenial to the working boys that used to congregate at the old Mercury office during the political campaigns of the past. Even the fact that Foster sits in [the] Editorial chair and the paper itself [is] practically under the control of the old "Mercury Clique" does [not] suffice. Our boys hate Tom Kinney thoroughly. They say they will have nothing to do with a man who employed the man as his Editor who did so much to defeat Gov. Pennington. . . . I have no faith in Tom Kinney as a Republican Union man. I believe that notwithstanding his fair promises and his humiliating concessions to the "Mercury Clique," he hates them and will hit them whenever he can. He plainly saw that something must be done to squelch the new paper enterprise, and the only way to do it was to accept unconditionally our terms. I know he thought the movement for a new paper was too formidable to be trifled with. And now he thinks he has effectively closed the door against any future attempts to start a new paper.[75]

Porter made no secret of his disappointment with the "arrangements" between Kinney and the Dodd committee. In his view, the pact proved unsatisfactory because Kinney, although bowing to the Clique's major demands, refused to transform his paper's offices into a clubhouse or turn his columns over to party propagandists. Whether in fact the "arrangements" made for a more partisan *Advertiser* is not easily determined. After Foster became editor the paper seemed to quibble less with administration policy and to take a more positive view of the Union war effort. A ringing endorsement of Lincoln's policies on the eve of the November presidential election capped weeks of favorable editorial comment.[76] Yet the tide was so clearly running in favor of the North during the war's final year that the *Advertiser* may well have taken a more affirmative stance regardless of the threat of a rival paper. It may be more than coincidence, however, that the *Advertiser* was without Republican competition so long as Foster remained editor. On June 18, 1866, the *Evening Courier*, Newark's first Republican paper published since the *Mercury*'s demise, appeared on the streets. None other than John Y. Foster was its editor.[77]

4

A Not Unexpected Step

The Civil War was the stuff of every editor's dreams. Popular interest was overwhelming, and it was not unusual for a paper's circulation to quadruple after an important battle. Unfortunately, the quality of American journalism was unequal to the challenge. Because of what one historian has called the "prevailing low code of journalistic ethics," the war was reported with little objectivity, only a minimal regard for the truth, and a frenzied partisanship.[1] The *Journal*, *Advertiser*, and *Mercury* furnish no better example of such journalism than their coverage of the Twenty-sixth New Jersey Infantry, a nine-month Essex County regiment that saw limited service with the Army of the Potomac in 1862 and 1863. Recruited only after immense effort to forestall the draft threatened by President Lincoln in the summer of 1862, the Twenty-sixth was the last truly volunteer outfit raised in Newark and its suburbs. "[T]he flower of Essex County" (so christened by one of its officers) departed Newark for the seat of war in high spirits, confident it would be assigned to garrison duty far behind the lines. Armed with antique muzzle-loading muskets, bereft of meaningful training, the men of the Twenty-sixth were aghast when they were ordered to the front during the Battle of Fredericksburg, then reassured when staff officers, fearing for the unit's safety, stationed them out of harm's way in a protected area. After stumbling through Virginia's "sacred soil" on Burnside's abortive January Mud March, the men faced their first real combat when a regiment of Vermont volunteers challenged them to an epic two-day snowball fight. When the Twenty-sixth finally came under actual fire at Chancellorsville, a majority panicked and broke for the rear. The unit was as poorly led as it was trained and equipped: the Jerseymen had the ill luck to be commanded by a soldier of fortune from New York State who was cashiered in June 1863 for drunkeness on the battlefield. Discharged on the eve of Gettysburg, the Twenty-sixth marched home to a hero's welcome, ignoring Governor Parker's plea to reenlist for the duration of the emergency. The regimental career was brief, awkward, and of little significance to the Union war effort.

Notwithstanding its wilted laurels, the Twenty-sixth New Jersey enjoyed lavish, sometimes daily coverage by Newark's papers, coverage units that fought longer and better would have envied. Partly this was due to the public's insatiable hunger for news of husbands, sons, and brothers at the front, partly also to the literary types—the chaplain and several enlisted men—who joined the unit. In the main, however, Newark's editors focused on the regiment because the political imperatives of the moment demanded it. New Jersey politics were at their most discordant during the months the Twenty-sixth Regiment wore the Union blue. The fall 1862 elections had resulted in a Democratic victory so sweeping that the Copperheads bragged they would soon control the state. It was at the same time the darkest hour of the Union war effort. Lincoln seemed ineffectual, his administration was in turmoil. In the field the Union commanders in the East, McClellan, Burnside, and then Hooker, blundered away the mighty Army of the Potomac less than sixty-five miles from Richmond. New Jersey Copperheads rejoiced. Unionists despaired. Responding to the crisis, Foster of the *Mercury* called for the sternest resolution; Kinney at the *Advertiser* was by turns warmly supportive and mildly critical of the administration; Fuller saw the war a failure, and cried for peace. News of "the flower of Essex County" proved a convenient vehicle for each man's purpose.

The story of the Twenty-sixth New Jersey begins five days after the fiasco at Bull Run, when President Lincoln appointed thirty-five year-old George B. McClellan commander of the disorganized and demoralized Union army at Washington. Lincoln needed a man who could bring order out of confusion, who could put together in reasonable time an army to invade Virginia. McClellan, who had spent the early war months successfully chasing Confederates in western Virginia, was the only Union general who had won any battles, a sufficient recommendation for the beleagured president. McClellan set about his task with vigor and great ability. During the summer and fall of 1861 he fashioned from the ragtag elements that had run away at Bull Run an army that would one day be counted among the finest in history. The Army of the Potomac was McClellan's creation: Under other commanders, and at other times, it would fight heroically and achieve greatly; under McClellan the Union's best-trained and best-equipped army squandered its power.

In the spring of 1862 McClellan won Lincoln's endorsement of a scheme to move against Richmond from the east rather than the north. The first elements of the Army of the Potomac left the Washington area for Fortress Monroe, Virginia, a Union-held enclave on the southeast coast of the Old Dominion, in mid-March. Using the fort as a base, McClellan planned to move inland through the flatlands between the York and James Rivers known as the Peninsula, attacking the Confederate capital at its least protected point. Instead, with over 100,000 troops under his command, the "Young Napoleon" wasted the summer and his army in a succession of inconclusive battles at Yorktown, Fair Oaks, and the Seven Days' that ended in Union retreat.

The failure of the much-heralded Peninsula campaign came at an awkward moment for the administration. Both the Western and Eastern armies demanded increased manpower but the North, after nearly a year and a half of fruitless warfare, had grown immune to patriotic appeals. Congressional authorization of a months' advance pay for three-year volunteers and a two-dollar premium did little to stimulate recruitment. On June 28, 1862, Secretary of State William H. Seward traveled to New York City for a conference with the governors of Pennsylvania and New York, carrying with him a desperate appeal from the president. "[L]et the country give us a hundred thousand new troops in the shortest possible time," he wrote, "which will substantially end the war." The president assured the governors that for all the military reverses of the first eighteen months of the war, despite all the home front criticism, the administration was not disheartened. "I expect," added Lincoln, "to maintain this conflict until successful, or till I die, or am conquered, or my term expires, or Congress or the country forsakes me."[2] Seward told the Union governors that if they could raise additional troops, and enroll them without delay, Richmond itself could be taken and the Confederacy subdued.

The Union governors welcomed Lincoln's assurances: By chance, their meeting with Seward coincided with the Seven Days' Battles, one of the greatest bloodlettings of the Civil War. On June 25, 1862, the Army of the Potomac was within the sound of the churchbells of Richmond after a ponderous march up the Peninsula. Suddenly General Robert E. Lee attacked McClellan's right wing, north of the Chickahominy River, turning the Union troops to the defensive. Convinced that he was outnumbered two to one, McClellan sought to disengage from Lee's smaller force, fighting a series of battles at Mechanicsville, Gaine's Mill, Glendale, and Malvern Hill as he retreated to a new base on the James River. During seven days' hard fighting that ended on July 1, 1862, McClellan lost 15,849 men, killed, wounded, and missing.[3]

McClellan's heavy losses stunned the North. Lincoln, hearing the news, was "as nearly inconsolable as I could be and live." The New York stock market fell. The value of the Union greenback plunged. As the casualty lists began to appear in the newspapers, Henry Ward Beecher, the Brooklyn minister, spoke for many: Lincoln, he said, had "[N]ot a spark of genius. . . ; not an element for leadership. Not one particle of heroic enthusiasm."[4]

The enormous casualties of the Seven Days' Battles were not yet fully known when the Union governors asked Lincoln to call upon the states for "such additional number of men as may in your judgment be necessary to garrison and hold all of the numerous cities and military positions that have been captured by our armies."[5] Lincoln responded on July 1, issuing a call for 300,000 volunteers, chiefly infantry, to serve for three years. "I trust that they may be enrolled without delay," he told the governors, "so as to bring this unnecessary and injurious civil war to a speedy and satisfactory conclusion."[6]

During July, volunteering lagged disastrously. When details of the Seven Days' Battles finally reached them, the people of the North neither rushed to the colors, as they had after Bull Run, nor panicked, as many had after "Stonewall" Jackson's brilliant victories in the Shenandoah Valley during the spring of the year. Instead, there was a depth of gloom hard to measure and then, in mid-July, as the pine coffins of the Union dead came north for burial, a reluctant appreciation that victory was not to be achieved cheaply or quickly or gloriously. Disabled veterans on furlough from the front, their empty sleeves and wooden crutches mute evidence of the slaughter, were everywhere, spreading their stories of the horrors of the camp and battlefield.[7]

In August, Lincoln authorized Secretary of War Edwin Stanton to issue the North's first call for a draft, 300,000 militia to serve for nine months unless sooner discharged. Stanton's order was not without precedent—the Confederates had already resorted to conscription in the spring of the year—and good Union men, Democrats as well as Republicans, applauded the move. "This decisive step is not unexpected," said the *Daily Advertiser:*

> The public apprehension of the dangers and necessities of the hour has led to a general conviction that only by means of a draft could a proper military force be brought into the field, as soon as will be necessary.
>
> The great demand for labor at the North, in the harvest field, in manufactures, and in the various ramifications of business—indeed all the elements of our prosperity operated to retard the progress of voluntary enlistment; and meantime the golden moments were passing away while the dangers that environ the nation were thickening with fearful rapidity.
>
> The questions, therefore, which the Government was called upon to decide, were, "Whether the convenience, comfort and business prosperity of individuals should be consulted, or the National existence be preserved? Whether the rebels alone should be allowed to use an engine combining the elements of celerity and force . . .?" And the Government could not be long in choosing. It has determined that the Nation must be first preserved and all personal interests postponed to that end. . . .

The draft "will prove not unsatisfactory to our people," claimed the *Advertiser*. Besides confirming the determination of the government to bring the war to a successful conclusion, the draft would spread the burden equally:

> Instead of confining the hardships as well as the glory of the war to the poorer classes, it will operate to engage all classes and occupations and interests of our people in the exercise of a duty which is incumbent on all; and a degree of earnestness will in future be imparted to the war, which has hitherto been the great lack of the body of the loyal States.[8]

Stanton's order of August 4 was not quite a draft in the modern sense. The Lincoln administration could not bring itself to that, not just yet at least. As before, volunteer regiments could be raised by the states, and under a complicated accounting formula, if enough nine-month men were enrolled before

September 5, no one would have to be drafted after all. The August 4 order was nevertheless a powerful stimulus for recruitment: no state government wished to have anything remotely to do with the draft if it could help it, prompting officials from governor to mayor to redouble their efforts to raise the volunteers needed.[9]

In early August, after New Jersey Governor Charles S. Olden announced that the state would pay a cash bounty of six dollars per month to each volunteer, recruiting began to pick up. Olden's promise of a bounty would be a key factor in enabling New Jersey to meet its quota, predicted the *Daily Advertiser* on August 11:

> Our people argue that as they are liable to be drafted, at any rate, in which event they will receive nothing beyond mere soldier's pay, it is to their advantage to close with the proposition of the Governor and secure the State bounty in addition. . . . The term of service being so short, only nine months, and the prospect being that the drafted men will not be required for active service, but to perform garrison or camp duty, many look upon the matter in the light of an agreeable episode in their lives, attended by the spice of excitement.
> The opportunity is one which should not be allowed to pass by unimproved by our thousands of young men and others, whose chances of being drafted are comparatively great, and who may now have the merit of volunteering, together with the advantage of increased pay.[10]

The ever-present threat of Stanton's draft hung like a sword over the head of every Jerseyman of military age. Their discomfiture was not eased when the respected *Daily Advertiser* called for the immediate imposition of a draft the moment voluntary enlistment slackened:

> If volunteering falters, there should be no tenderfootedness about drafting. It has been resorted to by the rebels with tremendous effect, and there should be no hesitation on our part from any sentimental notions as to the honor or dishonor involved. Private interests and feelings must be postponed to the public necessities, and these require an immediate and overwhelming accession to our military strength. . . . If not resorted to, and if further delay is encountered out of regard to a false delicacy, we shall be outnumbered at every point, and the national safety put in immediate peril. The sole thing to be considered is how to increase our army—how to beat the rebels in the struggle to secure an overwhelming force, and to this all minor considerations must give way. . . . It is our national existence we are contending for, and no measures should be neglected which will ensure it. Let there be a draft then, and that promptly, is the suggestion of wisdom and the requirement of necessity.[11]

Unionists across the nation harbored serious doubt that New Jersey could meet its quota of 10,478 "nine-monthers"—the state's reputation as a hotbed of

Copperheadism seemed an assurance of failure. Understandably, the *Daily Journal*, memories of its brush with a criminal indictment the previous fall still fresh, treaded gingerly on the subject of conscription. The prospect of the draft, said Fuller, "brings home forcibly to every family the question of war as it has never before been presented, and many individuals who . . . have been violently patriotic, now begin to question the foundation of their sentiments, as their courage 'oozes out' when their own names . . . are enrolled for the draft."[12] The *Journal* foresaw opposition to the presidential order:

> Some people anticipate trouble when drafting goes into operation, many persons regarding an honest opposition to the principles and theory of the war as a sufficient cause for exemption from the service, but it is unlikely the Administration will allow such an excuse to prevail, although it is generally regarded as a correct principle that those who approve of the war and its objects are the right men to fight it out.
>
> The following notice to exempts will be interesting. It was posted in a store down town: ATTENTION CONSCRIPTS! Certificates of disability issued to those who don't wish to be drafted. Price $500.[13]

The state's quota was filled without unusual difficulty, however, although not until the deadline had passed; the absence of a draft muted Copperhead opposition to the president's call. New Jersey's nine-month men volunteered for reasons as diverse as Jersey's seacoast and mountains. Some were prompted by the example of friend and neighbor, others enlisted out of pure patriotism. Many joined the ranks to avoid the stigma of the draft, while thousands more stepped forward for economic reasons: with state and local cash bounties added, a soldier would easily earn more than he could ever hope for in the factory or on the farm.[14] Ira S. Dodd of Orange, one of those who answered Lincoln's call, remembered later that "the chief impulse was the imperious spirit of the hour which had begotten the feeling in every man's breast that until he had offered himself to his country he owed an unpaid debt." When a regiment was actually being organized in the neighborhood, added Dodd, "this was brought home with redoubled force." When friends and neighbors came forward, "very shame made it difficult to hold back."[15]

Essex County, with an 1860 census count of slightly under 100,000, was assigned the modest quota of 1,160 men. As September 5, the day the draft was to begin, drew inexorably closer, public officials, clergymen, merchants, bankers, and newspaper editors cajoled, exhorted, and pleaded. Let us avoid the draft at all costs, they cried, as they bent their joint effort to the patriotic cause. Clergymen throughout the county mounted their pulpits, casting aside their usual two-hour Sunday sermons to urge enrollment without delay. In Irvington the Reverend Moses Cummings, sometime preacher at the First Christian Church and outspoken critic of slavery, thundered of duty in terms no man could misunderstand.[16] An ardent Unionist, the Reverend Isaac Newton Sprague of Caldwell's First Presbyterian Church "in personal interviews often made it exceedingly irksome for any able-bodied man who remained at home."[17] At the Presbyterian Church in Bloomfield, after the minister there spoke "on the state of the country," several "well-known residents announced their intention to go."[18]

Cash bounties, some raised by cities and towns, others by private citizens and committees, were a powerful inducement. Newark's Common Council grandly announced on August 19 a bounty of ten dollars per man. On August 30 the newspapers reported that W. E. Skinner, a Newark attorney, had contributed $250 to be divided equally among the members of a company being raised by Captain William H. Halsey. In large part, the bounties were raised at war meetings held in every part of the county: Bloomfield's citizens subscribed $15,000; Clinton Township, far less populous, raised $2,400 in a single evening. A "large and respectable meeting" of residents of Newark's Sixth Ward convened "without distinction of party" at the Broome Street Democratic headquarters on August 25, resolving unanimously

> that the loyal citizens of the Sixth Ward in meeting assembled, being anxious to avoid the necessity of a draft, pledge themselves to second the efforts of the [Marcus L.] Ward Committee and all others in raising funds necessary to increase the bounty to volunteers. That while we deplore a fratricidal war, we pledge ourselves to stand by the Government in maintaining the Union and Constitution as bequeathed to us by our fathers.

A list "opened for subscriptions," said the *Daily Advertiser*, "was responded to liberally, and the meeting adjourned with hearty cheers for the Union."[19]

In Orange a committee headed by the local bank president raised $18,000 in less than a month. On the day the Orange volunteers were sworn in, Charles A. Lighthipe, president of the Orange Bank and treasurer of the finance committee, went down to Camp Frelinghuysen with $18,000 in cash, and an equal amount in town certificates. "The money was put up in neat packages of $100, in Orange Bank bills, and as the name of each volunteer was called, he came forward, signed a receipt and received his pay."[20]

Newark's insurance companies caught the spirit of the hour. Mutual Benefit Life Insurance Company announced in mid-August that for an additional premium of five percent on all existing life policies, it would cover "risk arising from entering into the military or naval service of the United States" north of Atlanta, Georgia. For an additional two percent, volunteers could be insured against death occurring south of that point.[21]

Noted for its thriving boot, shoe, and hat industry, Orange, the largest town in Essex County after Newark, raised two full companies for the new regiment. There were some anxious moments, according to the Orange *Journal*:

> Monday last [September 1] was an exciting day in Orange. It was the time appointed to marshal the brave volunteers of Orange and send them down to

Camp Frelinghuysen. Early in the morning flags were flying, the old "revolutioner" belched forth its thunder, and strains of martial and band music, lent their inspiriting strains to the scenes of excitement. Men, women and children thronged the streets, and many a sad farewell was taken, and a "God bless you," uttered, as the men were formed on the Green opposite the Park House at about noon.

Upon inspecting the ranks, however, it was ascertained that there were some fifteen men short; although 75 more men had enrolled themselves than were really required to fill the quota! At length the company was formed into line by Capt. Cairns, and marched up and down Main street, in the hope that the few required would "fall in;" but such was not the result. The afternoon was spent in endeavoring to procure the requisite number without effect, headquarters being established at Willow Hall. All day crowds thronged the hall, and many serious and ludicrous scenes were enacted. At about six o'clock in the evening it was thought best to adjourn till 7 o'clock the next morning when after reading the roll, and it being found that only 9 men were wanted, the company were dismissed, each man rising in his place and promising to be on hand at the time named the next morning, and determining to do all he could to fill up the ranks.

Tuesday morning dawned upon us clear and cool, after a refreshing shower during the previous night; but many misgivings were expressed as to our ability to procure the necessary number. . . . The belief was quite generally entertained that we should yet have to submit to the draft, notwithstanding the efforts which had been made to avoid it, and the large number of men who were already on hand and ready to go. Thus matters stood till about 11 o'clock on Tuesday, when the desired number of men having been obtained, the large company were formed in line, and led by Rubsam's brass band of Newark, proceeded in fine order to Camp Frelinghuysen, at Roseville.[22]

Newark filled its volunteer quota of 534 men by agonizingly slow degrees. Alarmingly sluggish in early August, recruitment picked up only after it became obvious that a draft was inevitable if the quota could not be met. The city's Republican press worked as hard as any recruiting officer to fill the ranks with daily news articles and stories calculated to promote enlistment. During August and early September the *Mercury* ran no fewer than seventy articles on the subject, using every argument imaginable to spur the volunteers forward:

Every unmarried man who has no one but himself to support, and who has strength to shoulder a musket has but one path of duty now, and that leads to the field. Thousands of men are leaving wives, children, business—everything at their country's call. Shall the young men who have nothing to leave ignobly hold back? Let every young man think of this. Honor and Manhood are not now in the workshop—behind the counter; they are in the field. . . . Young man, that excuse must be indeed weighty which keeps you from the field to-day.[23]

A special appeal to the city's Irish and Germans appeared in the *Mercury* on August 12:

Black hearted traitors are striving to mislead you, and prevent your enlisting by representing to you that this is an Abolition war—that it is designed to elevate the black race, to your downfall. Irishmen, when any one dare approach you with this infamous lie, tell them with scorn that for such a cause as they claim this to be, [General Thomas F.] Meagher would not fight, nor [General Michael] Corcoran languish in heroic captivity. . . . Germans, when you are thus approached, point to the noble and war-torn [General Franz] Sigel, and tell those who insult him, and you by defaming the cause in which he fights, that where he leads, you know it is safe to follow.[24]

Any *Mercury* reader still hesitant about enlisting could take comfort in the notion, expressed by the paper in early August, that "the man of nervous temperament" who "enters a fight with trembling knees" does "the sternest and most brilliant fighting" when "the fierce wine of battle pours in tumultuous surges through his veins." In any event, added the paper, "few of the new soldiers called into service will see any fighting at all."

The very enormity of the preparations makes it almost certain that they will not be needed. Men must not fear that the battle storm is to beat upon them as heavily and disasterously as it has upon the noble columns who line the James river. The great contest has been practically fought and won. Now it but remains to strike one overwhelming blow, and the war is over.[25]

The *Daily Advertiser* beat the drums as loudly as the *Mercury*. At midmonth the paper carried an urgent letter that posed the question on everyone's lips:

Volunteering or drafting? This is an important question for the citizens of Newark to decide upon, and one which will test the loyalty of the residents of our beautiful city. Several neighboring cities have determined that drafting shall not be resorted to there, and to avoid the necessity they are straining every nerve and using every lawful means to urge on recruiting. In some places all stores are closed early in the afternoon so that all can engage in the good work. From the proud millionaire to the humble day laborer, no one is idle. Rich men give freely of their money both as bounties to volunteers, and as a fund for the support of the families of those who have bravely left their fire sides to strike for Freedom and the Right. And while these things are going on, will Newark, which can boast of so many opulent citizens, of so much wealth and patriotism, will Newark, the pride of our glorious little State, hang back and refuse to give freely from her abundant coffers?

Patriotism in the Southern cities, the writer continued, put Newark to shame.

In Mobile . . . every able-bodied man, except one, has shouldered a musket and has marched forth to defend his bogus Government against the rightful one, and from that one, who is too cowardly to go, every face is turned, every respectable door is shut. Such is the feeling there, and should we be less active in defending our native land, than they are in trying to destroy it? Oh! let us arise in our strength and shake off our sloth! . . . Let us resolve that the city of Newark, and the State of New Jersey will not submit to the ignominy of drafting, and we will be saved the disgrace, if we are only willing to work well, to act bravely. Let us determine, trusting in the God of Battles, that our infamous foe shall be utterly crushed and annihilated. Let us determine that we will conquer, and glory will perch upon our glittering arms, and triumph where our starry banners wave.[26]

Bounty money and a great deal of it had to be raised, another practical Newarker told the *Advertiser*, if the city hoped to "avoid the stigma of a draft."

Will not our banks, insurance offices, and other monied corporations and monied men, and every man who is liable to be drafted, come forward and furnish the necessary funds? There are those willing to volunteer, but they have to leave situations and throw themselves out of business; shall we ask them to do it? Let those of us who are not liable to draft come forward and say to those who are, we will help to sustain this burden.

Let a public meeting be called; let our citizens come up at once and say we will stand by you, and raise all the funds necessary to secure at once our full complement.[27]

Not everyone was eager to enroll. Some, convinced a draft was inevitable, hastily obtained substitutes. Another correspondent of the *Daily Advertiser* who signed himself "A Young Volunteer" condemned the slackers:

It is generally known that a number of the young men of this city have formed an association, assuring to each of their members a substitute in case he shall be drafted for the war. The majority of them are in comfortable circumstances, strong and able bodied, ranging between the ages of 20 and 30 years, and being unmarried, without family cares and responsibilities, they are the very men upon whom it properly devolves in this national crisis to step forward and fill up our depleted ranks. But instead of nobly doing this, instead of even waiting patiently to find whether or not the Government would require their services, their fears of the draft seems to have obtained so great an ascendency as to have induced them to adopt this eminently unpatriotic course, a course which is not only mortifying to many of their friends, but positively injurious to the cause of enlistments in our city. . . . Should not then the formation of such societies cease? Will not our loyal and true hearted ladies frown upon them, and by their powerful influence, make these young men feel, as they should, heartily ashamed of themselves.[28]

Whether due to bounty money or the "powerful influence" of the ladies, Newark edged slowly closer to its quota. "Recruiting in this city is brisk, and some of the companies are nearly full," reported the *Daily Advertiser* on August

30, adding: "It is believed there will not be any draft here." Captain Halsey had some 120 men on his roll book, reported the paper, "and [he] has no doubt that over 100 of them can be relied on. He will take the first 98 that are sworn in." Captain Israel Cozine, who had erected a barrack on the lower end of Military Park to receive recruits, had 41 men enrolled.[29] Some men still held back for fear the choice positions in the new regiment would be open only to the favored few. Not so, announced James J. Brooks:

> I propose helping to raise a company in which there shall be no parcelling out of offices, no recognition of services in raising the company, no election of officers until the company is full and every member sworn in. Let every man who cannot see honor in the wounds a drafted man may receive in defence of his country, or who believes with me that a draft on any community evinces a lack of patriotism in that community, enlist and help and report progress at the war meeting to be held at the Fifth Baptist Church . . . to-morrow night.
>
> Only four days remain for work. Remember the $75 bounty makes our pay nearly NINE DOLLARS PER WEEK.[30]

September came and went with Newark's quota unfilled. The deadline was extended to September 5, yet the *Daily Advertiser* fretted that a draft could not be avoided:

> Recruiting in Newark has been comparatively slow since yesterday, owing in some measure to the lack of accommodation at the rendezvous. Many who have enrolled their names here in the city will not report themselves in camp, and if the proper quarters are not furnished we may yet have to feel the rigor of a draft. . . .
>
> On Saturday the quota must be filled either by volunteers or drafted men, and as less than two days remains in which to work, the greatest efforts should be made immediately. . . . Another effort is to be made here this afternoon and evening, and all the stores and places of business are requested to close at 4 o'clock, and the citizens assemble in mass meeting on the Park.[31]

At the last moment the additional men needed were enrolled. On September 9 the commissioner of the draft certified that Essex County had met its quota. "This finally settles the matter," said a much relieved *Daily Advertiser*, "so far as the last call is concerned, and our citizens can once more rest easy, though it is but little satisfaction to those who have spent their time and money to procure exemption papers."[32] All in all, New Jersey raised eleven volunteer infantry regiments. By mid-September the men were in camp and by October 10 all had left the state for the field. Numbered from the twenty-first to the thirty-first, New Jersey's nine-month regiments would serve in Virginia, asigned to the First, Second, Sixth, and Ninth Corps, Army of the Potomac.

5

A Glorious Day for the Patriot

Nine-month regiments raised in northern New Jersey rendezvoused at Camp Frelinghuysen, located in Newark's Roseville section. Rendezvous no. 4, as it was officially known, was nothing more than a large field sloping gently to the Morris Canal, alongside Bathgate's Woods. The canal, already declining in importance, afforded bathing facilities for the men, the fields offered ample room for drill.[1] Hastily built wooden barracks and large canvas tents provided rough but adequate accommodation for several thousand soldiers. Colonel Cornelius Van Vorst was commandant.

Volunteers from Sussex and Morris Counties had already reached Camp Frelinghuysen when the first recruits from Essex began to arrive. By noon on September 2 nearly 1,500 men were in camp, far more than Colonel Van Vorst had anticipated. "The accommodations are not sufficient for the large number of men sent in," reported the Orange *Journal*, "and last night 371 were quartered outside—a portion of them in Frey's factory . . . and the remainder in the malleable iron foundry in Nesbitt street. In a few days, however, additional barracks will be erected and this inconvenience avoided."[2]

September 2 also saw the formation of several companies of the as yet unnamed regiment.

This morning a number of companies were organized, the men electing their own officers by ballot. Every man is obliged to be sworn in as a private, and in the case of the non-election of those who have been recruiting with the expectation of receiving a commission, they are compelled to serve as privates. This caused considerable hesitancy among a number of expectant Captains, who had but few men, but while they have their choice in taking the oath or not, the order is imperative.[3]

The comfortable shade of Bathgate's Woods, the cool waters of the Morris Canal, and the light, almost nonexistent military discipline made life at Camp Frelinghuysen "delightful." For nearly a month the rendezvous "was the centre

73

of Essex County life: Thousands of persons visited there daily; women, boys and girls trudged over the hot and dusty roads carrying baskets of provisions for the men of their homes."[4] The *Advertiser* reported daily on events at Camp Frelinghuysen:

There are now over 2,000 men at the . . . rendezvous, and the order which prevails is a source of gratifying remark and surprise by the large number of visitors who are admitted every day. Twice a week Dodsworth's Band, of New York, furnish music for the dress parade, after which some of their choicest pieces are performed. Last night a serenading party from Bloomfield, accompanied by a number of ladies, visited the camp, and after favoring the inmates with a variety of songs, were admitted, and partook of a bountiful supply of such refreshments as could be afforded. . . . Next week the men will receive their uniforms.[5]

As the hard realities of military life began to intrude, the heady enthusiasm of early September wore thin. Dissension surfaced first over the choice of officers for the regiment, now designated the Twenty-sixth New Jersey Volunteers. On September 16 the *Daily Advertiser* reported that "considerable difficulty" surrounded the election of regimental field officers.

The Citizen's Committee, in order to secure competent military men for the various positions, have done all in their power, expecting at the same time to act in concert with the line officers, but their exertions have given offence to a few, and virtually caused a division, which resulted in objections, from one side or the other, to every candidate proposed. Caucus meetings have been held each day, but up to noon to-day, they had failed to agree.

The enlisted men, meanwhile, accused Marcus L. Ward's Public Aid Committee of reneging on its promises.

A misunderstanding has occurred between the married men of this city and the Aid Committee, in regard to furnishing their families with assistance, at least till their first months' pay was received. The volunteers assert that when they enlisted they were distinctly promised that their families would receive a certain sum per week, and that now the danger of a draft is averted, the contract is not carried out. On the other hand the Committee say they never authorized any such promise, as they have not the funds necessary to carry it out. The matter as it now stands, has caused a general dissatisfaction, and unless it is reconciled some difficulty may occur when the men come to be mustered in.[6]

By midmonth all such difficulties had been resolved. The men of each company chose their own captain, the captains elected the major, lieutenant colonel, and colonel. When their first choice for colonel was rejected by state authorities, the officers elected a New Yorker, Andrew J. Morrison, to the command of the regiment. A cavalry officer, Morrison was ignorant of infantry tactics and lacked any experience in actual command. "He was, however, an imposing individual," wrote a noncommissioned officer, "a fine horseman, with a decidedly military bearing and a self-assurance which temporarily concealed his defects."[7]

On September 18 the Twenty-sixth New Jersey was mustered into the service of the United States. Soon after uniforms arrived rumors began to circulate that the Twenty-sixth was about to be ordered south. At dawn on September 20 hundreds of men, determined to visit their families one last time, broke from camp. The New York newspapers, including the *Times*, carried the story:

> There were some 2,300 soldiers in the camp, and . . . they had been promised a furlough to enable them to visit their homes before marching to the seat of war. The furlough was promised for Wednesday last; when the time came, they were requested to wait until they got their uniforms. The uniforms were furnished on Friday, when, to their surprise, they were informed that they were under marching orders, and could not have a furlough at all. This caused much ill-feeling in camp, but the soldiers, although they were determined to have their promised furlough, yet decided to proceed in a quiet and orderly manner. They therefore held a mass meeting, and appointed a Committee to wait upon the commanding officer and inform him that they should leave camp yesterday morning, with or without a furlough, and that they would all return again at any reasonable time that he would fix. Morning came, and, as the Colonel in command had decided that he had no power to grant furloughs while they were under marching orders, about a third of the men . . . skedaddled.[8]

The skedaddlers "rushed the guard and started an undignified dash . . . toward Orange Street, a number of officers following and commanding them to halt. Clouds of dust enveloped the mass of human beings running at top speed and the race was soon declared in favor of the enlisted men."[9] Captains Samuel Dodd and William Morris persuaded most of their companies to remain until they could depart "in a more soldier-like manner."

> Col. Van Vorst was finally prevailed upon to grant the men furloughs until 9 o'clock Monday morning, although he protested that he had no authority so to do. Furloughs were accordingly given to the remainder, and they departed quietly. It was stated in some of the evening papers that during the stampede of the skedaddlers one of the men was shot in the arm by Maj. Babcock. This is a mistake. The Major fired his pistol, hoping to intimidate the men and induce them to return, but it was not loaded with ball and nobody was hurt. The affair did not partake of the nature of a riot in any respect, and there is no doubt that nearly all the skedaddlers will quietly return to camp to-day.[10]

New York City's Copperhead press had a field day with the story. Said the New York *Evening Express:*

Several commissioned officers of the Twenty-sixth and Twenty-seventh Regiments of nine-months' volunteers who took French leave from their quarters at Newark, last Saturday, are hunting up some of the runaways in Jersey City. It was not expected that they would find many of the skedaddlers here, except at the ferry, as very few of the self-dissolving regiments were enlisted in this county. At the ferry, however, it was thought, many of the men might be intercepted while making their way to New York. This morning several of them were apprehended there and as they were disposed to be obstreperous with the officers who took them into custody, some animated scenes occurred, much to the delight of the throng that pass over the ferry during the early hours of the day. The tenacity of the officers was greater than that of the soldiers, and they were in all cases taken to police headquarters, from which they were soon afterward forwarded to the encampment from which they deserted. About the streets, there was a lively lookout kept for the runaways, by the citizens and boys, who entered into the "sport" of soldier-catching with much zeal. The diversion proved very agreeable to the boys, whose zest for it so far exceeded their opportunities for enjoyment in the chase of the real "game," that a false cry was often made over any biped habituated in the least *a la militaire,* just for "the fun of the thing."

The police picked up very few of the runaways, notwithstanding this extraordinary vigilance, most of the arrests being made by the officers of the nominally disorganized corps.[11]

The *Daily Advertiser*, reporting the desertion of over half a regiment, was unperturbed:

Non-commissioned officers, who left without consent, will probably be reduced to the ranks, as also one or two commissioned officers. We are informed by the commandant that the best of feeling prevailed between the men and those in charge of the rendezvous, and that no rowdyism or spirit of violence prevailed, though he does not approve of the stampede, and will take proper measures to punish the offenders. The volunteers from Morris and Sussex counties, with but few exceptions, and all of Capt. Morris' company of this city, took no part in the "skedaddle," though the latter have since received furloughs. To-day the city is filled with "blue coats and brass buttons," and the various daguerriat saloons are carrying on a brisk business.[12]

Men of Companies G and H, the two companies raised in Orange, led the skedaddle. Two days after they left Camp Frelinghuysen they met by prearrangement at the Orange Common and "having engaged a brass band, proceeded to camp and passed in review before the Colonel's quarters."[13] Neither the *Mercury* nor the *Journal* reported the skedaddle; the *Advertiser* downplayed the embarrassing affair:

The late "skedaddle" at the rendezvous in Roseville has caused considerable excitement, and been the occasion of gross exaggeration by a portion of the New York press. Now that the excitement has subsided, we learn that only about 250 left in the morning without permission, chiefly from the Orange and Caldwell companies, and a number of stragglers from the various Newark companies. During the day the remainder of the 26th Regiment, except those on guard, were furloughed until this morning, and the latter as soon as relieved also received passes. This morning they all returned, some of the Companies headed by martial music, and to-day everything is as quiet as if nothing of the kind had occurred. At the time of the stampede, Capt. Babcock (Acting Major) fired a pistol in the air, but we can learn of no person being shot.[14]

During the time the regiment was at Camp Frelinghuysen, twenty-four men deserted, more than half of them from Company K, a Newark unit. Billeting volunteers only a few miles and in some cases only a city block or two from their homes led to other problems as well, according to newspaper accounts:

During the last week or two some drunkenness has been observable among the men, and the manner in which rum was smuggled in remained a mystery. Suspicion having been aroused, however, yesterday afternoon watch was kept at the gate for the offender, and not without success. About 5 o'clock a resident of Orange drove in with a wagon containing a barrel of onions. In overhauling it four or five dozen bottles of the vilest sort of liquor were found packed in sawdust, and the whole very nicely covered with onions. The party was arrested and taken before Col. Van Vorst, who ordered him to be locked up in the guard house over night, when he would make a charge against him. During the night, however, he managed to escape, and will very likely keep clear of the camp for some time.[15]

A telegram received on September 23 ordered the regiment to break camp on Friday morning. Furloughs were halted, muskets distributed, and Colonel Morrison, though yet to make his appearance, was expected momentarily. There was precious little time left for important last-minute details.

A very handsome sword, with the usual accompaniments, was presented to Capt. Geo. W. Harrison . . . at his residence in Orange last evening. The presentation was made on behalf of numerous friends by Capt. L. A. S. Robinson, of the Orange Blues, in a few brief and well timed remarks, to which Capt. Harrison responded in an appropriate manner, with a pledge that if he ever had occasion to draw the sword for the defence of his country, he would not disgrace his name, or prove unworthy of the confidence reposed in him by the donors.[16]

A final dress review vastly impressed the *Daily Mercury*'s reporter:

There is a marked improvement in drill in many of the companies, and though a military eye would of course note many defects, to the unprofessional observer the evolutions were gone through in a very creditable manner, the marching and wheeling being executed with considerable precision. The fact that some of the companies contain a proportion of men who have been tolerably well drilled in our various militia and firemens' volunteer companies, will account for this creditable display after so brief an enrolment, and also renders certain the rapid improvement of the regiment in military knowledge. The display was witnessed by an immense throng of spectators, and the charming music of Dodworth's Band added much to the pleasure of the occasion.

The *Mercury* had every confidence that the men would cover themselves with glory:

The men are all in the highest spirits, and express themselves as anxious to exchange the comparative comfort and abandon of camp life for the more rigorous discipline and increased privation of active field service. They have enlisted, they say, with a full appreciation of what they have to expect, and are prepared to do their duty with willing hearts. The best feeling prevails in camp, and we can assure our gallant volunteers that their city, county and State are proud of them, and look upon them as constituting as fine a body of men as has ever been sent into service.[17]

All too soon September 26, the day of departure, arrived. Beginning at dawn "an immense crowd of visitors" thronged Camp Frelinghuysen, "rapidly increasing in numbers until fully five thousand spectators were on the field."[18] As the time of departure drew near, reported the *Mercury*, fairly bursting with pride,

flags began to be displayed from every possible point where a flag could fly— from the tall city staff, from all the public buildings, from church towers, from private dwellings, suspended across the streets, in the windows, on vehicles and horses heads—everywhere floated, and glowed, and wreathed itself in resplendant folds, the beautiful banner of the stars. Vast crowds of people surged along the streets and early took possession of every window and door-step . . . from which a good view of the pageant might be secured, and as the hours passed on the crowd increased, the lanes and by-ways contributing their drops of humanity, the larger streets into which were emptied the contents of our immense manufactories, and of every private dwelling, became great affluents of life, all converging to the central flood which filled Broad street with tumultuous billows. People, people, were everywhere. . . . People fringed the roofs, and paved the streets. People swarmed and clustered and hung like bees in windows and hoist-ways, and adventurous boys, the future statesmen and soldiers of the land, scaled perilous heights and descended again, like squirrels.

Scores of Newark firemen had enlisted in the Twenty-sixth. Their comrades who remained behind formed a guard of honor, the *Mercury* continued:

The fire department having determined to parade as an escort to the regiment, met at their respective houses at ten o'clock, and from thence marched to the Park, where the line was formed, the display, though very fine, being both sad and inspiriting—sad, for the thinned ranks of most of the companies told how fearfully the war had decimated the rolls of our gallant firemen, the regiment on the march numbering itself, hundreds of the truest and bravest of their number, and inspiriting because it told of men gone to the fight for Liberty and the Union, trained in danger's school, and ready to accept the toils and perils of the soldier's life.[19]

Both the *Advertiser* and the *Mercury* treated the regimental departure as the major news story it was, each devoting a full column to the day's events. The *Journal*, on the other hand, reported the story cursorily, almost begrudgingly. "The regiment was recruited entirely in this county," said the paper in its warmest passage, "and is one of which Essex may be proud."[20] The usually staid *Advertiser* grew moist-eyed as it chronicled the departure. It was, it said, "a glorious day for the patriot to go forth in defence of his country."

The scene at the camp last evening and this morning was one of great excitement. It was constantly thronged with relatives and friends of the volunteers, some of whom were engaged in giving to their loved ones tokens of regard, while those who were more thoughtful brought articles of comfort. Many a man went forth from among us to-day bearing with him trifles wrought by the loving hands of wife, mother, sister or sweetheart, which will be lovingly looked upon when far away, and bring to recollection the home that has been left. Amid the bustle of camp or the din of battle mayhap he will press still closer to his heart these tokens and offer a prayer for the safety and welfare of the giver. The tears which were shed; the silent pressure of the hand; the sad countenance, index of the more saddened heart; the parting kiss, and the affectionate aideu all indicated how great a sacrifice was being made by our soldiers in behalf of their country.[21]

At noon the regiment fell into line for the march from Camp Frelinghuysen to the Chestnut Street depot, led by Rubsam's brass band and an escort of exempt firemen with their prize steam engine, its whistle screaming. "Another thousand of our stalwart patriots were about to follow the thousands that had gone before to battle valiantly for the right," gushed the *Advertiser*, "and our citizens gathered to greet them with a hopeful and loving farewell and to cheer them with their fervent prayers and aspirations."

The ranks of the regiment were full . . . and a more sturdy and effective looking body of men, even New Jersey, famed as it is for hardy soldiers, has never sent forth. As they passed our office, covered with dust, swinging along at a rapid pace, they looked like veterans, and we doubt not will do substantial service. Many a touching episode occurred along the march, to which we can scarcely linger to do justice. Here was a brave and sympathizing woman trying to keep up with the rapidly moving ranks and carrying a large pail of water, from which she administered to the wearied soldiers; here a boy was carrying a musket for some tired comrade in the ranks who was overburthened by his knapsack and luggage; and eddying along the sidewalks and in the streets there were tender partings, which, though made in the broad day, were too holy to be made more public by our recital.[22]

Only one incident marred the day. Near the corner of Orange and Broad Streets, Lieutenant Colonel Thomas A. Colt of Irvington, his horse frightened by the cacophony of fire whistles, churchbells, music, and cheers, was thrown from the saddle and painfully injured. Ignoring his family's pleas to stay behind, Colt boarded a carriage to follow his regiment to the depot.[23]

The *Mercury* ended its story on a lofty note:

> The regiment took the cars at the foot of Chestnut street, where the leave takings were renewed, and for the last time. The train moved off amid great cheering, and thus another New Jersey regiment went forth to meet the foe. May the breath of battle blow lightly over them, if blow it must, and may we, when they return, nine months hence, miss very few from the ranks which marched away to-day so full of strength and hope.[24]

The *Advertiser* and the *Mercury* both petitioned the Almighty to keep watch over the departed regiment. "God bless our noble firemen-soldiers, and all, who march to-day, or ever, to battle for the Right," implored the *Mercury*. "Our hearts go with them, and our prayers and blessings follow them." The *Advertiser* begged God to "shield and protect them amid the dangers they may encounter, and hasten an honorable peace, and their speedy restoration to their families."[25]

6

The Flower of Essex County

The *Advertiser*, the *Mercury*, and, after it broke a four-month silence, the *Journal*, followed the progress of the Twenty-sixth Regiment closely. At one time or another each of the papers had a correspondent in the field; by and large, however, what the newspapers printed was written by the soldiers themselves. Charles S. Woodruff of Newark, a private in Company B and a former printer (probably with the *Mercury*) wrote for the *Mercury*. The regimental chaplain, the Reverend David T. Morrill, was a regular contributor to the *Daily Advertiser*. Sergeant Amos J. Cummings of Irvington, the unit's most accomplished writer, corresponded first with the *Mercury* and later, after politics reared its head within regimental ranks, with the *Journal*. Several unidentified soldiers added their voices as well. Scarcely a day passed without some news from the regiment.

Leaving Newark the Twenty-sixth traveled by railroad via Philadelphia and Baltimore to Washington, where it went into camp on Capitol Hill. There it remained until October 1, when it was ordered to Frederick, Maryland, "making the journey in open cars on which any degree of comfort was altogether impossible."[1] After a week and a half at Frederick, the unit marched to Hagerstown, Maryland, joining the Army of the Potomac as part of General Henry Briggs's brigade, Second Army Corps. First news of the regiment since its departure from Newark appeared in the *Daily Advertiser* on October 2:

> After leaving Newark nothing specially interesting occurred until we reached Philadelphia, where we had a good supper furnished at the Volunteer Refreshment Saloons, to which the boys did ample justice.
>
> In marching to the depot we had to run a gauntlet of extended hands and the good-byes and words of cheer of the people rang upon our ears, creating a perfect din, until we arrived at the depot. The Philadelphians have hearts that beat warm and true in the cause of liberty and humanity. What a contrast we met in Baltimore! There the men looked sullen and downcast, and I sought in vain for a smile of welcome, excepting from an old colored woman, who

seemed to be particularly jubilant and gave vent to her enthusiasm by clapping her hands and hammering her fat sides most lustily.

We reached Washington on Saturday at about 5½ P.M., and were quartered at the Soldiers' Retreat. Our accommodations were not the best, for we had to lie down on the hard floor, but having had very little sleep the night before most of us slept as soundly as if we were on beds of down. On Sunday morning we marched to Capitol Hill, where we are now encamped. . . . Most of the men have made the very common error of all green soldiers, and overloaded themselves with clothing and other articles. . . . The boys are all in excellent spirits, and anxious to strike a New Jersey blow for the UNION.[2]

Washington in the weeks following the Union victory at Antietam was a revelation to the Jerseyans, most of whom knew of civil war only through the newspapers. Washington's hospitals and churches, even the insane asylum, were filled with moaning wounded. Almost daily the hospital ships docked at the Sixth Street wharf; the cemetery next to the Soldier's Home was a scene of continual activity.[3] The few days the regiment spent in the national capital offered "a wholesome lesson," wrote one soldier. "It sobered us; it took away all lingering sense of insubordination, and taught us the relentless power of the mighty machine of which we had become a part."[4] On October 1 came orders to leave Washington:

We left . . . crowded together upon coal or dirt cars, scarcely having room to sit down, but they were the best accommodations I suppose that could be obtained. However, this did not prevent some remarks not very complimentary to the Baltimore & Ohio Railroad. . . . As we passed we were often cheered most enthusiastically by the inhabitants along the road, but these manifestations of loyalty do not prevent the precaution of having the road, and especially the bridges, thoroughly guarded by Union soldiers.

We arrived at Frederick on Wednesday morning at about daybreak. The regiment is now encamped about a mile outside the city, on the farm of a loyal Marylander. . . . The situation is pleasant, and water is plenty for all purposes. The weather, since we have been here, has been delightful. . . .

The regiment is now furnished with small shelter tents, which will accommodate but two men, each man carrying half. Yesterday we received our overcoats. . . .

Yesterday afternoon, just as the regiment was mustering for dress parade, the first mail for the 26th since we left home arrived. . . . It was with the greatest difficulty the men were kept in the ranks until the letters could be regularly delivered.[5]

After spending ten days at Frederick, the regiment took up the line of march to Hagerstown.

The day being cloudy and cool we marched along at a rapid pace arriving at Middletown about 6 o'clock, when the order was given to halt for the night.

Our tents were soon pitched, camp fires were lighted, and after doing ample justice to the contents of our haversacks we spread our blankets and lay down for the night. At daybreak our slumbers were brought to an abrupt termination by the roll of the drum. It was the Sabbath, but its rest and quiet was not for us, we must reach Bakersville before night, so after eating a hasty breakfast of hard crackers we pushed forward.

The road we took was the one Stonewall Jackson passed over on his retreat from Frederick [after the Battle of Antietam]. Traces of heavy skirmishing were observable all along the road. . . . Near the roadside I observed a number of graves of our men who had fallen, and who were doubtless buried where they fell. At the head of each grave was a small piece of board, on which was marked the initials and sometimes the full name of the deceased, and the regiment to which he belonged.[6]

Nearing Boonesboro, Colonel Morrison halted the regiment, throwing out a guard. Several days earlier, Confederate cavalrymen under the command of J. E. B. Stuart had passed through the Union lines, crossed into Pennsylvania, and entered Chambersburg, receiving the surrender of the town. Now, with 1,200 liberated horses in their bag and an angry pack of Union cavalry at their rear, they were pounding south to the Potomac and safety. Stuart's raiders were reported close by, Morrison told his men, and every man must be ready for action at a moment's notice. "He told us that we must not load our muskets," recalled Sergeant Dodd, "that he greatly preferred the bayonet."[7] Fortunately Stuart's cavalry were some two hours behind the Twenty-sixth.

Each regiment in the Union army was authorized to elect a chaplain by vote of the field officers and company commanders. In many units the men barely tolerated their chaplain, complaining that they were battle-shy and prone to laziness. Others performed their duties well, earning the grudging respect of the men. Some wrote letters home for the illiterate or tended the sick and wounded. A few, carried away by the excitement of the moment, charged the enemy with their men, performing deeds of great heroism.[8] David T. Morrill, minister of Newark's Fifth Baptist Church, joined the regiment on October 21, carrying in his baggage letters from home and several hundred hymnals. His first report appeared in the *Daily Advertiser* on October 24:

On reaching the regiment yesterday I found the men, with very few exceptions, in good health and spirits. They are very glad to see any one from home, especially if he brings messages and letters from loved ones there.

So long as the regiment remains here it will be very easy of access to friends. One can leave Newark at half-past six or eight P.M., and reach here about noon the next day, resting in Harrisburg four or five hours meanwhile. The expense is some eight or nine dollars. One can come within three-fourths of a mile of the camp by railroad. Packages by express will readily reach the regiment so long as it is here. . . .

If we do not move soon, will those who have manifested so deep an interest in the moral and religious welfare of the Regiment forward tracts and late religious newspapers . . . ? I hope the promised Testaments will be forwarded at once. The two hundred soldiers' hymn books that I brought were equally divided among the companies and while I write I can hear "the voice of praise ascending high."⁹

Anxious families at home often first learned of the illness or death of a son or brother through Chaplain Morrill's published correspondence in the *Advertiser:*

A sad accident occurred on the morning of the 21st . . . to a young man in Co. I . . . named Isaac M. Jacobus, whose parents reside at 69 State St. He and another young man were engaged in examining a revolver, when it was accidentally discharged and the bullet entered the abdomen, just above the lower rib on the left side, passed through the body, and is thought by the surgeons to be lying between the two lower ribs. He was immediately carried to the camp hospital, where he was examined by Surgeons [Luther G.] Thomas and [William W.] Bowlby, assisted by the Brigade Surgeon. The wound was pronounced serious, though not necessarily fatal. The health of the camp in other respects is good, there being only two cases of fever here, both of which are considered convalescent.¹⁰

The *Daily Mercury's* war correspondent traveled to Maryland in late October to inspect firsthand the Jersey regiments stationed there. His report of the Twenty-sixth, the first unit he visited, warmed many a loyal Newark heart:

On Thursday, at noon, I arrived within the Federal lines at Hagerstown, and at once devoted myself to the rather difficult task of hunting up, from among the many regiments quartered there, the gallant 26th New Jersey, in whom so many of our citizens are interested. After making many inquiries without gaining the desired information, I sauntered into the Washington House, resolved to refresh the inner man, and then renew my efforts to find the 26th. . . .

On being shown into dinner, among many officers and soldiers of every grade, to my infinite satisfaction I found that the Assistant Quartermaster of the 26th was my nearest neighbor at table. He greeted me warmly, and as he was going to return to camp soon after dinner, I was but too glad to accompany him.

The camp I found located about a mile from the town, on high ground, and well supplied with water. . . .

My arrival was the signal for a rush of the boys to see me, for there were few in the regiment that I did not know, from Colonel Morrison down to the humblest private in the ranks. I found at the colonel's tent, Rev. Mr. Haley, of the Roseville Baptist church, and Mr. William King, of Orange, both on a visit to their friends in the regiment. . . .

I had originally intended to stay but an hour with the 26th, but the time slipped away so pleasantly that it was almost the hour for dress parade, when I recollected that my original programme was to visit the 1st N. J. Brigade, some ten miles away, yet that night. But Colonel Morrison would not listen to my leaving the camp so soon, and promised, if I would remain until morning that he would send me to Bakersville in an ambulance. Upon this promise, I determined to remain and certainly I had no cause to regret it. At 5 o'clock the regiment had a dress parade, in which the rapid improvement of the men, and the soldierly qualities of the colonel, were made equally apparent.

Just as the parade was dismissed, muffled drums were heard coming nearer and nearer, and soon a little funeral cortege came slowly along through the camp, and wound its way toward a dark piece of woods a short distance beyond. While the sad train was passing, the camp, that a moment before was all bustle and life, was hushed to silence; each man seeming to feel the solemnity of the moment; for a soldier soon learns that with him life is indeed uncertain. I took the arm of Assistant Surgeon Thomas and followed the funeral procession to the lonely woods, where a grave had been prepared, and where with uncovered head I listened to the good chaplain, who, most fervently prayed for the far-off parents of the lad they were about to consign to his last resting place. . . .

On returning to the tent of Col. Morrison, we found a bountiful repast spread out, and can assure you we never partook of a meal that we relished more. The supper was but just finished, and segars in puffing order, when a corps of manly voices outside the tent commenced singing a beautiful air. It proved to be a glee club of Germans belonging to the regiment, and for an hour they entertained us with songs of fatherland, and those other inspiring choruses which the Germans know so well how to sing.

No sooner had the singers retired than the more familiar voices of certain members of Companies A, E, H and I, struck up a lively air, and for some time they continued to sing many of the choicest gems—some sentimental, some patriotic, and some comical.[11]

McClellan's victory at the Battle of Antietam in September proved to be a hollow one. Lee's decimated army, staggered by the loss of some of its best troops, might have been utterly destroyed and the war shortened perceptably if only McClellan had renewed his attack. But for forty days the Army of the Potomac lay immobile, while Lee regrouped. Lincoln urged movement; McClellan preferred caution. As October's ideal fighting weather went sliding by, McClellan called for more troops and supplies—although a strength report on October 20 showed 133,433 men present for duty.[12] Lincoln's patience with his young general wore noticeably thin. When a message arrived in Washington that half of the army's horses were broken down from fatigue and disease, the president could endure no more. "I have just read your despatch about sore tongued and fatigued horses," he telegraphed McClellan. "Will you pardon me for asking what the horses of your army have done since the battle of Antietam that fatigue anything?"[13] Still McClellan did not move.

The Twenty-sixth spent the month of October drilling, marching and waiting. Wrote Private Woodruff:

We are drilling almost constantly, and are improving rapidly. Yesterday we had a regimental or battallion drill, lasting three hours. We yesterday received guns to replace those that were out of order. About one-third of those we brought with us from Newark were worthless. Those we have received are the same style of gun—the old fashioned, smooth-bore muskets, and we are afraid we shall not get any better very soon. Col. Morrison, however, says he will rely principally upon the bayonet.[14]

The weather turned much colder—water froze in the men's canteens—as the Twenty-sixth prepared to cross the Potomac River. On October 29 orders came to leave Hagerstown.

The standing order, "Prepare to march," was yesterday morning followed by an order to "March in an hour." There was "hurrying to and fro," and mounting knapsacks in "hot haste." One of the saddest events connected with breaking camp and marching along is leaving the sick comrades behind in hospitals among strangers. We left ten behind who were carried in ambulances to the Court House Hospital, Hagerstown. . . . One has consumption, another the dysentery; the rest have typhoid fever. Some are convalescent, and the others are in the earlier stages of fever. The night before we left we had a prayer meeting for the purpose of thanking "the Preserver of men" for his remarkable preservation of the regiment while in that camp. Death did not come near our camp, while in the adjoining camp, out of about an equal number of men, there were four deaths.[15]

That evening, their last on Union soil, the men pitched their tents "in a wood of gigantic trees of primeval growth." The Reverend Morrill was deeply affected:

In an hour or two there had as by magic sprung up a "white walled" city of scores of streets and hundreds of houses. The moonlight, the huge trees with their dim shadows, the numerous camp fires brightly burning surrounded by groups of soldiers, the light shining through the canvass roofed tents, all taken together, formed one of the most picturesque scenes that I ever beheld.

Our rations were soon despatched and I proceeded to distribute some of the thousand tracts received from the American Temperance Union as a donation from the Presbyterian Church in Boonton. . . . They will, I trust, do something to decrease intemperance which so fearfully aggravates the horrors of war; . . . for the credit of the Regiment I must say that I have not seen a drunken man since I joined the Regiment, and have heard of only two.

This morning the men are receiving their ammunition, which looks as if we [are] soon to move on and over.

In a few weeks at farthest there will a pressing and pinching want of mittens—soldiers' (one fingered) mittens. Will every mother, wife and maiden interested in the Regiment send one pair? Don't say "be warmed," but knit and send the mittens.[16]

The Twenty-sixth was 998 men strong as it crossed the Potomac to Virginia, the capital state of the Confederacy. October's idleness had made many of the men anxious "to strike a blow for the Union." The hard reality was that the regiment was far from ready for battle. Said one officer:

We were fully and well equipped, with the important exception, however, of our guns, which were old, altered muskets, and totally unfit for active service. In respect to men, the regiment was composed of the flower of Essex County. True we had been been hastily brought together, and some had been enlisted who were too old or too young or otherwise unfit for service, but the number of these was not large, and the great body of the regiment was composed of young active men, mechanics and farmers, men of character and intelligence for the most part. Out of such material the very best soldiers might have been made. Of our officers, Colonel Morrison was almost the only one who had seen service, and he had been a cavalry officer, so that his duties as commander of an infantry regiment were new to him. Many of the officers were, up to the time of their appointment, unacquainted even with the company drill, and it was inevitable from the way in which they were chosen that some of them should prove unfit for the positions which they occupied. We had to go through that weeding-out process which all our volunteer regiments went through with; but for us the process was a costly one, for we went through it, not in a winter camp, but during an active and trying campaign, when good officers would have been everything to us. We were emphatically a green regiment when we entered upon active service, and we learned our drill, not on the parade ground, but by long marches and finally on the battle field. We had one great advantage. We were brigaded with veterans, and with veterans, too, who had won a high reputation in the Peninsula and Maryland campaigns. Their example was our real teacher in the school of war.[17]

7

Foot-sore, Shoulder-sore
and Very Much Fatigued

Implicit in the government's summer call for volunteers was the promise that the men would see light duty as garrison troops. The *Mercury* and the *Advertiser* had virtually assured their readers that little active service should be expected of the "nine-monthers." And until October became November, men of the Twenty-sixth nursed the hope that a nine-month regiment could hardly be of any real military value. Such at least was the reasoning of many. Yet the exigencies of war defy reason and the shortening days of autumn were to have a sobering effect. "We had dreamed," wrote Sergeant Dodd, "that we were to be employed in garrison duty to relieve older and more experienced troops. Now we knew that we must take our share, raw as we were, in the toil and peril of the coming campaign."[1]

November was a sobering month for the nation as well. Lincoln had finally made up his mind. McClellan, for all his brilliance, suffered from a serious case of "the slows." Always certain he was outnumbered, forever calling for more troops and supplies, he had used the Army of the Potomac—the largest, best equipped army any nation had ever put in the field—defensively, for limited ends. Lincoln had come to understand that the South would not be beaten until its armies were destroyed, its people convinced their cause was hopeless. McClellan could not see that, and because of it his usefulness was at an end. On November 7 McClelland was relieved of command, replaced by Major General Ambrose E. Burnside.[2]

Burnside took command reluctantly, doubting his own ability to lead so great a host. Friendly with McClellan and popular with the men, he had achieved some success in North Carolina. He also enjoyed a reputation as a fighter, which was exactly what Lincoln wanted. Aware that the president demanded action, Burnside formulated his plan. He would move eastward quickly, through the Virginia countryside to Falmouth, then cross the Rappahannock River at Fredericksburg, seize the town and make it his base for a lightning strike at Richmond. Lincoln approved the plan. "He thinks that it will succeed if you move very rapidly," General Henry Halleck wired Burnside, "otherwise not."[3] Burnside regrouped his corps into Right, Left, and Center Grand Divisions, ordering his division and corps commanders to move by forced march. Between November 17 and 19 the Army of the Potomac reached Falmouth, occupying the heights opposite Fredericksburg. The Twenty-sixth New Jersey, now part of the Left Grand Division commanded by General William Franklin, left Hagerstown on October 31, marched to Berlin, crossed the Potomac on pontoons to New Baltimore, and thence proceeded to Aquia Creek, some few miles from Falmouth. There it waited, knowing nothing of Burnside's plan other than rumor and surmise.

On the evening before the long march began the Twenty-sixth received orders to be ready to leave camp at dawn with knapsacks, tents, and two day's rations. Private Woodruff took a moment to pen a short and somewhat inaccurate note to the *Daily Mercury:*

> I suppose you would like to know what has become of the 26th. . . . We are ordered to proceed immediately to Washington, where we are to store our knapsacks, and march immediately, we know not whither. It is reported among the officers that we are to take transports and sail to South Carolina. This evening each man received a Testament with a gilt edge, and a red morocco cover. . . .
>
> The health of the regiment is very good, and the men are happy and contented. We have only had a very few desertions, and they who have deserted were not true patriots, but merely mercenaries.[4]

Sergeant Cummings's first letter to the *Mercury* was full of good humor.

> After nearly two weeks sojourn at Hagerstown, our Brigade received orders to move, and on Thursday morning, after a rigid picket duty of twenty-four hours, we filed off in the direction of Williamsport, within a mile of which we encamped in a splendid grove of oaks, beneath which we found camp-fires already burning, as a force of fifteen thousand men had left it only a few hours before our arrival. The 26th were here much surprised at the Brobdingnagian character of lice left behind by those preceding us, as they held un-lice-nsed sway, and roamed the woods in swarms until our arrival.[5]

The regiment marched a hard fifteen miles that day. "The middle of the day was exceedingly warm," wrote the Reverend Morrill to the *Advertiser*, a note of disapproval already apparent, "and the men were so heavily loaded that some of them gave out by the way."[6]

> We were marching in company with Vermont veterans and the difference in the powers of endurance between new levies and veterans is marked. There are two or three reasons; one is, that new men overburthen themselves with unnecessary baggage which the old veteran has learned to dispense with.

Another reason, is that many men enter the army that ought never to have been accepted. Laxity in the Examining Surgeons ought to be a punishable offence. It is a crime against the man and the Government. The idea of frail young men carrying a gun and from thirty to fifty pounds all day, is absurd in the extreme . . . .

We encamped for the night in a magnificent forest such as I have seldom seen, except in this country. But it was only for the night. We had some time to put up only a few tents, but the majority laid down on a bed of leaves with the lofty boughs waving over our heads.[6]

At six the next morning the unit was on the road again. Chaplain Morrill, entitled to a horse by virtue of his rank, was no less exhausted than the foot soldiers.

The only thought that reconciled me at all was that perhaps we were hastening on to help our brethren that were in the death throes of battle. As we came through Crampton Pass and heard the continual sound of cannon we thought that this might be the case, and the thought roused many a weary and lagging soldier.[7]

That evening, after marching some ten miles under a sweltering sun, the Twenty-sixth made camp two miles to the southeast of Boonesboro. Sergeant Cummings, a robust twenty-four years of age, was as weary as the rest.

That moonlight night your correspondent wrapped himself in his blanket at the foot of a whispering oak, and for the first time since leaving home heard the hoarse murmuring of the katydids and the shrill chirrups of crickets. The regiment had been marched with but a slight rest during the day, and the most of the boys, fatigued in body if not in mind, discarded the trouble of pitching their "shelters," raking the fallen leaves in beds, and dropping thereon in chatting squads, fell asleep around their blazing campfires.[8]

On Sunday the line of march took the men past the Antietam battlefield, explained Sergeant Cummings:

At half past four o'clock on Sunday morning, the boys sprang to their feet at the sound of the reveille, and after snatching a hasty cup of coffee were again on the march, leading the brigade. It was the only time the 26th has had the honor of being the vanguard. With but little delay we marched over a portion of the ever-memorable field of Antietam, on which a Union farmer pointed out to me a well into which the bodies of seventy dead Rebels had been buried. . . .

Through Rotersville, through or over Crampton Pass, through a pleasant little village nestling at its foot, in which the church bells were calmly tolling the hour for Divine service amid the sullen booming of artillery which was heard to our right in the direction of Winchester during the entire day, the 26th wound its way, the tail of the brigade twisting itself along the tortuous road in our rear. Acting Gen. [Henry] Whiting, Colonel of a Vermont regiment in our brigade, rode at our head, and seemed bent on "bushing" us, if possible. Rests were, like angel's visits, few and far between, and many a weary Jerseyman either slung away his knapsack in toto, or distributed a portion of its contents by the roadside, which exactly suited the cormorant tastes of the Vermonters in our rear. Many an interchange of opinion concerning Col. Whiting revealed the estimation in which he was held by our panting files, and if one-half our wishes that day had been gratified he would have gone to—somewhere several thousand times. Toward night the men began to fall out of the ranks, and your correspondent, with several of Companies B. and A. formed what we called a "Starlight Bridgade," and limped into camp at Berlin, on the Potomac, six miles below Harper's Ferry after nine o'clock, footsore, feverish and altogether fit subjects for a benevolent Almshouse-keeper. I first saw the Potomac by moonlight, as it wound its course between the steep hills which line the boundaries of Virginia and Maryland at this point. On its shallow bosom, directly in our front, and above the blackened ponderous stone piers of what was once a bridge in reality, floated the first pontoon-bridge which had presented itself to the 26th. Beyond lay the densely-wooded and frowning hills of Virginia. But "its no use talking." We were sore and exhausted, and dropped ourselves upon the stony ground amid many thousands blackening the river side. The night became cold—very cold. Aeolus had kicked the North wind from his cave, and he was revenging the insult by swelling his cheeks and venting his cold breath upon the men. It was the coldest night that we ever experienced. It was almost impossible to sleep, and half the night we lay awake with fever burning our cheeks and ague shaking our limbs, while our visions of hot whiskey skins floated before us.[9]

The Reverend Morrill, with better sources of information than the enlisted men, perceived the outlines of the army's new plan.

We are within sound of the distant cannon's roar. There is a massive and rapid movement of the whole of the vast army in this vicinity. It is thought to be a race for Richmond, through Thoroughfare Gap. Since "the race is not to the swift," may we not hope to win this time? The weather is most delightful and the roads very fine, and we are admonished by the familiar proverb, "Make hay while the sun shines," to improve diligently every passing hour.

The flattering unction that some have laid to their souls, that the "nine months men" were only expected to do garrison duty is being rapidly dispelled. It looks a little as if we were expected to do three years' duty in nine months.[10]

The countryside through which the regiment marched was sparsely settled, poorly cultivated, and sadly ravaged by the passage of contending armies. Yet there was still some property to be confiscated, especially if its owner were a Rebel. The chaplain was saddened by what he saw:

There are others besides the "black men that have no rights that are respected." When a man condemns "Yankee men and Yankee money"—spelling condemn, d——m—as some do, it is the signal for indiscriminate and immediate confiscation, especially if rations are scant and the men hungry. The land is fine and the scenery magnificant, but it will take a quarter of a century to repair the desolation war has made.[11]

Morrill had an eye for the humorous side of war as well as anyone.

A pretty good instance of Diamond cut Diamond, or rogue catch rogue, occurred last night, in this wise: The Vermont boys, with whom we are brigaded, are adepts at plundering, as I suppose all the old Regiments are, and last night they were leading off in that direction, when some Jersey boys taking some guns and one of them the Colonel's sword, went out and pretending to be a provost guard fell in with some Vt. boys who were carrying off a yearling which they had taken and killed. They made them "stand and deliver" and ordered them to repair to their quarters, telling them if they were caught again they would at once be reported to Gen. McClellan—the Jersey boys meanwhile appropriating the plunder.[12]

The men, wrote Sergeant Cummings, were dog tired, some ill with fever, as another day's march began.

Once again the reveille. Every man was on his feet, and many after the Doctor. A pill settled my case, and ere the sun was up we had passed over the pontoon bridge, and were climbing the steep Virginia boundry. We had reached our Division, and now hoped for easier marching. On the top of the hill we halted in a large field, and a rail fence was soon used up in cooking our coffee, while Vinton's Brigade, and the Division artillery, took the front. . . . Before meridian we passed through Lovettsville, which your readers will easily find on their maps, and from thence, with slight interruptions by the army telegraph wagons, the corps of which were stretching the thin rubber-coated army telegraph over the rocks and fields lining our march, we reached Wheatland, two miles beyond which we struck over the fields and the whole brigade encamped in a grove of small trees, near a field of unshocked corn, the stalks of which we immediately gobbled up and piled against the trees as a burrow for the men. Colonel Morrison slept in one, another served for a hospital, and any quantity of privates availed themselves of the opportunity, and secured similar places of refuge. There were no white men occupying the houses in the vicinity, they having either joined or been forced into the rebel service. The Vermonters—in fact, all the old regiments—pitched into the chickens and sheep in the vicinity, and soon returned laden with fresh meat, and that of the best kind, while the poor green 26th lay with hungry stomachs, with the exception of a few rabbits which they ran down in the woods and fields adjacent. We could hardly realize that we were in an enemy's country. The 1st and 2d New Jersey lay in a grove to our left, and many a camp fire in our camp was surrounded with a knot of eager listeners to their adventures.[13]

Because the supply wagons were delayed, wrote Cummings, provisions began to run short. Each man was alloted two hard crackers as his daily ration. Yet still the march continued, seemingly without end.

The reveille again. Again a rousing of the aching limbs, and a rubbing of the smoke-filled eyes. One cup of steaming coffee, (that's what they call it,) and with unwashed faces and hands, greasy from rations of salt pork, the 26th again grasped their miserable smooth-bore Harpers Ferry and Springfield muskets, and trudged along the weary road, their snaky line of bayonets glistening in the morning sun. This was a hard day's toil, and the boys were much fagged. Again your correspondent joined the "Starlight-Brigade," and again found our camp on a wooded-hill. The campfires again gleamed, and to some purpose, as the boys "began to learn the ropes" from the Vermonters, and fresh meat made its first appearance in our camp. Cabbages, potatoes, etc., were unearthed, and many a Secesh homestead, in the vicinity, found itself minus of eatables that night. Pig-headed Whiting fired at some of the boys on a foraging excursion, but we did well, nevertheless, and many an empty stomach of the previous night, lay calmly reposing in full glory on the night of Wednesday, November 5th, 1862.

Morning came, and with it the inevitable reveille, dispelling the home dreams of the weary soldier. No marching until noon. The 26th was hungry and out of rations. It must be filled, and filled it was with meat, but crackers were non est—half box for one company. At noon, the whole of Franklin's corps, to which we belong, moved simultaneously in a southeast direction, in heavy columns, over the fields and along the roads. It was a magnificent sight. The hills, valleys and plains were perfectly black with moving masses of humanity. Night came, cold and starless. Our regiment was halted by Division, in a bleak open field, surrounded with the worm-rail fences so common in this country. At the order "Stack arms!" the rails vanished like lightning. We were then again ordered to fall in line, and moved off into a dense grove during the darkness, which was only relieved by the fires of those fortunate enough to precede us. The sky threatened rain. Fires were built, coffee and meat vanished, and we crawled into our "shelters" just as the big drops of rain commenced beating the long roll over our heads. Yet, even in such cases, hospitality burned bright within our hearts. Two stragglers of the New Jersey 21st, unable to find their regiment during the darkness, came into our camp and were furnished with a cup of coffee and a hotel gratis. We were in dreamland that night, for the soft patter of the rain over our heads carried us back to childhood, when we slept in grandmother's garret, and listened to the drops dancing on the shingles above us.

The reveille, and "Fall in for roll call, Company E," from the Orderly. It was our sixth day's consecutive march. To say that we were tired would be useless. For myself I can truly say that I was done for, and had serious intentions of calling for a corporal and six men to bury me. But we must surge ahead with the great sea of humanity rolling toward Richmond, and our footsteps were once more wearily turned southward. We passed through Purcellsville, Uniontown, Upperville, and various collections of houses, pig-styes, and hen-coops honored with high-sounding names, within sight of the Thoroughfare Gap, the Bull Run Mountain, and Manassas Gap—a steady tramp, tramp, over stony mountains, over wide plains, and through deep gullies, marching through brooks and over ruined arches—no inhabitants, no life, no hay, no fences of any account—one wide credit of desolation balancing the debit of Virginia's Secession. One can have no idea of the ravages of war until he sees the reality. . . . Before night, we crossed the Manassas Gap Railroad, and encamped in the bosom of the Sixth Army Corps, at White Plains, or Salem Station. Tents were hastily pitched on the hill-side, and then the 26th rested from its long march. We were in the woods, and the dead leaves were quickly scratched into our tents, on which despite the weather, which had suddenly grown very cold, we enjoyed a sweet sleep, redolent with hazy recollections of home.

On the morning of the next day, Saturday, Nov. 8, we found a fierce snow storm whirling its milky flakes into the crevices of our tents and whitening the bare fields and mountains around us. It was a day of gloomy thoughts and chilly reflections. Even Company A had sobered down, and the members became as silent as quakers. The snow fell quite steadily until night-fall, leaving the ground in a convenient state of muddiness for the 26th New Jersey to go on picket duty, which they improved on the next day, without rations. Passing through the debris of a camp some of the boys secured some salt pork and old beef bones which had been left behind, and the second reserve spent their midnight hours in endeavoring to roast or boil a supper from them. What would the folks at home have said could they have seen us? The next morning we were called in without seeing any of the enemy, although we afterwards learned they were closely watching us. Upon reaching camp we were given fifteen minutes to strike our tents, pack our knapsacks, and get our rations, after which the regiment was reformed and acted as a rear guard to our corps, bringing in a train of cattle with us. They say "Stonewall" talks of attacking us. We are ready for him.[14]

The Twenty-sixth New Jersey reached New Baltimore, Virginia, on November 9 "after a weary Sunday march." Chaplain Morrill was outraged. The army, he wrote the *Daily Advertiser*, must not profane the Lord's Day if it hoped to be victorious.

It seems to be the fate of this Regiment to march on Sundays. I do not know, however, that it is peculiar to it, as I heard a veteran of the 2d N. J. say to-day, who had been in service 18 months, that he had never seen a Sunday since he entered the service. Men may think as they will, but how can we expect the blessing of the God of battles when we so persistently and so universally profane his day and name as is done in the army?[15]

The Twenty-sixth camped near New Baltimore for nearly a week, enjoying a welcome respite from the hardships of the march. "There is no enemy in sight," wrote Cummings, "and his whereabouts is of course to us unknown."

> The New Jersey Brigade, Gen. [Alfred T. A.] Torbert, is in our front, and it is computed by competent judges that there are three hundred thousand Union troops between us and Culpepper Court House. As far as the eye can reach it discloses fields and forest-covered hills dotted with the camp-fires of our army. Our encampment is situated on an oak-crowned knoll, over which we are jumbled in an almost undistinguishable mess with the 2d, 3d, 4th, 5th and 6th Vermont regiments, which form the rest of our Brigade. We were reviewed yesterday morning by Gen. McClellan . . . accompanied by a brilliant train of officers, among whom the slouched hat and militaire whiskers of Burnside were conspicuous, after which our new Brigadier, Gen. [Albion P.] Howe, put us through a brigade drill, and with a graceful wave of his hat, dismissed us. The 26th have improved rapidly within the last few weeks, and for rapidity of movement and efficiency of drill, compares favorably with some of the old regiments. The colonel is a great favorite with the boys, and under his eye the regiment never can fail to earn a brilliant reputation in the battle-field. One of the boys this morning expressed himself as willing to "go through Hades with his hat off for Col. Morrison," and that terse expression is an index to the feeling of the whole regiment.[16]

Life in camp was not altogether unpleasant; at worst it compared favorably with the battlefield. During these waiting days of November, the regiment lived in shelter tents and slept upon the ground, at least until it learned how luxurious a bed could be made from pine branches, dried grass or corn stalks.[17] Music was one of the favorite diversions of the Civil War soldier, only slightly less appreciated than hot black coffee in the morning. Whether on the march or in camp, the men entertained themselves with the popular and patriotic airs of the day. While the Twenty-sixth had no band, its glee clubs entertained brigade-wide. When General Alfred T. A. Torbert of the New Jersey Brigade visited Colonel Morrison, the glee clubs of Companies A, E, and I were there to serenade him. Sergeant Cummings recounted the homey interlude for *Mercury* readers:

> The entrance to the Colonel's tent was a scene for a painter. Before it blazed a tremendous camp fire lighting a circle of eager listeners. . . . At the entrance sat the General wrapped in a military cloak, with his army hat drawn over his eyes, and enjoying one of the Colonel's cigars. To his left was Col. Morrison and one of the General's aids, Colonel [Charles] Stoughten of the 5th Vermont, another favorite of ours, and various other military dignitaries, while his left disclosed the good-natured phiz of Chaplain Morrill, who seemed to laugh as much as anybody, and the easy, manly Captain Morris twirling his moustache with his usual careless sang froid. Gen. Tor-

bert was much amused at hearing "Robinson Crusoe" sung in Tom Osborn's best style. Amid other pieces sung for the General's entertainment were "The Star Spangled Banner," "Alabama again," "The Jewish Maid," "Vive l'America," "Bingen on the Rhine," "Rosa's Wedding Day," "Rip, Rap, Set 'em up Again," the whole concluding with the grand chorus of "America," which brought out the deep bass voice of Col. Stoughten. After refreshments by the Colonel, the party sang "Columbia the Gem of the Ocean," and separated for the night.[18]

Neither Colonel Morrison's cherry campfire nor the gay songs of the glee club could dispell for long the certain knowledge that a winter campaign, a thing dreaded by Yankee and Rebel alike, was in prospect. The Reverend Morrill was uneasy.

> Our regiment and in fact all the troops in the vicinity, are encamped in the woods, consequently fuel is abundant. The falling leaves and nipping frost warn us that grim visaged winter is close at hand. We are living in hopes that tents better adapted to the inclement season will soon be furnished the Regiment.
>
> At this point I mention the suggestion that friends at home who contemplate sending on warm clothing to the regiment would do well to hurry them up as they will soon be greatly needed. Three very important articles in the soldiers' diet, namely, rice, beans and sugar have been stopped for the present, the reason assigned for stopping them is the difficulties of transportation, but this does not satisfy the men, and as might be expected considerable dissatisfaction is felt in consequence.[19]

Several days later the chaplain wrote again to the *Daily Advertiser* in the same gloomy tone.

> We are still encamped where we were when I wrote last, expecting every hour of every day to hear the word "March." It seems a pity that during these golden Indian summer days we should be in camp, so near the verge of winter and the horrors of Virginia mud. I suppose, and that is about all any one can do in regard to army movements, that we are waiting for Gen. Burnside to get well seated in the saddle of his predecessor and to become familiar with the forces and position of this vast army. Still another reason is the lack of food. We cannot move without rations. However willing we may be to subsist on the enemy, in this region it is an impossibility to any great extent. The armies during the past two years have swept over this region like devouring locusts, leaving scarcely an edible thing behind them. It is only two or three days since the Railroad was put in running order, and though taxed to its utmost capacity it has not as yet been able to bring enough . . . pilot bread and crackers for the daily consumption of these numerous legions.

Morrill's rapidly dwindling enthusiasm perked briefly when General Albion P. Howe, the new brigade commander, inspected the regiment.

He seems a thorough soldier and disciplinarian, and is winning golden opinions from all those men who like to see and are willing to undergo all that is requisite to make good soldiers. But there are far too many who shrink from burdens, shirk duty and desire to save or serve themselves rather than endure what is necessary to save and serve their country. The stern realities of war sift out and blow away much chaff that passes for the good wheat of patriotism amid the peaceful scenes of home. I sometimes ask myself shall we ever again see that self-forgetful, self-denying patriotism that for seven years animated the hearts of our Revolutionary fathers, amid trials and privations that as yet we know little or nothing of.[20]

Enlisted men, worn by the long march through the ravaged Virginia countryside, could only grumble at their fate. Officers had the option of resignation. "The unfit ones began to drop off," wrote Sergeant Dodd. "First our lieutenant-colonel, then our major was smitten with what the men called 'cannon fever.' Their health failed suddenly, their resignations were offered and accepted and we were well rid of them."[21] The winnowing process continued through the winter months; four captains, the major, and the lieutenant colonel all resigned before mid-March.[22] Fortunately, the vacancies were filled by men of good caliber. Captain William W. Morris of Company A, promoted to major on November 19, was perhaps the most widely admired officer in the regiment.[23]

On November 15 came the long-expected order to break camp. Once again, complained the Reverend Morrill, the unit was to march on a Sunday.

> Whether war inverts all the laws of God's kingdom or not I cannot say, but it has thus far with us inverted the laws of the Sabbath. We have rested weekdays and worked (marched) Sundays. To-night the men are to receive an additional supply of ammunition sufficient to make 40 rounds per man. This looks like earnest work. We start for Fredericksburg, and the knowing ones at headquarters ominously shake their heads and say that in a day or two there will come "the tug of war."[24]

That same day President Lincoln issued an order calling for "the orderly observance of the Sabbath by the officers and men in the military and naval service."[25] Chaplain Morrill learned of the directive four days later:

> There was a good deal of displeasure manifested by the men because they were deprived again of their Sunday rest. Riding along I conferred with several chaplains of the division in regard to memorializing the generals respecting the better observance of the Lord's day. . . .
> Feeling thus, you can imagine how glad I was yesterday to see the general order concerning Sabbath observance issued by the President as Commander in Chief of the Army and Navy. In the name of thousands and hundreds of thousands, I say "God bless Abraham Lincoln for this order." Oh that the order had come earlier! but better late than not at all. God alone knows how terribly the discipline and character of the National forces has suffered and

the cause they defend been imperiled by the almost universal profanation of the day and the name of the "Most High."[26]

Before breaking camp at New Baltimore, "the sick that were unable to accompany us" were sent to the hospital at Warrenton. The march to Aquia Creek was an exhausting one, wrote Private Larter:

After three days of the severest marching ever experienced by us, and I think by any troops in our army, we have reached this place. We left New Baltimore on Sunday last, and marched to about three miles beyond Catlett's Station, where we encamped for the night, having undergone the most rapid marching all day. So also on the second and third day, we marched almost on a double quick. We reached this place yesterday about noon, foot-sore, shoulder-sore, and very much fatigued. We are now right near Aquia Creek. It is supposed we will remain here two or three days to get supplies.[27]

Chaplain Morrill's low tolerance for the rigors of camp life was put to its first test as the skies above filled with storm clouds. "The men were very weary when they had pitched their tents, gathered their wood and cooked their supplies," he told the *Advertiser:*

Still quite a number were gathered around a large fire, where we sang and prayed, and I talked about this anomalous way of spending the day of rest. . . . We were aroused by the reveille at 5 o'clock next morning and marched at 7. Nothing of an unusual character occurred that day; there was the usual amount of groaning under the burdens of knapsacks and falling out by the way.

We are 10 miles from Aquia Creek Landing where we are procuring our supplies, and some 16 miles from Fredericksburg. We are now in the left wing of the army under Gen. [William B.] Franklin. The rainy season has commenced and the roads are becoming horrible. . . . The leaves have not all fallen from the trees, and the persimmons have not yet been fully ripened by the frost. . . . To-day has been showery, reminding me of April at home. The showers have been accompanied by thunder and lightning, and now while I write the rain comes pattering down upon the roof of our tents. . . .

Mr. Green, the sutler reached camp yesterday, 10 days from Newark, having passed through many dangers and difficulties in pursuit of the Regiment. He narrowly escaped being captured by the Guerrillas that hang upon our rear. Seven of his craft were taken a little in advance. His arrival was most welcome to many of the men. The saying of one for the time seemed true. "Sutler is king."

It is not hunger, but a craving for a change of diet that make soldiers willing to pay anything for something different from the three articles on which they subsist, pork, beef and crackers. It is a cry of nature almost as loud as hunger, and it is desirable that whenever possible the Government should heed it and furnish a greater variety of food. The most prevalent disease in camp—that which so terribly debilitates the men—chronic diarrhea—is without doubt partly occasioned by the lack of variety in diet.

We have just received notice of the first death that has occurred in our Regiment. George Elwood, Co. D, from Caldwell died Nov. 6th, of Typhoid fever, in the U.S. Hospital at Hagerstown, Md. Death the great reaper has begun among us to gather in his harvest. . . . The inadequacy of shelter tents to shelter the men in a severe storm has been fully demonstrated in this storm. The men in the main strive to make the best of it. As one man in the Division was drummed out of camp to the tune of the "rogue's march" amid the jeers of thousands for cowardice, I overheard some say that they "would rather bear it some longer than to be thus disgraced."[28]

The heavy rains, explained Morrill, turned the usually dusty roads to mud.

I have often heard the expression, "By the powers of mud!" I never realized before that mud had any particular power, but I know now that it is one of the great powers of the earth—a power that almost paralyzes the power of 300,000 armed men. But it must hinder our enemies in some measure if not to the same extent that it does us. . . .

In regard to the religious interest in the Regiment, it is not all that I should like to see it, though there is some, which is evidenced by the interest felt in the prayer meetings which are held almost every evening, and pretty well attended, considering the disadvantages under which we labor. One word to those fathers, mothers and wives who have written to me asking me to look specially after their sons and husbands and write them in return. I receive your letters thankfully, will do what I can gladly, but cannot promise to write generally or punctually. Few of you have any idea of the difficulties which attend correspondence in camp. Do not construe the fact of my not answering your letters into indifference in regard to the request they contain.[29]

After nearly a week of rain during which the men suffered miserably from exposure, the weather turned dry and very cold. The Reverend Morrill persuaded Colonel Morrison to honor Lincoln's recent order.

For the first time since I have been in the Regiment we made the attempt last Lord's day to observe the Sabbath. True it was not such a calm and quiet day as most of us have been accustomed to spend at home. The sounds of drum and fife are not as suggestive of worship as the sound of the "church going bell." And the continual sound of the wood choppers' axes, made by those who had forgotten . . . to chop enough Saturday for two days, reminded us all more of a working week day than a resting Sunday.

We had regimental inspection, at the close of which the regiment formed a hollow square, when I read some of the articles of war, after which we sung and I made an address and offered prayer, and after we had sung again the regiment was dismissed. It was pretty cold for out-door service, but it was the best that could be done. The men had the rest of the day to themselves, with the exception of a little while taken for dress parade towards night.

An evening prayer meeting called by the chaplain was interrupted by rowdies from a nearby regiment.

We suffered it rather than resort to the rigors of military law, which make it a punishable offense. But one of our number was determined to inflict summary punishment upon the chief offender. He came in a towering rage, swearing that he would whip the first man he could find that would be guilty of such a sacreligious [sic] act as disturbing a prayer meeting. I told him I was glad to see his respect for religious worship, but did not think it was necessary to swear and fight to maintain it. But he thought otherwise, and in spite of all my persuasions and calls for interference, he could not be stopped in his efforts . . . until he had most thoroughly thrashed the offender and made him promise to do so no more. By this time I had succeeded in getting the officer of the day to make his appearance, but he could lay hold of only the one who had been the champion of unmolested worship. It was the general opinion of all that he hardly deserved to be punished as the law directed, so he was let go. His seemed to be a righteous indignation, though rather unrighteously manifested. The idea has been current in camp that after we laid in 13 days rations for man and beast . . . that we should march again. But nothing definite is known here. . . . There was considerable heavy firing heard yesterday in the direction of Fredericksburg, with what result we do not know.[30]

Aquia Creek Landing on the Potomac was now the army's base of supplies. Government steamers arrived daily, filling the new warehouses with the necessaries of a winter campaign.

All our supplies reach us by way of Aquia Creek Landing. They are brought from the landing here, a distance of twelve miles, in wagons. By reason of the bad roads, when we first arrived, it was with the greatest difficulty that they could be brought up fast enough but as they have been improved somewhat since, we have our usual supplies.

About a week since sixty men were detailed from the 26th to guard a supply train to the landing and back, your correspondent being among the number; it was a day or two after a heavy rain, and we had a good opportunity to witness the difficulty of moving wagons over Virginia roads, or rather through Virginia mud. Sometimes the hub would be buried completely in the sacred soil. What will be the condition of these roads after two or three weeks rain, such as sometimes visits these parts, shall have fallen, we can form some faint conception. In no place scarcely are the roads wide enough for two teams to pass each other, consequently all the supply trains have to return by another route. It generally takes about two days to make the trip.[31]

The Twenty-sixth New Jersey Volunteers celebrated Thanksgiving Day as best it could. "Throughout the limit of the corps, good humor and mirth prevailed; the sick forgot their pains, and the homesick ones, for the time, looked bright, as they yielded to the general feeling of happiness."[32] Wrote Chaplain Morrill:

The day was so fine, the air so bracing and the sky so clear and the sun so genial that he who did not involuntarily thank God must have had a most thankless heart. There was an almost total exemption from drill which invariably pleases soldiers. At the close of regimental inspection a hollow square was formed and the Governor's proclamation read, and being assembled in our accustomed place of worship, viz., around our flag staff, I mentioned a few of the reasons we had for thanksgiving. . . . The arrival of the sutler with fresh supplies furnished some variety for the men. The officers dined on pork and beans—the "et ceteras" being omitted.

But that which afforded the most joy to the Regiment on that day was the sight of many old friends and acquaintances. The 2d N.J. Brigade and Clark's (late Beam's) Battery went past us on their march to Falmouth to join General Hooker. . . . There was many a glad meeting of those long separated by the vicissitudes of war. It was a solemn sight, however, to see the desolations war had made in those regiments. When they went from home they were 900 to 1,000 strong, now two or three hundred effective men were all they could muster.

The day after Thanksgiving orders came to move the regimental camp to "a more eligible site." Rumor had it, said the chaplain, that the army was going into winter quarters:

The order involved the usual military paradox—"Make yourselves comfortable for 40 days, and be prepared to move at an hour's notice." The idea of going into winter quarters I am sorry to say, is by far the most popular. I concede that a winter campaign must be horrible here; but can it be attended with a greater loss of health and life than our summer campaign was? To me it seems that masterly inactivity will destroy us as a nation, and masterly activity can do no more.

In all this division of the army the men are as busy as ants in preparing comfortable (?) quarters for the winter. I doubt whether there is a style of hut or habitation used in any part of the world that has not in some respects its counterpart here. On the whole, I think the Barbarian style predominates. Necessity, the mother of invention, has a most numerous progeny here. Our camp is most beautiful for situation. It is in a fine grove, on a gentle and gradual declivity, laid out in regular streets, which are covered with arbors made of boughs. Between the main body of the camp and tents of the field and staff officers, there runs a rivulet, which furnishes water, and gives a picturesque variety to the scene. In front of the Colonel's tent there stands a fine flag staff, from the top of which every day floats the red, white and blue. On either side of the avenue there is a row of fine trees. A fine rustic bridge crosses the rivulet. The whole was planned by the Colonel, who has in the opinion of all shown good judgment and taste. If it should be asked, "Why so much pains should be taken with a camp which we may be ordered to leave in an hour?" I answer that it serves to counteract idleness, which in all respects is the soldier's bane.

The move to a more permanent camp led many of the men to believe that there would be no winter campaign after all. "To move or not to move seems to be the question now," wrote Chaplain Morrill. "All quiet along the Rappahannock from present appearances seems likely to become stereotyped, although appearances are oftentimes deceitful."[33]

8

Ghastly Heaps upon the Bloody Field

When General Edwin V. Sumner's Right Grand Division reached Stafford Heights east of Fredericksburg in late November, it found only a token Confederate force holding the city. Anxious to seize the unexpected opportunity, Sumner requested immediate permission to cross the Rappahannock and occupy the city. Burnside refused. Two days later General Joseph Hooker, commanding the Center Grand Division, arrived at Stafford Heights. A rapid dash across the river would secure the town and open the road to Richmond, he argued. Burnside would have none of it. His carefully drawn plans called for the army to cross the river on pontoon bridges; any advance, he insisted, must wait their arrival.

Stored near Harper's Ferry, the pontoons were to be brought down the Potomac and then ferried overland to Falmouth. Both the pontoons and the army were to arrive at Fredericksburg simultaneously, or so the directives read. But garbled orders and general confusion prevailed over Burnside's plan. By the time the pontoons finally reached the banks of the Rappahannock, General Lee had reinforced the Fredericksburg garrison with over 35,000 of his finest troops. Burnside, expecting to surprise his enemy, knew that was now impossible. For two weeks he hesitated, not knowing what to do.[1]

Meanwhile, the Army of the Potomac, 130,000 men strong, waited in its camps on Stafford Heights, coping as best it could with bad weather and even worse roads. On December 4, the Twenty-sixth moved several miles closer to Fredericksburg, wrote Cummings, camping that night about a mile to the west of the Aquia Creek railroad.

> The weather was very cold, and the morning of the 5th found us shivering in a fierce storm of sleet and snow. On the morning of the 6th we struck our stiff and icy tents, and after a vain attempt to dry them, were once more underway. The fields were white with snow, and the road was a perfect compost of mud and water. We marched eight or ten miles on this day, mud up to our knees, night finding us in a snow-embowered woods and the

103

thermometer near zero. Selecting their tent sites, the boys dried the ground by building fires thereon, and crept into their shelters at a late hour, after drying their wet stockings—for everybody had wet feet on that day.[2]

Chaplain Morrill called the December 6 march "one of those things that only those who try them know, it can neither be imagined nor described."

Heretofore, when groaning about marches and marching in the presence of Peninsular veterans, they have been accustomed to say, "O, this is nothing to the Peninsula." But they acknowledged that they had never experienced the like before. This of course inspirited the men in their tramp-tramp, splash-splash through the mud—for men will endure much more when conscious that they are really doing something.

As we proceeded we found the snow deeper and the mud deepening, and I will not trust my reputation for veracity in stating the depth of the mixture of mud and snow; suffice it to say that we made four and a half or five miles from daylight until two o'clock P. M., when we reached our present camping ground, in a heavy timbered wood. When we came in, the most of the men had either damp or wet feet. They had first to clear away the snow (three or four inches deep) and build fires, so as to dry the ground on which they were to sleep. The day was quite cold, as may be inferred from the fact that the snow did not thaw sufficiently to fall from the trees, and as night came on the cold blasts from the North began to blow and we realized the significance of those words that trip so lightly on many tongues that know not what they say when they speak of a "winter campaign." Wood was plenty, large fires were built, and around them, wrapped in their blankets, the men lay down to sleep or shiver as best they could. But cold drove sleep from many eyelids that night. The baggage train could not reach us, and there was only one small fly [tent] for all the field and staff, and so some of us must needs lie down without any other cover save that which God ever and always spreads over his creatures. Among that number I found myself. The sensation was strange I confess, and the scenery novel. The earth around lay wrapped in a blanket of white, the camp fires burned brightly, the full-orbed moon shone clearly, and the stars sparkled in the cold night air like diamonds of the first water, as I gazed upon them through the trees hung with snow crystals. I managed to pass a tolerable night. . . . But I had more blankets than most of the men.

The sound of the axe awoke me from sleep, or I might rather say that every time I awoke during the night I could hear the sound of the woodman's axe. . . . It did not sound much like the Sabbath, but it was plainly a work both of necessity and mercy. All military duty was omitted, save a brief company inspection. But the men were very busy in endeavoring to make themselves comfortable; the day was so cold that the snow did not at midday melt on even the south side of trees and fields. And we could hear it in the winds, and feel it in our bones, that even a colder night was approaching. Our teams, with the exception of one that we left fast in the mud, reached us in the morning, having been 24 hours in coming four or five miles. This was owing to the energy of our Quartermaster who engineered a new road and sat in his saddle all night, meanwhile freezing one of his feet. The most of the teams of the division were stuck in the mud, and in that condition were frozen in, where they now remain. The ambulance train, filled with the sick, became fast, and but one of two things remained, either to put them out in the mud to get along as best they could, or remain there during the long, cold, cheerless night. Our sick choose the first alternative, and well they did, for two Vermont soldiers in our brigade died in the train there that night.

The rigors of the march left the chaplain with little patience for home-bound patriots.

To sit at home by a snug fire in the political club-room, or the Editor's sanctum and cry "onward to Richmond" on a "winter campaign," is one thing and to move onward and take part in this campaign is a more widely different thing than any one who does not participate in it can imagine.

As a single illustration, sixteen horses could not move one piece of artillery on Saturday—this was after one day's storm. And the bread for those Divisions whose teams could not reach them, was brought two, three and four miles yesterday on men's backs. We have been scant for the last 24 hours until this afternoon. Some men have had only two or three crackers a piece, because the men could not carry it and the teams could not haul it. I do not write these things because I am discouraged or would dishearten any one else, or because I desire the army to turn back or tarry, but that others may know in part what is now being endured by hundreds of thousands.[3]

The following day the regiment moved to a better camp site. A heartier type than the chaplain, Cummings glossed over the hardships and bitter cold. His letter to the *Mercury* was downright bouyant:

We removed to a dense grove of small pines, half a mile distant, where good water was handy, and where the cold winds of winter would be broken in their endeavors to break us. Streets were cut through the pines at right angles, bowers were formed, and three days transformed the dense wilderness into a perfect paradise. The ground was high and healthy, and the usual good judgment of our colonel was evinced in its selection. It was the finest thing of the kind that we had witnessed since leaving home, and there were many sighs of regret when the order came [later] to abandon it.[4]

One evening after supper the Twenty-sixth's irrepressible glee club turned out to serenade General Francis Vinton of the Third Brigade. Meeting at Colonel Morrison's tent first, "the boys gave him a taste of their quality, which favor he reciprocated, as usual." Properly insulated against the biting cold by the Colonel's "favor," the glee club trudged merrily over the snow-covered fields under the command of Major Morris. Sergeant Cummings described the happy scene:

Arriving at our destination, the General warmly greeted the Major and Adjutant White, who is always around on such occasions, threw open the flaps of his tent and welcomed the party in true soldierly style, which improved our voices, if not our feelings. Ranged in a semi-circle around a log fire cheerily blazing in front of the tent, the boys sang for over an hour. . . . The General is a West Pointer, and is probably the youngest of his rank in the army, being but twenty-four years of age. His hair was cropped close to his head, which surmounted an elegant figure, alive with true military dignity and suavity. In short, he looked as if he could fight. He was also a musical amateur, and placed an extra violin and violincello at our disposal. "The Raw Recruit," sung by Divine, pleased the General greatly, and the Dutch song of Charley Collins threw him into open laughter, but "Robinson Crusoe" and "Nicuragua" capped the climax. . . . On our return we gave a secesh family "The Star Spangled Banner" in regular Jersey style, and midnight found the "Sergeant" creeping into his shelter, the worse for wear, waking in the morning and finding his cartridge-box in his watch pocket.[5]

Adjutant John White's stock of whiskey might fortify a soldier against the cold; it could do nothing for his empty pocketbook. "There is," said Sergeant Cummings in a rare moment of criticism, "a great deal of dissatisfaction in the regiment on account of the non-payment of dues."

We have not received a cent as yet, and the families of many of the troops are now actually suffering for the want of money. We should be paid, by rights, every two months. Some of the Vermonters have gone five, seven, and even nine months without receiving a red. There have been very bitter feelings on the part of the men toward the government on this account, and this outrage toward us should be allayed as soon as possible. The brigade is to be paid off this week, it is understood; but the 26th New Jersey is to be left out, on account of some slight informality in the muster-rolls. "Red Tape" again— anything for an excuse. They have found the names of some men on the rolls who are over forty-five years of age, and this is seized upon as an excuse for delaying the pay of the whole regiment indefinitely. . . .

Another word in reference to our arms. In company E there are fifteen muskets unfit for service, and it is nothing but murder to ask such armed men to accompany us to the battle field, and stand fire without firing in return.[6]

On December 9 the regiment received orders "to provide ourselves with 20 rounds more of ammunition per man—making 60 in all . . . to have 3 days' cooked rations in our haversacks, and be ready to march at a moment's notice." According to the Reverend Morrill,

the impression prevailed that the long expected hour of conflict had come. The report was current that at 12 M. the pontoon bridges were to be thrown over under cover of artillery, and on them we were to pass over and to engage in that great struggle which may finally decide the fate of the American Republic. I think the tidings was welcome . . . to the most of the men.

On Dress parade Col. Morrison made some brief remarks to the Regiment, the purport of which was that heretofore he had been wont to consider himself a citizen of New York, but after to-morrow wished to be considered a Jerseyman; that it gave him pride and pleasure to think that during the time he had been in command he had never found it necessary to confine a single man in the guard-house; that he desired to share the perils and the honors of the Regiment.[7]

Lee's army at Fredericksburg had grown to nearly 40,000 men by December 9, most of them entrenched along the heights west of the city. More graybacks arrived hourly, ultimately swelling the Confederate host occupying the heights to some 80,000. Burnside's senior officers, peering nervously across the river, feared the rebel positions were impregnable. "If you make the attack as contemplated," one outspoken officer told him, "it will be the greatest slaughter of the war."[8] Burnside was obstinate. His plan called for a frontal assault across the river over pontoons and a frontal assault it would be. On December 9 the Right, Left, and Center Grand Divisions were alerted for the long-expected move. On the following day battle orders were delivered: Sumner's Right Grand Division was to cross directly opposite the city; Franklin's Left Grand Division would cross some distance below, then flank the heights; Hooker's Center Grand Division would be held in reserve.

Burnside's plan, already shambled by hesitation and delay, suffered near-complete collapse on December 11, the day of the crossing. Although pontoon building to the south proceeded on schedule, Confederate sharpshooters concealed in the stout brick buildings of Fredericksburg laid down so deadly a fire that Union engineers were unable to complete the pontoon bridges opposite the city. A terrific cannonade that reduced Fredericksburg to smoldering ruin failed to dislodge the sharpshooters. Not until dusk, after Union volunteers paddled across the river and cleared the enemy street by street, were the pontoons completed. Another day had been lost.

Finally on December 12 the bluecoats poured across the Rappahannock to take up positions below the Fredericksburg heights. Lee, making his headquarters on the heights west of the city, marveled at the audacity of the Yankees—and waited, sure that his artillery, well placed, and his infantry, dug in, could repell any attack. Burnside too was pleased. At last his army was across the river; moreover, balloon reports confirmed that half of Lee's vastly smaller force was still downriver. That the two Rebel armies might join together before the Union soldiers captured the heights was improbable.[9]

Assigned to the Second Brigade, Left Grand Division, the Twenty-sixth New Jersey broke camp on Stafford Heights before dawn on December 11. "Hastily packing our knapsacks and swallowing a cup of coffee, we started off almost on a double-quick for a distance of four miles."[10] Halting beside the road, the men were ordered to load their muskets.

We were scarcely on the way again before cannonading commenced, and as we drew near the river it became more and more distinct, until we could hear the howling of the shells following the reports. On we went, until reaching the brow of a hill, the valley of the Rappahannock burst upon our sight. At our feet lay an extensive plain, through the midst of which we could trace the course of the river. In the back-ground, the Heights of Fredericksburg stood out against the horizon. To our right, the plain narrowed, and just where the hills met the river, lay the little, quaint old city. That view would have been remarkable at any time, but as we saw it, it was more than remarkable. The hills over which we were passing were grim with batteries, while on the plain beneath, the long dark lines of the Union army stretched for miles away into the distance. On the opposite bank we could catch glimpses of the rebel host, and from the hills directly in front of us their batteries peered out, half masked by the trees. To the right, the cannonading was becoming more and more terrible, and the smoke from the rebel guns hung like a pall over the devoted city. We soon had descended into the plain, and taking our place in the line, lay waiting on our arms. Presently the battery on the hill behind us commenced firing, sending the shells wizzing over our heads. . . . Sometimes the firing almost ceased for a little while, and then was renewed with re-doubled vigor. At sundown, a detachment attempted to cross the pontoon bridge which had been laid in front of us. As they went down the river bank, the sharpshooters on the other side opened on them. Then a battery, dashing down to the river bank, opened on the sharpshooters, and the flashing guns and shells bursting in the gathering darkness, made the scene indescribably grand.[11]

Confederate sharpshooters holed up in the ruins of Fredericksburg delayed the entire Union advance; the Twenty-sixth "stood or sat in the mud" for eleven hours, until 8:00 p.m., when it was ordered back some two miles to high ground where it bivouacked for the night. Early the next morning, wrote Cummings, the troops were aroused and before nine o'clock "were quietly trotting over the pontoons."

Passing the houses on the river bank, which bore witness to the accuracy of our pieces on the previous day, we were formed in division to the left under cover of a slight acclivity. An hour passed without much music in our front, but suddenly the whizzing of a shell was heard which exploded a few feet to the right of us. Before this the boys were intent on mounting the rise of ground, and gazing at the rebel batteries to our front and right, and this had undoubtedly drawn their fire; but after this their curiosity appeared to be satisfied, as they sought the shelter of the hill, and dodged the shells which poured among them quite freely for awhile, although the most of them failed to explode. One struck under a mounted horse on the hill, and spattered the major and company H with mud. The regiment appeared rather tremulous at first, and but few of them lay in their places, preferring a position, to their minds, safer; but becoming familiarized to the peculiar sound of the missile, they grew apparently unconcerned, and carelessly sought the protection of their knapsacks in the ranks.[12]

Much of the heaviest shelling came from Rebel batteries to the right. The flash of their guns, Cummings told the *Mercury*, was plainly visible to the Jerseymen.

Our batteries were hastily planted on the mound in our front, and soon opened a sharp fire upon the enemy's position, which continued with slight intermission throughout the entire day, the roar of which was interwoven with the sharp musketry of our skirmishers to the left. Toward dark the firing slackened, and soon entirely ceased. An occasional shot from the pickets was heard during the night, but nothing of account, and the 26th fell upon the muddy field wrapped in their blankets, and gazing at the brightly winking stars until sleep closed their eyelids.[13]

On December 13 the battle for Fredericksburg began in earnest. Soon after the morning fog lifted Sumner's Right Grand Division was ordered forward. First one wave of bluecoats and then another charged across the open river plain, only to be staggered by overwhelming Confederate firepower. Lee, they found, had consolidated his forces—now indeed his position was impregnable. Six charges were ordered. Six were mounted courageously. Six failed utterly. Only darkness put an end to the slaughter.

Some distance to the south Franklin's division, comprising more than half the army's full strength, watched the carnage with growing frustration. Hobbled by confusing orders, cautious by nature, Franklin sent out one division to test the Rebels, watched as it was beaten back, then waited. Throughout that bloody day, as Sumner's men hurled themselves against the Confederate positions, only three of Franklin's eight divisions were used offensively and one whole corps, the largest in the army, saw no action at all. Like most of Franklin's men, the Twenty-sixth were passive witnesses to one of the Union's saddest defeats.[14] The day began early for the regiment, Cummings as usual enjoying every moment:

Before the flush of morn the pickets were actively blazing away, and in a few minutes the opening roar of Beam's battery in our front brought us to our feet, and blankets were rolled up in a hurry. Simultaneously with this the batteries along the whole line of the army commenced operations, and the effect was deafening. The fields were covered with their pyramidal spires of white vapor, and the rattling re-echoes of the discharges among the distant hills were grand in the extreme. The rebels were not loth [*sic*] in replying, and their shell were soon flying among the 26th in every direction, knocking over our stacked arms and wounding some of the men. It was almost miraculous that so many escaped unhurt. One shell struck in the rear of company E and covered the right of company B with mud. Luckily for us it did not explode.

Had it done so, the loss of life would have been fearful. Another struck a stack of muskets, exploding one, and shivering others in splinters, tearing great holes in the blankets near by, and injuring no one of the many lying beneath. Another struck in Company K, and seriously wounded Corporal John Sloat . . . whose ankle bone was fractured. Sergeant Rigby, of Co. K, was also slightly wounded, a piece of shell striking him on the hip. Over us, into us, skipping through us and around us, fast fell the storm, and still none were killed. Some of the boys left the ranks and ensconsed [*sic*] themselves behind a pile of cracker boxes—among them three Sergeants. The most of the boys, however, stood the fire nobly.[15]

As the day wore on the shelling grew even heavier. Yet the Twenty-sixth, most of the men hugging the muddy plain, remained in place, protected somewhat by a slight embankment.

Column after column filed past us on the way to the front, and one regiment after another of our own brigade fell quietly into their ranks and moved off to battle, until we were left alone. We awaited our turn, a little nervously, perhaps, but still quietly and hopefully. We knew that we were not in fighting trim. Our Colonel was away sick, and Major Morris, our only field officer, had as yet had no opportunity to prove himself the brave officer we afterwards found him. Our muskets were useless, and our drill, as yet, was very imperfect. But every one seemed to feel that we could fight in spite of all this, and we felt half anxious to be led to the front.[16]

Sergeant Cummings's breezy account of the battle, printed ten days after news of Burnside's defeat reached Newark, must have set *Mercury* readers to wondering whether the Rebels had been victorious after all:

During the afternoon of Saturday at intervals the musketry firing was absolutely terrific, volley after volley ringing over the fields, and starting the battery supports from their reclining position. Anon the loud cheers of our brave boys while charging the enemy's batteries were distinguishable, and created unbounded excitement among those held back. From every eminence in our front the rebels were hurling their iron tempest upon our devoted masses, and the fields around us were furrowed with the hissing shell and screeching round shot. About 5 o'clock in the afternoon the rebels attempted a bayonet charge on Beam's battery, which was situated directly in front of the Twenty-sixth. With their peculiar cheer they came surging in one extended regimental line, shoulder to shoulder, toward the slope on which the battery was planted. They were met, however, by the Third and Fourth Vermont, of our brigade, and after a desperate fight rolled back into the woods, with the loss of their colonel, some prisoners, and many killed and wounded. A few of them threw down their arms, and ran into our ranks, declaring themselves to be tired of the war, and their intention of serving no longer.[17]

Appearing in the *Advertiser* nearly two weeks after the battle, Morrill's letter struck a vastly different note:

It was in the middle of Saturday afternoon, when the shelling was most terrific, that some of the Regiments, being under the hill near the river, began to show some signs of fear. One brigade was ordered to march up and a brass band was ordered out in range of the shells and told to play. It played several patriotic airs, and among other tunes it played "Dixie." The tune has always seemed light and gay to me before. But no dead march ever seemed more solemn to me than Dixie then. Between the roar of cannon and the crash of musketry these brazen throats cried "Away, Away!" Away to gaping wounds—away to dying groans—away to death or victory—and away the column marched with steady step towards the place where the fight raged most furiously. In the rear of the column there was the stretcher-bearers' corps—a corps that I had never seen shoulder their arms and march in the ranks before. I cannot say that the music gave much spirit or courage to me. . . . But that it had an inspiriting effect upon the soldiers was most plainly manifest.[18]

Late in the day the Twenty-sixth received its orders. According to Cummings, the men

fell into line with alacrity, and not a cheek blanched. Although the shells of the enemy were falling around us—not like hail, but still very briskly—the companies formed as coolly as if we were going on dress parade, and in two minutes we were steadily marching in divisions towards the front. General Howe observed us from the roof of a house near by, and knowing the colors, sent an orderly peremptorily ordering us to resume our position, saying it "was nothing but murder to send men to the front with such miserable pieces." In this opinion of the general's we all coinsided [*sic*]. From General Howe's headquarters, a few rods to the right of our position, the brilliant charges of Hooker's brave troops upon the rebel batteries and earthworks were plainly distinguishable. The poor fellows fought like tigers, but in vain, and were at last compelled to withdraw decimated by the infernal fire of the rebels. Again and again they rallied, and at one time carried a line of rifle-pits, and drove the enemy to the protection of their earthworks, but in vain endeavored to carry the heights above them. The enemy's batteries rose on the hill above them, one over another, like a pair of stairs, and simultaneously belched their fires upon our devoted columns, while the answering fire of our batteries across the river had apparently but little effect upon them. . . . The number of wounded horses dashing over the plain throughout the day, riderless and bloody, particularly struck my attention. One splendid white horse dashed past the regiment early in the morning with bloody neck and haunches, apparently perfectly wild with pain and fright, and swam the river, rushing over the steep on the opposite side, and disappearing in the woods on their summit.[19]

At sunset the firing ceased. "The prevalent opinion," wrote Morrill, trying hard to be objective, was "that there was no decisive advantage on either side. What little ground we had gained was fully counter-balanced by our greater loss of men from engaging a sheltered enemy."[20] Though more than 12,000 Union soldiers lay dead or wounded on the plains near Fredericksburg, Burnside at a meeting late that evening told his incredulous officers that he intended to renew the fight the next day. He would personally lead the charge, he announced, at the head of his old corps. Thoroughly sickened by the day's butchery, his division commanders persuaded Burnside that further combat would be futile. On December 14 an exhausted Army of the Potomac rested on the plains, suffering still more casualties from a fearsome Confederate bombardment. On December 15, during a heavy rainstorm, the survivors retreated across the Rappahannock to their camps on Stafford Heights.[21]

Reports of the slaughter at Fredericksburg were slow to reach the North. On December 15, the day the beaten Union forces crossed the rain-swollen river, the *Daily Advertiser* thought it "safe . . . to indulge in more cheerful anticipations than ever before."[22] Twenty-four hours later news of the carnage resounded like a thunderclap across the state. Reviewing the battle reports, the *Advertiser* blamed "the cruel collapse . . . of a campaign from which so much was expected" on the delayed pontoons and missing supplies—and by inference, on the administration itself. Neither General Burnside nor the valiant men under his command were at fault:

> Whether [Burnside's] change of base was the result of his own convictions or was made in obedience to orders, the opinion is general that it was performed with celerity and ability, and that it had every promise of success at the time. The criminal neglect which held his army in a mighty paralysis on the banks of the Rappahannock, without supplies for subsistence, or means of crossing, or for fighting when across, is universally conceded to have been the prime cause of all the subsequent misfortunes. . . . Who were responsible for this delay—the key to all the subsequent disaster—is the question which now demands an answer. And it is due from the Government to a generous and patriotic people that the causes which led to it be probed to the quick.

The armchair generals at the *Advertiser* believed the administration had "too many irons in the fire." Union troops, said the paper, were "too widely diffused" on too many fronts. Instead, urged the *Advertiser*, Washington must "hurl the whole concentrated power of the Republic against a vital part of the rebellious Confederacy."[23]

The usually optimistic *Mercury*, forced to concede that the army's "retrograde movement" had produced "a profoundly dispiriting effect upon the public mind," placed the blame squarely on Burnside's "essentially foolhardy and imprudent" plan of attack:

> When the news was flashed along the wires that the assault had been finally commenced, every heart leaped with joy, not doubting for one moment that

victory would crown our standard. Necessarily finding all these high hopes destroyed . . . , it could not be otherwise than that every true and loyal heart should be filled with sorrow and alarm, and the sky should grow dark again, with no bow shining from its depths. Yet it is far from wise to despair of the republic because of a single reverse. The fuller details of the battle which resulted so disasterously, while they reveal immense losses, whole brigades shattered and broken, and regiments almost obliterated, with thousands of dead and wounded lying in ghastly heaps upon the bloody field—afford no ground at all for questioning the bravery of our troops or doubting their success, had any proper mode of attack been adopted. The sole cause of our defeat, it is now conclusively established, lies in the fact that the plan of operation was radically wrong.[24]

The *Daily Journal* carried full details of the tragedy on the Rappahannock. Fairly gloating over the sad news, the paper dismissed the war as an "unquestioned failure," demanded an immediate armistice, the recall of General McClellan as Lincoln's principal adviser, and the opening of negotiations with the South.

Gen. Burnside and the grand army of the Potomac are probably on their way to Washington or to winter quarters. Disorganized, dispirited, routed, it would seem impossible to bring it again into effective fighting order this winter. . . . So it may fall back again for the defence of the national capital, where if it had originally remained, the country would have been spared its bitter record of calamity and disgrace, if not of ruin. Fanaticism has done its work; it has established its power for devilish mischief, and while it reigns we despair of peace, liberty, law and order.[25]

The *Journal* blamed neither delayed pontoons nor Burnside's plans: the "abolition incapables" and "fanatics" in Washington were the sole cause. "In the name of the people of New Jersey," cried the paper, "we renew our demand for peace." It was "folly" to persist in the notion that the Union could be restored by military measures, or that the South could ever be conquered. "These positions, if admitted, as we think they will by all except the fanatics and the fools, lead to the conclusion that the Union and the Constitution can be preserved in whole, or in part, only by peaceful measures, by compromises, or by a Convention of the people."[26]

The full brunt of the North's rage fell not upon Burnside or his discredited plan. Lincoln—his enemies and even some of his friends called him thickheaded and ignorant, a man of highly questionable abilities—was held responsible. Mindful of the national mood, despairing of yet another failed general, the president could only counsel patience. "Gentlemen," he told a group of ministers who called upon him to urge more vigorous prosecution of the war, "suppose all the property you were worth was in gold, and you had put it in the hands of Blondin to carry across the Niagara River. Would you shake the cable or keep shouting out to him, 'Blondin, stand up a little straighter! 'Blondin, stoop a little more!' 'Go a little faster;' 'Lean a little more to the north;' 'Lean a little more to the south'? No. You would hold your breath as well as your tongue, and keep your hands off until he was safe over. The government is carrying an immense weight. Untold treasures are in their hands. They are doing the very best they can. Don't badger them. Keep silence, and we'll get you safe across."[27] If the slaughter at Fredricksburg convinced many in the North that the Union cause or the president or both were hopeless, it did little permanent damage to the Army of the Potomac. "Every private soldier knew that the Battle of Fredericksburg had been a costly and bloody mistake," wrote one newspaper reporter, "and yet I think on the day or the week following it the soldiers would have gone into battle just as cheerfully and sturdily as before. The more I saw of the Army of the Potomac, the more I wondered at its invincible spirit which no disasters seemed able to destroy."[28]

The Twenty-sixth suffered only three casualties at Fredericksburg, all from flying shell fragments. One other, Private John Dries, explained Cummings, died of typhoid fever.

> Dries was sick at the time we broke camp preparatory to crossing the river. Procuring a pass from his captain, he kept up with his regiment as long as possible, but finally grew very weak and fell out by the roadside. Seeing an ambulance passing, some hours afterwards, he importuned the driver for a ride, but was refused, although the vehicle contained naught but three great dogs. After this Dries crawled out of the snow beneath the shelter of some thick pines, and was found there in a dying condition three days afterward by a teamster of the 104th New York volunteers, and carried to the hospital. There being no shelter for him he was transfered to the tent of a teamster, where he soon died.

While searching for Dries's body, Sergeant Cummings passed through a field hospital.

> The rebel wounded and our own frequently lay side by side breathing their last. The hospital headquarters were situated in a large white frame house on the Northern bank of the river in which a small army of surgeons were busily engaged, night and day, in dismembering our poor, wounded braves, the shrieks and groans of whom were frequently heart rending. As we entered one tent they had just amputated the leg of a wounded Pennsylvanian. The operation was performed at the thigh joint, and the subject of it died in less than a half hour. As fast they expired they were buried in their blankets—three or four in a grave—on the river bank, their friends (if they had any) generally placing a piece of a cracker box at the head of the grave, detailing thereon their names, companies and regiments. This was generally done with a lead pencil, however, and the action of the weather will soon efface it. At the entrance of one of the tents, we observed a small pyramid of legs, arms, hands and feet—the result of hospital operations. But sickening as were the scenes in the hospital, they had not the influences upon one's nerves as the

scenes on the field. Some of the dead were mashed into one complete jelly, their remains stringing over a distance of five yards, while others lay on their backs, hands clenched and toes turned in, a picture of stern determination and resolve which death alone could conquer. These were generally shot through the heart. Those shot in the head presented a horrible appearance, the blood and oozing brains hiding their features.[29]

The field hospital of the Second Division was a large stone mansion set a little below the pontoon bridges on the south bank of the river. Although exposed to enemy fire it was the only shelter available. Its owner, "an old secesh bachelor, very aristocratic in his notions," remained under guard in a downstairs room.[30] Injured slightly, Chaplain Morrill entered the hospital just before it was removed to the other side of the Rappahannock.

> I joined the "limping brigade" this morning, having sprained my knee, and went into the hospital to be assisted instead of assisting. We were comfortably resting on our beds of straw, when about 11 o'clock an order came to be ready to move all the wounded and hospital stores at 3 A.M., farther back to some more secure position. . . .
> When we learned that the whole army was to be withdrawn to this side of the river, there were phantoms of Bull Run, and the Peninsular retreat, floated in many brains and uttered by many tongues. McClellan men lifted their heads and anti-McClellan men hung theirs. A sad and anxious look was written on every face. . . .
> It was a hard thing for men whose legs and arms had just been amputated, to be . . . tumbled into ambulances and jostled two or three miles over rough roads. . . .
> At two o'clock the ambulances filled with the sick and wounded, started on the suffering journey. It was the first night I ever spent in an ambulance, the wind blew a gale and the rain came pouring down, and we were shut up for five or six hours. It was painful for me, what must it have been to the severely wounded? We moved back some two miles from the river, and when morning came we found that our whole force had retired to the wooded hills.[31]

At dusk a soldier from one of the Vermont regiments brigaded with the Twenty-sixth was carried into the hospital. One arm had been shattered by a minié ball and he had wounds in both hips, wrote Morrill.

> He came reluctantly from the field, lamenting that he could not "ping the rebels again," and exalting that he had given them 19 or 20 shots (he was a skirmisher) before they had crippled him. Wounded in three places as he was, he was still full of fight, breathing out threatening and slaughter against them. He was coaxed to lie down on the amputating table and chloroform was administered to him, and the arm was taken off close to the shoulder. During this time he made a noise like a maddened bull. It seemed to me that the chloroform controlled everything except the fighting faculties which had become so excited that they were beyond control. After his arm was off and his

other wounds dressed he lay there complaining of its being cold, and convulsively twitching the stump.[32]

The gruesome scenes reported so graphically by Cummings may have shocked *Mercury* readers but his jaunty tone helped ease the pain of Burnside's mortification. Morrill by contrast was outspokenly critical of nearly everything connected with the campaign. The *Advertiser* had vigorously questioned the administration's conduct of the war; its field correspondent desponded of victory. In a letter that enraged Newark Republicans, a discouraged chaplain spoke his feelings plainly:

> The five days' battle may thus be summed up. We marched over the river and we marched back again, minus 10,000 killed and wounded. . . . We went over hopefully, we came back despondingly. We not only mourn the loss of the thousands of unreturning brave, but the moral effect of a victory. This would be equivalent to 50,000 men. There is nothing, so far as I can see, humanly speaking, that this army so much needs as confidence, hope. Men may disguise the fact, but they cannot deny it, that the army is sadly disheartened. The prevalent feeling is that we cannot conquer a peace; that we are no nearer subduing our enemies under our feet than when we first began; that the rebels fought better on Saturday than on the first Bull Run battlefield. Some may question the policy of writing this, if true; but I believe otherwise. If from the beginning "the truth, the whole truth, and nothing but the truth" had been written, we should be in a different condition from what we are to-day. It is one thing to say how the army ought to feel and another to say how it does feel. While I write from the army I mean to state what is. If the two armies could settle it, it would be settled without any more bullets or blood. In obedience to popular clamor we undertook an almost impossibility, and consequently failed.

Morrill's already low spirits sank further when he learned that two of his children were "hopelessly sick."

> I have made every laudable effort in my power to get leave of absence for a few days, that I might see them once more, either living or dead; but all in vain. War is hard and unrelenting; war has no bowels of compassion. Ordinarily a Chaplain is considered by the officers a "fifth wheel to a coach," but let him ask leave of absence and he is one of the four indispensable wheels. I never felt it much harder to be subject to the powers that be, than now.[34]

Soon after reaching its old camp on Stafford Heights, the regiment was ordered on a picket along the north bank of the river. A number of the men, explained Morrill, were "to all intents and purposes barefoot, their shoes having been worn out since the last requisition was made."[35] Barefoot or not, wrote Cummings, the men enjoyed themselves.

By mutual agreement no firing was allowed, and [the men] held many an amusing conversation with the "rebs," who rather anxiously inquired when we were coming across the river to visit them again. They appeared to have plenty to eat and drink—especially the latter. Some of them laid down their arms and crossed the river for the purpose of exchanging tobacco for coffee— a request quickly acceded to by our boys.[36]

The closing days of December brought some of the most severe weather of the campaign. Wrote Cummings:

The weather is very cold, and the cry for winter quarters is growing clamorous. Night before last one of the Vermonters in our brigade was frozen to death within his tent. Many of the Twenty-sixth doze over a blazing camp fire during the night, in preference to taking their chances within the tents. . . . Axes are much needed by the boys at present, and it is almost impossible to secure one. They would be much more serviceable to us than our arms, as with them we could protect ourselves from the rigors of winter.[37]

As December drew to a close the Twenty-sixth New Jersey waited on Stafford Heights, uncertain whether they would be ordered to winter quarters or on to a new campaign. It was, wrote the chaplain, his composure returning, a period of welcome inactivity.

The two most notable events that have broken the quiet of the camp within the last few days, have been the arrival of Marcus L. Ward and Wm. H. Kirk. The former is proving himself more and more worthy the title he bears, "soldier's friend." He came on to see what could be done to hasten the arrival of that day, which to the soldier and the soldier's family is most welcome— pay day. Mr. Kirk was most warmly greeted by all, and especially those to whom he brought letters and parcels. It has been so long since any civilian on a similar errand has been able to force our lines that we have begun to conclude that they were as impregnable as those of the enemy. . . .

While writing the above the order has come to "be ready to march on 12 hours notice, with 3 days cooked rations in haversacks, and 2 days light rations to be carried with 60 rounds of ammunition." Any one reading the above is at perfect liberty to exercise his ingenuity in determining what the order signifies—Whether it means "on to Richmond" or "back to Washington." If he reaches a definite certain conclusion he will do more than we are able to do here.[38]

9

Lilliputians in a Great Mud Pie

"It appears to me the Almighty is against us," a somber Lincoln told a friend in late December 1862, "and I can hardly see a ray of hope."[1] The blundering and bloodshed of Fredericksburg still rankled the Northern mind. Generals U. S. Grant and Nathaniel P. Banks toiled uselessly in the west, "stuck in the mud," one newspaper said. Secretary of State Seward had tendered his resignation, General Burnside his, and in Congress the resurgent Democrats, led by Ohio Representative Clement L. Vallandigham, castigated the president mercilessly. Despite nearly a million men in arms, twice that of the Confederacy, the Union had failed miserably to subdue the rebellious states. Frustration, anger, and recrimination all arose as a tide that threatened to engulf the president, his administration, and the Union itself. Such was the state of the nation as the year 1863 began.

After his resignation was rejected by the president, Burnside grew even more determined not to sit out the winter in camp. January was still young when preparations for a renewal of the contest began. Its tents pitched near Belle Plain, Virginia, the Twenty-sixth Regiment was "on the tiptoe of expectation," said Chaplain Morrill, "in regard to the when and the where we are to move." New Year's Day itself was celebrated quietly, continued the chaplain:

> Some of the more fortunate feasted on turkey procured at fabulous prices, but the greater part dined on the plainer and cheaper fare furnished at Uncle Sam's free lunch, which is open at all hours. Never before have I seen the virtue of temperance . . . reign so supreme on New Year's day.
>
> Some of the men acknowledged that they never before entered upon the second day of a new year with such clear heads and furless tongues as Jan. 2d, 1863.[2]

On January 2 the regiment's sick were sent in ambulances to Falmouth for transport by steamer to Washington. "This ordinarily signifies active movements," wrote Morrill somewhat ominously. The chaplain was already in a

118

black mood when this newest intelligence arrived. Only a few days earlier he had been the unhappy recipient of several letters from home upbraiding him for the tone of his recent correspondence to the *Daily Advertiser*. Morrill felt compelled to defend himself:

> I would not publicly allude to the subject were it not for the fact that the error, . . . if such, was a public one and as such demands a public confession. . . .
>
> If anyone denies that the army "came back despondingly from Fredericksburg," that it "needed confidence—hope," that it was "sadly disheartened," that "If it was left to the army to settle it it would be settled without bullets or blood, or the attempt made," I am willing to risk the case on its testimony fairly taken. I have found those (a few) who questioned the policy of making public the statements, but never one who did not assent to and affirm their truth. . . .
>
> I came to the army with considerable confidence and hope, fully persuaded that the army was eager for the fray and confident of success. What was my surprise to hear the veterans of ten battles—officers and men—frequently express the opinion that we could not settle the contest by the sword; that they were weary of the war. I immediately began to conclude that the true feeling of the army had not been fairly represented by the press: which after all gives cast and character to public opinion. It seemed to me in this great contest for truth we ought to be willing to know the truth; that in the end we could not expect to be successful by ignoring the truth or concealing the truth. The most of our military movements in this department of the army have been influenced if not controlled by the pressure of public opinion uttered by and through the press. To this there is no objection, so long as the press gives a true . . . sound. That it does not in many instances, I appeal to the experience of thousands, who will bear me witness to-day that their ideas of the army, and of the war, heretofore, gathered from the usual channels have been erroneous. . . . This war in part originated in a partisan press, it has been fed and fanned by public misrepresentation, and shall it be continued and concluded thus? I should be sorry to discourage anybody's patriotism, but I see an evil and a wrong greater than even that. I see the true feeling of the army concealed or misrepresented, and the army made the suffering slaughtered victim of such misrepresentations.
>
> Under the common opinion that the army is clamorous to be led "on" and confident of success and "spoiling for a fight" the public press says "on" and military commanders take up the echo and say "on," and "on" the soldier goes to defeat and death. "On" he must go and "on" he will go. If to-day the order should come to cross the Rappahannock where we did before (and it is not an incredible thing) we should go, and I should go. . . .
>
> This is some of the hardness required of those who would be good soldiers. But in the name of all that is true and humane I protest against having the public believe that we are anxiously eager to hear that order, or confidently expect victory. If the army must obey public opinion, is it not right and proper that its true feeling should enter into the formation of that same public

opinion? There will come a day of retribution for partisans and presses which stifle and pervert the true feelings of this mighty host of armed men.[3]

Morrill's post-Fredericksburg correspondence reflected not only his own but a great body of opinion within army ranks. Soldier morale was at its lowest ebb of the war; defeatism was rampant. Nearly every man who had been at the front any length of time could have echoed the chaplain's censure of the partisan press. Peace Democrats at home in New Jersey seized on Morrill's letters as evidence the war could not be won. The *Daily Journal*, which had ignored the Twenty-sixty Regiment since the day it departed Newark, reprinted portions of the chaplain's reply to his critics under the headline, "Gloomy Condition of the Army of the Potomac." Newark Republicans, who much preferred Sergeant Cummings's ebullient reports in the *Mercury*, were convinced the chaplain was as badly infected with Copperheadism as the paper that printed his letters. Morrill's condemnation of "partisans and presses" doubly infuriated them, prompting a move to have the chaplain dismissed from the service.

In mid-January when Colonel Morrison returned from an extended sick leave, he was received by the men, said Cummings, "with great enthusiasm." The sergeant was an unblushing fan of the colonel: "Cheer after cheer, given with a will, testified their affection and devotion for him. The colonel looked pale and thin, but bestrode his horse with his usual ease and elegance—for there is not a finer horseman in this whole army than this same colonel of ours."[4] When Morrison resumed command the regiment had been in camp for nearly a month. Despite "all the moving rumors" to the contrary, wrote Morrill, the men looked forward to remaining at Belle Plain at least until spring.

> The men are more cheerful and comfortable than they have been at some other times, though they have not stockaded and made themselves as comfortable as some of the older regiments. . . . It is surprising to the uninitiated to see what comforts and luxuries (?) an old soldier can make out of the simplest and rudest materials. . . . The rations are regularly distributed and now and then the men have some rice and potatoes which form a most agreeable and healthful change of diet to those whose variety of food consists of the numberless dishes that can be compounded out of . . . pork, beans and crackers.
>
> A few days since a sad accident occurred on the picket line. Some of the pickets were posted at a house where there was a family residing. A little boy took up one of the soldier's guns which was loaded, but had no cap, and begging a cap from some other one, put it on and snapped it unthinkingly at his sister who was killed by the discharge.[5]

While the Army of the Potomac lingered idly in its cantonments, its commander poured over his maps with renewed intensity. Appointed on the strength of his reputation as a man of action, Burnside intended to measure up. By the third week in January his plans were firm: the army would once again cross the Rappahannock, this time further north at Bank's Ford, then march south cutting the Confederate lines between Fredericksburg and Richmond. On January 20 the men were assembled to hear Burnside's grandiloquent order of the day: "The commanding general announces to the Army of the Potomac that they are about to meet the enemy once more. . . . The auspicious moment seems to have arrived to strike a great and mortal blow to the rebellion, and to gain that decisive victory which is due to the country."[6] The march toward the Rappahannock began well enough:

> We moved off at a rapid rate, and as we had lately drawn our winter clothing, our knapsacks were unusually heavy. On we went for about four miles. Then a short halt to rest; and then on again, across the railroad, through wood and valley, up hill and down, past many a deserted camp the column moved, until at last it halted in a corn field to allow the stragglers to catch up, for the rapid pace and their heavy loads had begun to tell on the men. Soon we started again at a more rapid rate than before, and now the regiments began to dwindle away and every deserted camp was filled with those who had fallen out of the ranks, utterly unable to keep up. We finally camped in a thick woods near Banks' Ford. It had been somewhat cloudy all day, but for weeks there had been no storms and the roads were in splendid condition.[7]

Soon, however, the weather turned angry. Wrote Cummings:

> We bivouacked in the woods, and hardly were our fires lighted before the rain fell in torrents. The men were as stiff as foundered horses, and, speaking personally, I can say that the intolerable aching of my bones was not allevieated by snoozing in the puddle of water in which I found myself long before daylight.
> Morning found us moving toward the river in a chilly January rain, mud up to our knees at every step, the wet pine, cedar, and laurel shrubs wiping our faces continually for over an hour, when our brigade was deployed on an open field.[8]

All day the icy rain poured down, transforming the roads into splashy creeks. Artillery, infantry, pontoons for the crossing, supply wagons, ammunition trains, ambulances, all bogged down in the knee-deep mud. The rain continued without let-up for thirty hours.

The Twenty-sixth was ordered to haul a train of pontoons:

> Our position was like that of liliputians [*sic*] in a great mud pie. The wheels went down actually over the hubs, and those of us were fortunate who did not get in over our knees. Some actually went down up to the middle. The horses, poor beasts, could of course do nothing to help us, and the train was literally stuck. Another regiment was sent to our aid, and with their assistance we dragged the pontoons almost over the horses' backs through the field to the hill where the others were drawn up.[9]

It was hard work, reported Cummings:

But at it the Twenty-sixth went—in the mud up to their waists, jerking at the long ropes attached to the pontoons in earnest, the colonel and adjutant dashing through the mud up to the bellies of their horses overseeing and encouraging the boys, now here, now there, first at one pontoon and then at another, unmindful of the rain and heedless of the mud. It was tough work, but the boys ripped it through bravely. Night dropped her curtains and found them still at it, wet to the skin, and clothed in a new uniform, for the mud had covered everything—even their heads and faces. Old "P.H.," with his customary bravery, had deserted us, and there was no prospect of the brigade being relieved. Under the circumstances, a council of war was held by the colonel of the brigade, and Colonel Morrison volunteered in an effort to have the men relieved if possible, if not, he would march off his regiment first in case the other colonels would follow his example. Not one of them faltered, for it seemed to be a case of life or death with the men, who had done the work of horses throughout the day, and, with wet feet and saturated clothing, were still manfully exerting themselves. General Woodruff was at last ferreted out, through the exertions of Col. Morrison, and the brigade released.[10]

Wrote an officer of the regiment:

We were then ordered back to the place where our arms were stacked. By this time it was dark. We were wet to the skin with the rain, covered with mud and chilled through and through by the cold storm. There was nothing at hand of which to make fires except green scrub pines, yet the men actually did make miserable smokey little fires with these, in spite of the rain, but to get warm by one of them was an impossibility, much less to cook our suppers. We remained for some time in this miserable plight, when the Colonel rode up and said: "Boys, take off your equipments; there are forty more of these boats to be got through to-night and this brigade must do it; so prepare for work!" This was adding misery to misery, but we waited and no orders to grapple the pontoons came, but presently the Colonel rode up again and told us to fall in, and we were going back to our camp. This news was received joyfully enough, and after stumbling along through the mud and darkness for about a mile, we found ourselves at the place from which we started in the morning. Soon rousing fires were going, by which we dried ourselves and cooked our coffee.[11]

On the following day, Sergeant Cummings wrote, "tents were struck long before daylight, and the faces of the regiment were turned homeward to our old camp."

The hardness of that march it is impossible to describe. At every step the mud would suck us in almost to the kneepan. Wagons were swimming in slush-holes, mules were entirely concealed in them, with the exception of their heads and backs, and men lay down upon the mushy "sacred soil" in scores, blowing volumes of steam through their extended nostrils. It is a miracle to me how we reached camp that day, but reach it we did (part of us) and here we are to-day, rubbing our sore shins, fixing our tents and preparing for "winter quarters."[12]

Said another member of the regiment:

The march [back to camp] soon degenerated into a grand straggle, for the men were literally worn out by the three days of terrible work which they had been through. The Twenty-sixth kept together very well until we reached Falmouth. There rations were served out; among them, as an extra favor, a whiskey ration, which did more harm than good. After leaving Falmouth, the regiment dwindled rapidly away, one after another falling out of the ranks, until a mere handful was left. The whole army straggled; here you could see a group of men from two or three different regiments cooly making coffee around a fire, while others were plodding leisurely along, some in groups, some singly. Now and then there would be a wagon stuck so that ten mules could not pull it out, or perhaps a knot of wagons, ambulances and artillery so entangled that it seemed as if they could never be separated. Many a poor fellow lay down by the roadside utterly exhausted and helpless, and the army seemed totally demoralized. Only twenty or thirty of the Twenty-sixth came into camp with the colors. For the next two or three days the stragglers kept coming in singly or in groups, and order was finally brought out of confusion. Though no notice was ever taken of those who fell out on the way home, a number of non-commissioned officers were reduced to the ranks for straggling on the outward march, but most of them were soon restored.[13]

January's Mud March demoralized a demoralized army. Desertions reached an all-time high, morale, an all-time low. Chaplain Morrill was thoroughly disgusted, although this time more circumspect in his criticism:

Gen. Burnside showed great pluck and perservance in persisting in his efforts after the storm had continued for some time. It seemed as if he were determined to conquer the elements and the enemy. It was not until long after many a commander would have given up that [he] abandoned the attempt. It seemed as if such persistence on his part and on the part of the men should have secured a different result, but God willed otherwise. He spoke so loud and distinct that every man in the army could hear and understand, at this time "thus far shalt thou go and no farther. . . ." Whether the move was a feint or a failure I will not undertake to say. It was attended with no inconsiderable loss of life in several respects.

But no ventures, no victories. The old motto is, "three times and out," so we have once more to go forth from this place for the Rappahannock and Richmond.[14]

Cummings derided the abortive expedition as "our second grand flip-flap toward the Rappahannock."[15] The men in the ranks, covered with mud and bone-weary, ridiculed Burnside's "auspicious moment." Some officers began to wonder aloud at the sanity of their commander. Said General Franklin: "I came to the conclusion that Burnside was fast losing his mind." General Hooker was more emphatic, if that were possible. The president, he said, was an imbecile, the administration was all played out and the country needed a dictator.[16] "It is said," wrote another officer, "that a very bad feeling has sprung up in the Army against Burnside growing out of his Fredericksburg failure and this latest sad attempt."[17] Humiliated once again, this time by the elements, infuriated by the abuse heaped upon him by his subordinates, Burnside took a steamboat to Washington, met in the White House with Lincoln, and demanded the immediate dismissal of ten of the highest-ranking officers in the army, including Franklin and Hooker. Lincoln pondered the matter for a day, then on January 25 relieved Burnside of command instead.

Burnside's departure would prove a turning point in the history of the Army of the Potomac. But that was all very far in the future. For the men in the ranks, wrote Private Woodruff in his first letter to the *Mercury* in some time, the paymaster's arrival was of more immediate importance:

> The paymaster arrived here Saturday and commenced paying the regiment Sunday, and continued Monday and Tuesday; but, at the rate he is getting along, he will not be done before Friday. We only receive two months pay this time.
>
> Mr. Rosseter arrived here Monday with small parcels for the boys. A number of boxes arrived Tuesday, and we are assured that they will come regularly three or four times a week hereafter from the Landing, the express company having established a station at Belle Landing. Our friends may now send on their boxes with confidence.
>
> Monday morning the Colonel called us up, and the Adjutant read a circular to the effect that the Colonel, in order to encourage order and cleanliness in the regiment, would give a supper, to cost at least one hundred dollars, to the officers and men of the company that should, by Saturday, present the best looking quarters, the most well regulated streets, and whose guns and equipment would bear the closest inspection.

Heavy rain continued to fall intermittently throughout the remainder of January, an irritating reminder of the wretched Mud March. Woodruff was obviously as discouraged as the rest:

> The rainy season seems to have fairly set in at last, and it rains most of the time, and the mud is so deep that it is almost impossible to move artillery, as it takes fourteen horses to every cannon.
>
> The pontoons remain on the banks of the Rappahannock, stuck in the mud. There let them lay forever.

Directly opposite the place where we proposed crossing, the rebels have stuck up a large signboard with the inscription, "Burnside's army stuck in the mud." Some of the rebel pickets called over the river to us, saying, "If you will wait a while we will come over and help you lay the pontoons." This kind of offer of assistance was not very graciously received.

As January ended, desertions were running at nearly 200 a day. Most of the deserters were out of the war permanently; only a few were caught and punished. The Twenty-sixth, wrote Woodruff, was not immune to the epidemic:

Monday, at dress parade, Jacob Wicker, of Company I, received his sentence for running away from the enemy. He ran away Sunday morning, Dec. 14th, when we lay in front of Fredericksburg, and did not return until the 17th, when we had re-crossed to this side of the Rappahannock. His sentence was to be sent to the Rip-Raps for two years, the first seven days of each month to be passed in solitary confinement, and the rest of the time at hard labor, and to lose all his pay except what might be due the sutler.[18]

10

The Finest Camp in the Army

Soldier morale had plunged to a new low by the time Major General Joseph Hooker assumed command of the Army of the Potomac. Of the 180,000 men officially on the rolls, nearly 85,000 were absent without leave. Scurvy and diarrhea plagued the troops; and the camps near Aquia Creek were little more than pigsties, with unbelievable filth and impenetrable mud everywhere. It was, said one soldier, a winter of despair.

Hooker tore into the army like a whirlwind. Fresh vegetables and soft bread supplemented the monotony of hardtack, salt pork, and coffee. Peremptory orders went out to regimental commanders to establish company kitchens, clean up the camps, and enhance elementary sanitation. Hospitals opened and the men were directed "to wear their hair cut short, to bathe twice a week, and put on clean underclothing at least once a week." A liberal furlough policy cut the tide of desertion while in the midst of all this reform, the paymasters came down from Washington, their carpetbags stuffed with welcome greenbacks.[1]

One of Hooker's first acts was to abolish Burnside's unwieldy Grand Divisions, replacing them with seven corps of infantry and one of cavalry. Whenever weather permitted, the rank and file were kept busy with a daily routine of drills, reviews and inspections. Even so minor a detail as corps badges for the men failed to escape Hooker's attention. The Twenty-sixth New Jersey, assigned to the Sixth Corps under command of General John Sedgwick, could now be identified by the white Greek cross sewn on its caps. Hooker's reforms had a near-miraculous effect on the army. As one enthusiastic soldier put it, "Cheerfulness, good order, and military discipline at once took the place of grumbling, depression and want of confidence."[2] Chaplain Morrill agreed. "Many changes are being introduced," he wrote, "all looking to the discipline and efficiency of the army. There seems to be a general girding up of the loins, preparatory to a more decisive contest than has yet been seen."[3] The troops, used to McClellan's boasting and Burnside's plodding, welcomed the new order of things. Hooker in turn spoke of his great pride and confidence in the men, calling them "the finest body of soldiers the sun ever shone on."[4] Although neither Lincoln nor Hooker nor the men of the Army of the Potomac knew it yet, the tide of the war had begun to turn ever so slightly toward the North.

Other than picket duty made unusually severe by the inclement weather, February passed quietly as the men of the Twenty-sixth busied themselves improving their winter quarters.

The competition among the companies for the $100 supper promised by Col. Morrison to the company having the finest street has made our camp one of the most beautiful in the whole army. . . . One of Frank Leslie's artists was here the other day, and he was so struck with it that he sketched it for that periodical. So it is likely that some of you will be able to see "Camp Fair View" without the trouble of making a pilgrimage of mud in "Old Virginia."[5]

A visitor from Newark was greatly impressed:

I have seen many camps here, but none can compare with the 26th N.J. Col. Morrison has taken a great deal of pains to embellish the camp by having it laid out in blocks, all around the streets of which he has placed pine trees some twelve feet high, which give it a beautiful appearance and look as if they had grown there. Every morning these streets are swept clean, and great attention is paid to sanitary measures, which has kept this regiment one of the healthiest in the service. Dr. L. G. Thomas, of our city, being the Surgeon, looks carefully after the health of the soldiers, and but few are in the hospital.

A deep ravine runs directly through the camp, and a beautiful stream of water winds its way through the ravine. The soldiers' tents are pitched on the side of the hill on one side of the ravine, and the tents of the Colonel and his staff on the opposite side, and it is a grand sight in the night to stand at the Colonel's tent door and view the camp on the opposite side. As far as the eye can reach, it seems as though you were opposite a large city, with the lights burning in the houses.[6]

Toward the end of February Camp Fair View cheered the arrival of a baking oven. The men, reported the *Daily Mercury*, could now enjoy a daily ration of "fresh, sweet bread."

The Bakery is situated in a round log house, about 18 feet square and 8 feet high; the three ovens are dug out of the bank outside of the house, and bake 160 loaves at a time, each loaf being a ration. It is calculated that these ovens will bake 2,888 rations in 24 hours. Accompanying this letter was one of these loaves, which, we having examined know that whereof we testify, and pronounce it fully equal to any that we have ever tasted.[7]

The Twenty-sixth Regiment was inordinately proud of its camp. A deprecating letter from another New Jersey regiment printed in the *Daily Mercury* prompted a hot reply from Sergeant Cummings:

Some days since I noticed a letter from one of your correspondents in the Thirteenth swearing at the camp of the Twenty-Sixth, terming us the "sickest set of mortals that he had ever seen" and averring that while the old regiments surrounding us had improved their camps, stockaded their tents, etc., the Twenty-Sixth had pitched their tents on the cold ground and there remained without an effort [to improve] their condition. One thing he omitted to state, viz: as regards the soberness of his informant when he visited our camp. The statement has not the imprint of truth on a single particular. We have stockaded our tents, taken the stumps out of our streets, and erected arches and bowers of cedars and pines until the camp is in reality what it purports to be—Camp Fairview, and I am reluctantly compelled to assert that although laboring evidently under the influence of an "eye-opener," the informant of your correspondent certainly did not take a fair view of Camp Fairview. Furthermore—although occupying the same camp, with the exception of a week, since the 4th of December last, we have only lost three men by sickness, none by desertion, and in no case have we turned our backs upon the enemy. Can the Thirteenth show as clean a record? Let their present disparity of numbers and past history answer. The Inspector General of the Army of the Potomac visited us a few days since, and complimented us with the remark that it was the finest camp in the army.[8]

Life at Camp Fair View, though a far cry from the comfort and safety of home, was tolerably pleasant for the Twenty-sixth New Jersey. "In many of the regiments, the sounds of the guitar and accordion could be heard every evening," wrote a surgeon attached to the Sixth Corps, "and on pleasant afternoons and evenings, parties assembled in the company streets and danced cotillions, and polkas, and jigs, to the music of violins."[9] Thanks to the chaplain, the men were furnished an ample supply of good reading:

> I proposed to have an out-door preaching service on Sunday, but was prevented by a severe rain storm. Not being able to preach, I turned Colporteur and went through every tent and called at every house in our Regimental city, and left a tract. Never before have I seen tracts received so gladly. Men were hungry for something to read, and this hunger gave a relish to tracts, which are not generally read with the greatest of zeal by the best of men.[10]

There was even time for a good-natured practical joke, reported the *Mercury*:

> It seems that the men in the 26th New Jersey regiment had repeatedly stolen the fresh meat from the Second Vermont boys, in the night, and appropriated it to their own use. Some of the Vermont boys thereupon killed a dog, dressed it neatly and hung up the quarters in the Quartermaster's department. The "Jerseys," mistaking it for mutton, stole it, as usual, and bore it off in triumph. The Vermonters were on the watch, and ascertained that it was served up next day upon the table of some of the Jersey officers. The joke soon became public, and the "Jerseys" are greeted, when they visit the camp of the Vermonters, with a "bow-wow-wow," by way of friendly salutation.
>
> If the story is true we submit that the Jersey boys must lose no time in "getting even" with the Greenmounters.[11]

One of Hooker's most welcome reforms was a system by which one man in each company could in turn take a ten-day furlough home. Major Morris left camp early in February for Newark. On February 12 the *Daily Mercury* reported his arrival:

Major Morris arrived in town last night upon a short furlough. He is looking well and hearty. The Major requests us to say that he will be found, for the next day or two, afternoons and evenings, at Dr. Thomas' office, corner of Elm and Mulberry streets, where he will be happy to answer any inquiries concerning the regiment. From Major M. we derive the following statement in regard to the present condition of the regiment;

The Twenty-sixth left Newark 1016 strong. We have had the usual camp diseases, such as diarrhoea and rheumatism; but a kind Providence has watched over us; and though we have had tedious marches, and in wet and cold weather have made our camps, to Him we must look that we are still a regiment little thinned by death. We have lost nine by disease—four having died in camp; the remainder are in a good state of health and spirits, unless we except eight, who are now in the hospital tent, convalescent cases. There are a few who will never be able to do much service, and had better not have [gone] out with the regiment. Efforts have been made to obtain their discharge, and repeated as often as possible, but owing to the peculiar powers of "red tape," and the fact that they are "only nine months' men," it is impossible to obtain their release, and so the poor fellows must linger out their term of service.[12]

When Chaplain Morrill returned to camp after his own brief furlough, he echoed Morris's complaint:

Upon inquiry I soon found that change true to her continually varying nature had been busy during my absence, and left her impress upon everything. Two of our number had had their "countenances changed" by death. . . . William Axtell, Co. A, died Feb. 6th of Typhoid Fever, and Stephen Jaggers of Co. E, died Feb. 8th of general debility. The last named was one for whom application was made for a discharge some two months since. The application was based on a certificate of the surgeon of the Regiment, stating that he would be unfit for service or die if he remained. But for some cause or other no notice was taken of this and some 20 or 30 other cases of the same kind. The wife of the deceased plead with me last Saturday night in tremulous tones to use my influence to procure his discharge. This I promised to do, but at the same time I remarked that my influence was only a "bubble on the billow." At this time when reforms are being introduced into the army, it does seem as if this wrong against the Government as well as against individual men and families should [not] be neglected. Let the people petition and protest until it is done. I have continued applications to do something in these instances, but while the law remains as it is I can do next to nothing.[13]

Visitors from home offered welcome relief from the monotony of camp life. Those lucky enough to procure a pass took the train from Newark to Washington, then boarded a steamer for the trip down the Potomac to Aquia Creek Landing. Newark City Alderman Nathaniel C. Ball, Auditor Smith Ward, and a Mr. Clements made the journey in midmonth. Alderman Ball, a Democrat, wrote up his account for the *Daily Journal*:

We arrived in Washington on Monday evening, and on Tuesday, through the kindness of the Hon. George T. Cobb and Senator [John P.] Hale, we obtained our pass to visit the Army of the Potomac. During the day we visited the places of interest, and while at the Capitol we were very kindly entertained by Senator Hale who showed us through the different departments. While there is much to interest one here, it makes the heart sad while viewing the statuary and paintings representing some of our past history, to think of our present distracted condition, and of the dark and uncertain future before us.

On Wednesday morning we left in the steamer for Aquia Creek. Our boat was loaded with stores for the army, and as if to impress one with the horrors of war, a large number of coffins were being sent down to be returned filled with its victims. The crowd of passengers was great; soldiers returning to the army, citizens going to visit their friends there, and among the number were a few females, willing to endure the hardships of travel in order to see a husband or brother.

As he journeyed down the Potomac, Ball was reminded of the "fanatic" in the White House:

We soon passed Alexandria and other points of interest, but as we neared this sacred spot, the residence of the Father of his Country, and passed by the tomb where now reposes his ashes, a great interest seemed manifest among those on board, all anxious to look upon the spot; and we felt in our hearts to pray that another Washington might be raised up in the hour of our country's peril.

About noon we arrived at Aquia Creek landing. This is the base from which this large army is supplied. A number of log buildings have been erected, and the stores are carried by rail to Falmouth station, from whence they are taken by teams. Belle Plain, some few miles below, being as we were told the nearest point to the 26th Regt., . . . we started at three o'clock in a steamer for that point, where we landed about four o'clock in the rain and mud. Having a trunk filled with stores for the soldiers which we had volunteered to take, we had great difficulty with it, but finally got it into a wagon going to the Brigade. Having on the boat met with the Chaplain of the 26th, Rev. Mr. Morrill, who was returning to the Regiment, and he being our guide we set out for the camp. But to describe our journey would be impossible; imagination cannot picture or pen describe truly that evening's travel. The depth of mud we could not determine, having gone down at times as deep as it was safe, and rise again; but as we struggled on the whole of the way was lined [with] encampments, and all the sympathy we received from the soldiers as we trudged through the mud, was every few minutes some one singing out to us "Why don't the Army move?" They had read the papers, and heard the cry "on to Richmond," and appeared to enjoy the fun of seeing civilians stuck in the mud. Darkness soon overtook us, and such darkness! Our troubles were now increased, the miles seemed much longer and our journey only about half accomplished.[14]

Chaplain Morrill, who was shepherding a box of medicine from Newark for the men, told much the same sad tale in the *Advertiser:*

At first we walked briskly and bravely, but by and by our feet came up more slowly, and we began to wish that the walk was over. We continued to ask direction and distances, but the farther we went the farther they said we had to go. We thought we had walked four miles and they said we had four still to go. The shades of night began to fall thick and fast, and the rain increased—the prospect was that it would be ours to beg a share of some soldier's narrow bed, or lie down untented in the mud. Goaded by these alternatives we plunged into the darkness and into the mud, over stumps and through runs. We were entangled in the bush heaps and tumbled over logs. First one would fall and then another until we all had our turn at tumbling. It seemed too bad to laugh, but that was better than to cry, and the circumstances demanded some vocal expression.[15]

After several hours of this, wrote Ball, the party neared its goal:

Our chaplain could not determine the right way, and we could get little information as to the location of the regiment, . . . but we were finally directed where we could see their camp and wallowing a short distance further we arrived at the tent of Mr. Green, the sutler, who kindly gave us some refreshments,—hot coffee, etc.,—and while partaking of them, Col. Morrison having heard of our arrival, sent for us to come to his tent, and in a true soldier's style received us to his log fire, when after changing some of our clothing we were made comfortable: but such a looking party as we were, we would have made a good picture for Frank Leslie's if taken by the "special artist—on the spot." I will only describe my own appearance, not taking liberties with the rest of the party. I had on a long overcoat of the fashionable style, and about one foot of the lower end was entirely covered with the sacred soil; my boots were no part of them discernable, and my pants, which I had thrust in my boots before setting out, were almost covered with mud, and the remainder of my garments that were not covered with yellow clay, were soaked in the rain, including my stovepipe hat, as the soldiers call it, and in this awful plight the Col. welcomed us to his quarters, and after spending some two hours by his cheerful fire we were separated for the night. I was taken by Quartermaster Bailey to his tent, where there was a large fire and a good bed, and the noble soldier not only gave me his bed but sole possession of his tent.[16]

Ball, who remained with the regiment several days, was impressed by Colonel Morrison, a fellow Democrat. "He is not only a good soldier but a true gentleman, and treats the men as such a man always will." The Twenty-sixth, wrote Ball, was "a model regiment, and the men will do their duty as soldiers when called upon, whatever may be their opinions about the government or its management of affairs."[17]

Ball's short visit stirred up a hornet's nest back in Newark. Soon after he returned home, an indignant *Mercury*, under the headline, "How Our City Officials Encourage the Soldiers," printed a note from a member of the Twenty-sixth:

> [T]he writer . . . affirms that a certain City Official in a late visit to the Camps of the New Jersey Soldiers endeavored to create dissatisfaction among them by offering to bet "forty dollars to twenty that they would be kept sixty days after their term of enlistment had expired." Our correspondent further says "if we would save our country and crush rebellion, would it not be best to commence at home?" If this be the encouragement men in high official position carry to the camps, we submit that their absence would be much better than their company.[18]

As the months dragged on some of the men of the Twenty-sixth lost their enthusiasm to "crush rebellion." In late February a soldier with the Thirteenth New Jersey Regiment complained to the *Mercury:*

> A friend of mine who has just returned from the 26th regiment . . . says that he is proud of the 13th for bearing the trials of camp life with so much patience and good humor, while they, the 26th, are continually grumbling and longing for their term of service to expire, instead of hoping, before they go home, the country may be saved and the Union restored. I cannot help thinking that this feeling is caused by such letters as their chaplain has written home.[19]

When Private Woodruff saw the letter, he was quick to assure *Mercury* readers that "[t]he boys are in the best of spirits."

> Another letter says we are the "sickest set he ever saw." That statement is a canard. I have not visited a regiment in which there was less dissatisfaction than there is in the 26th. The men all express their willingness to serve their term. On the contrary, there is the greatest dissatisfaction expressed by the 13th, and they all agree in saying that they "wish they were home." I have talked with a number of them and they all said they were sorry they had enlisted for three years.[20]

Even Chaplain Morrill's spirits had lifted somewhat. At least now, he told the *Advertiser*, there was a growing impression that decisive measures were in the offing:

> I think the feeling is gaining ground here, that however much the army may desire to escape the hardships and horrors of war, at present there is no

other alternative left but to fight. That we are "shut up to it" by the character and conduct of our foes, as well as our own self existence as a nation. That it is too late to heed the wise warnings that Shakespeare taught a father to give his son, "Beware of entrance to a quarrel." We have past that period. We are in a quarrel. "But being in, bear it that the opposer may beware of thee." It is not too late to heed this. While I cannot glory in war I am free to say that I am glad to see an increasing willingness to meet the necessity that Providence has permitted to be laid on this generation.[21]

Toward the end of February an unusually heavy snowfall blanketed northern Virginia, reported Chaplain Morrill.

The snow was nearly a foot deep on the level and in some places it was drifted to the depth of two or three feet. It was attended with some discomfort, but not much positive suffering among us. . . . Being unable to have public service I was again permitted to distribute some hymn books and tracts. . . . The men were glad to receive the hymn books, and the voice of song in many parts of the camp rose above the howling of the storm. At 12 o'clock M, when the storm was at its height, a cannon was heard and then another and another. We began to look one at another and ask "what does that mean?" "Are the rebels attacking us under cover of such a storm?" And then the Assembly was beat which some mistook for the long roll which is the signal for falling in in time of danger. Suddenly it occurred to us that it was the 22d of February—Washington's birth-day, and that the firing was a salute in honor of that event.[22]

A good snowfall was an event much welcomed by both Confederate and Union soldiers. If the accumulation were deep enough, snowball fights broke out almost everywhere, relieving at least for several hours the tedium of camp life.[23] The Twenty-sixth New Jersey was brigaded with four Vermont regiments, expert to a man in the art of snowballing. As soon as the snow stopped falling, the Vermont soldiers pounced upon the unsuspecting Twenty-sixth. Wrote Sergeant Cummings:

During the late heavy fall of snow the Vermonters twice made an attack on the encampment of the Twenty-Sixth, sending a perfect shower of snow balls at the head of every luckless Jerseyman, who made his appearance without his tent. The first attack was a complete surprise to us, but we essayed a sally from the camp, and drove the attacking party back to their reserves. Being heavily re-enforced they charged on us again, and after a desperate resistance we were driven back into our camp, fighting resolutely from the shelter of our tents until darkness put an end to the contest. Our casualties were quite heavy, but those of the enemy it is thought exceeded ours. A few days afterward the attack was renewed, but we took up a strong position on a hill in the rear of the camp, and repulsed every assault of the foe. The snow was crimsoned with blood from the olfactory organs of the Vermonters and the appearance of the battle field indicated the fierce nature of the contest. The enemy raised a flag of true, an armistice of a few hours was concluded, and then ensued that novel spectacle of war, men, who but a few minutes previous were engaged in one of the most sanguinary battles of modern times, harmonizing and fraternizing with clasped hands.

On February 25 the contest was renewed by the victorious Jerseymen. Sergeant Cummings regaled *Mercury* readers with his tale of the penultimate battle, the first ever fought by the "flower of Essex County."

Col. Morrison sent a challenge to Col. Seaver of the Third Vermont, to engage in the open field at 3 o'clock P.M. The challenge was accepted, on the condition that the Fourth Vermont should be included with the Third. This. was agreed to by the Colonel. Before the appointed time some of our men were detailed on fatigue duty, and at the time of the engagement we were only able to muster some three hundred men.

Nothing daunted by the superiority of numbers, Col. Morrison ordered Lieut. McCleese, of Company C . . . to fortify a small hill on our right, make as much ammunition as possible, and pile the snow balls in pyramids. This arduous duty was hastily performed. It was a strong position, a swollen brook at its base answering the purpose of a moat—too strong, in fact, for the Vermonters and they declined to attack us while occupying this miniature Chepeltepec. Commissioners were appointed, and after a parley, the Twenty-sixth was marched across the brook, and formed in line of battle on the field fronting the Vermonters. The hills were covered with spectators, and the eagerness to witness the novel contest knew no bounds. Companies A and B were thrown out as skirmishers. Company E occupied the right, C was given the centre and H rested on the left. The Colonel dashed over the field in all directions, encouraging the men to stand fast, amid the blue wreaths curling from a "brier wood" nonchalantly held in his left hand, and the Adjutant danced about on a spirited charger, apparently impatiently awaiting the hour of contest, the light of battle dilating within his eyes, and a quid of "navy plug" reposing beneath his cheek. Lieut. Woods, of the Ambulance Corps, and Lieut.—acted as mounted aids to the Colonel, while the "Sergeant" and John K. Shaw, an aspiring Newark youth of eighteen, acted as perambulating aids. The line being formed and everything in readiness for the contest, a red flag was raised as a signal and in a breath of time a strong body of the enemy drove in our skirmishers, and fiercely attacked our centre. At the same moment another strong force advanced against our right, but only as a feint; for they suddenly wheeled to the right, and joined their comrades in a furious charge on our centre. Major Morris ordered up Company E from our right, but too late to be of any advantage, and they were completely cut off from the main body of our army. Although flanked and pressed in front by overwhelming numbers, our centre heroically contested the advance of the enemy. Animated by the presence of the Colonel, they fought like veterans, and the white snow balls eddied through the air like popping corn from a frying pan. But the enemy were madly surging upon us in superior force and it was hardly within the power of human endurance to stand such a perfect *feu d'infer* any longer. Gradually the centre fell back inch by inch, the line then wavered to and fro, and finally the men broke in confusion and rolled down the hill followed by the victorious Vermonters. In vain the Colonel breasted the torrent; in vain the Major urged the men to stand fast; in vain did Adjutant White, the chivalric De Bayard of the 26th, implore the gods for aid.

The boys never rallied. Lieutenant Woods made an attempt to rally them and form them in hollow square on the fortified hill to the right, but he was mistaken by the boys for a Vermonter, and unceremoniously pelted from their midst. But the Colonel was not totally deserted by his men. The Vermonters seized his horse by the bridle, and made a desperate attempt to take him prisoner. The fight at this point was terrific beyond description. The men fought hand to hand. Colonel Seaver, the Achilles of the day, dashed through the combatants, seized Colonel Morrison by the shoulder and called upon him to surrender; but his demand was choked by the incessant patter of snow balls on his "physog." Around the rival chieftains the men struggled fearfully; there was the auburn haired Hodge, alias "wild Dutchman," fighting manfully; there was the fierce Teuton captain of Company E, dropping the foe right and left at every swing of his arms; but all in vain. Amid the wild excitement consequent upon the shouting—the rearing and plunging of horses, the Col. was drawn from his saddle and taken by the enemy. Most of his "staff" followed him as prisoners. A desperate attempt was made to rescue him, but it proved of no avail. Major Morris fared no better. Adjutant White, however, made a bold attempt to retrieve the fortunes of the day. Dashing into the dense ranks of the foe, he seized the bridle of Colonel Stoughton's Bucephalus, and gallantly attempted the impossibility of capturing the Colonel, who was the acting Brigadier of the attacking party. But [the] Adjutant had "caught a Tartar," for the Vermonters rushed around him like the waves beating upon some lone rock in the ocean, and vainly clamored for his surrender. He fought like an Ajax mounted on a "Black Bass," retaining his position in the saddle by resting his knee against the pommel. This was at last observed by a shrewd Yankee, who dexterously slipped between the two horses, detached the supporting knee, and the Adjutant fell from his lofty position like a tornado-stricken oak. This fall disheartened the Twenty-sixth, and only detached parties of a dozen scattered over the field persisted in an obstinate resistance. The "Sergeant" received a solid shot in the back of the head, and was borne to the rear a captive, and then "The bugles sang truce."

Thus ended the great battle of Fairview; unequaled in desperateness, and the theme of many a future poet's cogitations. Our loss was very heavy, and we were severely defeated. The spectators, acting on the well known principle of kicking a man when he is down, pitched into us most unmercifully when our centre was broken, and prevented us from reforming in line of battle. The slaughter of the enemy was fearful, and the prowess of the Newark ball players and firemen was displayed on their battered visages. Col. Stoughton was honored with a black eye, and the gallant Seaver fared but little better. The following is a fair recapitulation of the casualties on both sides:

Bloody noses, 53, bunged peepers, 81, extraordinary phrenological developments, 29, shot in the neck after the engagement, unknown.[24]

A steady rain melted the snow away as February drew to a close. "The boys are in good spirits," asserted Cummings, "and, although not particularly anxious to meet the enemy, will not shrink from the performance of their duty when called upon."[25]

11

The Winter of Discontent Is Passing Away

By early March, Hooker, although in command for less than six weeks, had succeeded masterfully in reviving the spirits of the Army of the Potomac. It took the enlisted men little time to realize that at last they had a commander who not only looked like a general but also acted like one. Hooker was decisive; he had plans, he spoke with confidence. And the men responded: "General Hooker enjoys the confidence of the troops under his command," wrote Private Woodruff on March 10, "and they . . . have more confidence and consequently more enthusiasm under him than under any other General."[1] Chaplain Morrill agreed:

> There is a growing confidence in Gen. Hooker. The "winter of discontent" is passing away with the natural winter and the time of the singing of birds is come. The birds tune their sweet treble lays in the morning and the frogs their hoarse bass in the evening, and though encompassed by mud, the showers are settling and the winds are drying the roads and fields. The elasticity of the American mind is strikingly exhibited in the hopeful spirit which, in the main, now characterizes the army.[2]

As the weather cleared, Hooker saw to it that the men were kept busy with a constant round of drills, inspections, and reviews. "The notes of busy preparation," wrote Morrill, were "continually heard."

> When the weather will permit at all the whole army is in a rigid course of drill. Every soldier that can do duty is ordered into ranks. No more soldier servants, orderlies, as they are called; their place is to be supplied by contrabands or officers are to serve themselves. If this order is rigidly enforced, as I hope it may be, it will increase the effective force of the army considerably.
>
> Every fine day we see the balloon up either on the right or the left, endeavoring to learn the whereabouts and whatabouts of the rebels. It is hoped that it will be used to more purpose than it has been before. We have hitherto

been lamentably ignorant in regard to the position and movements of our foes. A few days since we had a special inspection of our arms by the Corps Ordinance officer and they were again condemned. Whether we shall have others or not is yet undecided. The opinion is general among officers and men that it is hardly the fair thing to put them in the thickest of a fight with repeatedly condemned arms—with weapons almost as dangerous to those who use them as those against whom they are used.[3]

The epidemic of desertions that had plagued the army after Fredericksburg gradually abated. When deserters were apprehended, General Hooker ordered that their punishment be public. On Saint Patrick's Day, reported Morrill, the brigade was called out for the sentencing of eleven deserters:

The Regiments were drawn up in the form of three sides of a parallelogram. The acting General and staff were in front and the prisoners were then marched in under a guard to the centre of the Brigade. The acting Adjt. General then read the sentence to each one separately; each prisoner stepping forward a few paces and taking off his cap as his sentence was pronounced. Though they were all called deserters and tried for that offence, yet the guilt was not the same in all cases; some had come back voluntarily and others had been brought back under guard. So the punishment varied from forfeiting a few months' pay and having half their heads and faces shaved and being marched up and down in front of their Regiments with a label on their backs of "Deserter" to the tune of "the Rogue's March;" and forfeiting all their pay past, present, and prospective, and be sent to labor on some public works (Rip Raps for example) during the remaining part of their term of enlistment, have seven days a month of solitary confinement, and at the end of the time have the letter "D" branded on their left hip.

It was a sad and solemn spectacle. Its influence will be salutary. I believe that many went from that impressive scene more strongly than ever before, resolved to bear the rigors and run the risks incidental to being obedient and brave soldiers, rather than those which in these instances followed cowardly desertion.[4]

Despite Hooker's new order of things, life at Camp Fair View went on much as it had before. Packages from home were eagerly awaited, as always.

Friday afternoon the boxes for the regiment, which have been on the road a long time, came in, and then there was a general rush to get them. Some of them had been on the road two months, and the contents were covered with mould; chickens, loaves of bread, cake, apples and various other goodies were thrown away. All the boxes were inspected before they were given out, to see if they contained liquor or clothing; a number of soldiers having deserted recently, by having citizens suits sent in express boxes. A box was sent to some members of Company B, which contained a quart of whiskey, and it escaped the scrutiny of the box inspectors. It was sent by "Liberty, No. 1" to some of their members in the company. The arrival of the bottle was greeted with cheers for the firemen, and groans for the Inspectors.[5]

Company and regimental glee clubs remained actively in tune, the chaplain told his *Advertiser* readers:

> One of the pleasantest things that has occurred among us recently, was a visit one moonlight night from the glee club of the 2d N.J. They gave us one of the best serenades that I have heard since I left home. We have been accustomed to "lay the flattering unction to our souls," that we had some of the sweetest singers of the Army in our Regiment. But I think we shall have to yield the palm to the glee club of the 2d at least for the present.[6]

Morrill continued his good works.

> I received through Marcus L. Ward a few days since $27.64, a donation from the pupils of Miss Bonsall's school, "the eldest of whom is scarcely 9 years old," with the request that it should be "used for the benefit of sick and wounded Jersey soldiers," which request I will most cheerfully and carefully comply with. It is a pleasing thought to contemplate, that these little ones think of their fathers and brothers who are here suffering for their good. . . . There was many a "candy penny" in this contribution, many a childish sacrifice—but it will give a more enduring sweetness to think that their pennies and sacrifices have brought some medicine, food or clothing for some sick or wounded soldier in the Hospital, or on the battle field. I hope many other children of both larger and smaller growths will . . . do likewise.[7]

Reading was one of the more common diversions in the army. Newspapers, illustrated weeklies, dime novels, a few religious tracts, and an occasional "licentious" book passed from soldier to soldier. Like most of his fellow chaplains, the Reverend Morrill fought a hard but losing battle to improve the quality of the material his men read.

> Through the kindness of friends I have been able to furnish a very full supply of reading matter. From Rev. Mr. Davis, Assistant Minister of Grace Church, I received nearly 100 copies of "selections from the book of Common Prayer," and I ordered 500 copies of Dr. Fish's premium tract "Don't swear," all of which were very acceptable, and I hope will be very useful. The importance of an abundant supply of good reading matter for the army both secular and sacred cannot well be over-estimated. Satan seems to hate a vacuum about as much as nature is said to do. He does not allow a reading vacuum. He has scattered yellow covered leaves for the sickening of the army and even far worse . . . [a] kind that might appropriately be called black covered, though no cover could be colored so black as the contents of some of these volumes. Foul, fetid, reeking with the extract of nastiness gathered

from the hot beds of atheism and the sinks and sewers of licentiousness in all ages. If we would not have a debauched army we must gird ourselves for a greater work than we have done. Friends must write often and interestingly; in this way some "home influence" can be exerted. Useful and interesting reading matter must be furnished and that which is not religious, provided it be clean and healthful, to a certain extent, will be quite as useful as any, and in many instances even more so, because it will be read. I do not mean old musty-cast-off newspapers and magazines though these are read sometimes. But fresh magazines and newspapers such as men would read at home. The mail is the best channel of communication as a rule. If each friend at home would, in this particular, look after a friend here they would all be looked after and the multiplicity of hands would make light work.[8]

Morrill's readers obliged, sending the soldiers vast quantities of reading matter, especially newspapers. The *Daily Advertiser*, *Journal*, and *Mercury* as well as several German language papers printed in Newark were eagerly read throughout Camp Fair View. No matter that they reached camp 10 days to two weeks after publication: They relieved homesickness and kept the men informed of the progress of the war. Said Chaplain Morrill:

The army is not unmindful of events transpiring at home. The passage of the "Conscription bill" is approved here, as it furnishes a guarantee that sacrifices heretofore made shall not be in vain. And it makes it possible to fill up and keep full the old regiments, which every one here sees is essential to the proper and successful prosecution of the war. Military men here laugh at the thought or talk that it cannot be enforced. I know commanders of Regiments and Brigades that have expressed a wish to make a campaign in certain States in case conscription is resisted. In regard to letting (or making) the negro fight, there is not perfect unanimity. But the prevailing feeling is, let him fight, or make him fight; he ought to fight. He has as much or more at stake in this war than any one else. There is now and then one of the "dog-in-the-manger" sort of men, who declare that they "will not fight for the nigger," and will not let him fight for himself. But such unreasoning ones are not very numerous here, and it is to be hoped nowhere.[9]

By the end of March, the Twenty-sixth Regiment had been in federal service more than six months. It had seen no real action and none was in sight. Within three months it would march home to Newark, a prospect that filled Cummings, recently promoted to sergeant-major, with a measure of dread:

Twice have we left our present camp in search of the enemy: Once to participate in the disastrous engagement at Fredericksburg, again as active assistants in the expedition of January to [Banks] Ford, being detailed to drag the pontoons through small oceans of mud to a place of comparative safety. Since that eventful period we have remained in camp leading its usual monotonous life, varied with fatigue and picket duty, which in these days of ice, snow, rain and mud are not exactly spots of gold upon the pages of a private military history.[10]

Cummings, who joined the army for adventure, need not have worried. "Fighting Joe" Hooker had resurrected an army and proposed soon to use it. What his intentions were for the spring campaign, no one knew, but he boasted: "My plans are perfect and when I start to carry them out, may God have mercy on Bobby Lee, for I shall have none."[11] In less than a month Cummings, Morrill, Dodd, Woodruff, and their comrades in the Twenty-sixth would come to know the full meaning of their general's words.

12

A Trumpet Blast from the Twenty-sixth

The steadily improving weather of early April brought with it increasing pressure from Washington for prompt military action against Lee's Army of Northern Virginia. General Hooker responded with a flurry of activity. Surplus baggage was ordered to the rear, trenching tools and sandbags requisitioned and the Army Secret Service called on for up-to-date maps of Richmond's defenses. Hooker proposed that the War Department begin stockpiling huge quantities of siege equipment for early shipment to points near the Rebel capital. Later he urged Washington to assemble a flotilla of supply boats capable of delivering 1.5 million rations to the army as soon as it reached the Pamunkey River, twenty miles east of Richmond. "Go forward, and give us victories," Lincoln had written his newest general in January, and now it seemed that was precisely what "Fighting Joe" was about to do. The orders that flowed from headquarters daily gave no hint of Hooker's plan of operation; even his closest subordinates remained ignorant of his true intentions. Whatever Hooker's plan for the spring campaign, the Army of the Potomac clearly enjoyed the power to carry it to execution. By latest count 133,000 Union troops supported by seventy batteries of artillery faced a Confederate force across the Rappahannock of less than half that number. The odds favored the North and Hooker, his intelligence service at last operating efficiently, knew it. Hooker fairly burbled with enthusiasm, calling his army "one well worthy of the republic." It was, he announced to one of his many visitors, "the finest army on the planet."[1] The troops, Private Woodruff told the *Mercury*, were properly impressed.

> Yesterday afternoon our division was reviewed by the world renowned Joseph Hooker. The division was formed at two o'clock, and after waiting an hour, Gen. Hooker came in view. The band immediately commenced playing "Hail to the Chief." The 26th occupied the right of the line, and the artillery was posted immediately in our rear. After he rode past us we were marched around the field, past the general, and we had a fine opportunity of seeing the "idol of the army." As soon as we had passed, Gen. Hooker sent an

Aid to Col. Morrison to inform him that "the 26th marched the best of any regiment in the division." The review lasted about three hours, and passed off very satisfactory.[2]

To hear Joe Hooker tell it, catching Lee and capturing Richmond were as good as done. All too familiar with boastful generals, President Lincoln groaned when reports of Hooker's optimism reached him in Washington. "That is the most depressing thing about Hooker," the president remarked to a friend. "It seems to me that he is overconfident."[3] On April 3 Lincoln resolved to take a closer look at his new commander. He and Mrs. Lincoln, their ten-year-old son Tad, and a few close friends would, he telegraphed Hooker, arrive at Aquia Creek Landing on Easter Sunday.

Lincoln enjoyed his week-long visit immensely, spending long hours touring the hospital tents and camps and peering across the river with Tad at the Fredericksburg battlefield. If not particularly enlightening, conferences with Hooker and his staff were encouraging; in any event the president was obviously delighted to be away from Washington. By week's end Lincoln seemed satisfied, though still troubled by Hooker's superabundant confidence. On the final day of his visit Lincoln reviewed the Army of the Potomac. The Twenty-sixth, wrote Woodruff, was "aroused at 5 A.M. by the 'reveille.'"

We blacked our boots, and cleaned our guns and equipments with extra care, and at eight o'clock the line was formed and started, the "26th" being on the lead. We marched about half a mile, when an orderly rode up to the General with orders to return to camp, the review being postponed until the next day. Our General, however, thought it an excellent opportunity for a brigade drill, and he gave a "charge bayonets" at a "double quick." The "26th" advanced with a yell that would have put all rebels to flight. We were then dismissed for the day.

Yesterday we were again aroused by the drum at five A.M., and at eight A.M. we again started. We marched a distance of four miles. The road for the most part was very good, but there were two or three ditches to cross, and several low places where the mud and water was a foot deep, and by the time we reached the rendezvous we were pretty well spattered with mud.[4]

The grand review kindled Chaplain Morrill's flagging spirits. It was, he told the *Advertiser*, "most impressively sublime."

From the place where the President was posted to receive and return the salute of the passing corps, a magnificent scene was spread out before you. . . . The land lying in range of vision was vast. . . . In the distance was the battle field of Fredericksburg, sorrowfully sublime in the recollections it awakened to those who were engaged in its fearful scenes. Beyond that were those dark wood crowned heights, which for the most part concealed our enemies from our sight. It required little imagination to conceive that they looked sullenly over upon this mighty host that was gathering to scale the steeps and scatter their occupants. . . .

Such an army, under such circumstances amid such surroundings could not fail strongly to impress the most superficial spectator. But when the cause that called them forth was considered and the prize for which they were contending was estimated there was a moral grandeur connected with the scene that far transcended the material grandeur. It may be weakness, but I confess that I could not gaze upon that splendid pageant with eyes undimmed by tears. It is related of Xerxes that when from a height he looked down upon his mighty army and thought that a hundred years hence not one of that multitude would be living, he wept. How could I refrain when I thought of the number that in a hundred days or weeks would be "sleeping their last sleep" having "fought their last battle." But though they perish thus, they will not . . . have lived and died in vain.

The president, wrote Morrill, was accompanied by General Hooker "and a multitude of lesser military dignitaries."

I remember when a boy to have almost envied the man who had seen a real live general, but I have seen them if not "ad nauseant" [sic] almost "ad infinitum." In this regard I thought the President had a fine opportunity to see the creations of his own power. He is reported to have said that he could make one in "five minutes" and some of them look as if they had been very hastily constructed. As the colors of the various regiments were carried past him he stood uncovered and it would not have been inappropriate for all to have stood uncovered, as some of the torn, tattered and smoke-begrimmed [sic] banners were carried past. . . . By the magic alchemy of the mind, their fading colors were transmitted into unfading laurels won in their defence, and their smoke and dust chrystalized into the diamonds of sublime suffering and heroic daring. I envy not the heart that was so stolid as not to be moved by their sight.[5]

Lincoln was both pleased and profoundly moved by the spectacle. A newspaper correspondent present reported that the President "merely touched his hat in return salute to the officers, but uncovered to the men in the ranks." According to the Reverend Morrill:

As our Regiment passed, the President turned to Gen. Sedgwick, Commander of the corps, and was heard to say after casting his eye over it and gauging its size and appearance, "That's a splendid Regiment! what a front it presents." Size . . . adds much to the impression made by a body of soldiers, and I did not see another in the whole corps, that looked so large [as ours].

It was a striking illustration of the majesty of government to see all the vast army, enbracing officers of every grade and intellects of every calibre and degree of culture paying their respects to one who to all appearance was only a citizen of the republic instead of its President and commander in chief of all its armies. As military as all things were I was glad to be reminded that we still had a civil head.[6]

The grand review had refreshed the chaplain's waning patriotism. Not so the *Daily Journal*, which saw the day's events in a vastly different light. It was, wrote their correspondent with heavy sarcasm, "a magnificent display."

> The large field was covered with solid masses of troops as far as the eye could distinguish them. Drums were beating merrily; colors were flying; brass bands playing national airs; arms glittering in the sun, and officers riding here and there over the ground with an air of fussy importance. Then all was quiet suddenly, until a salute of twenty-one guns announced the President of the United States. He rode to the camp color and took off his hat. What a good time to cheer him! What an opportunity for sixty thousand men to proclaim their affection by one long continued spontaneous burst of applause! It did not come. He rode up and down the lines twice, in front and rear, and still no cheering—no enthusiasm—nothing but the cold formal military salute. There was one exception. A single regiment broke the silence, but it sounded like the voice of pity rather than the voice of admiration.

The frosty reception, said the *Journal*, ought to prompt some presidential soul-searching:

> He has reviewed the army; let him review himself. Let his aims, his plans, his vacillating policy, his innumerable blunders, pass in review before him. Let him review the past two years; and, in his midnight dream, he will see one long line of skeleton forms and weeping widows and orphans moving along in solemn silence, with no voice of consolation or sympathy for him. Let him look to the future, with its endless column of taxed and oppressed freemen, and he will hear, from the weary toiling masses of posterity, no word of cheering or blessing to gladden his heart.[7]

Thousands in New Jersey shared the *Journal's* caustic view of the president. Support for the administration slipped badly after the preliminary announcement of the Emancipation Proclamation in the fall of 1862, then slid to near-invisibility following the debacle at Fredericksburg and Burnside's farcical Mud March a month later. Republican politicians and presses battled vainly against the tide of discouragement and disillusion. The *Daily Mercury*, while conceding that public confidence in the war had ebbed, insisted that "if the power we now have in use be vigorously brought to bear, the rebellion can be crushed . . . before the first day of June." A "few decisive victories," it claimed, would "work an instant and magical change in the whole aspect of the situation."

> Let, then, the next three months be given to unceasing, unsparing war— using every means to cripple and subdue our foe. Let every patriot, from this

day forward, take new courage. Let the hands of the Administration be upheld, let it feel that it has the great loyal heart of the land beating in lively sympathy with its holy purpose—to save the Union; and let it listen to the majestic voice of the people which bids it instantly deal its heaviest and most crushing blows. Courage, good hearts, the day [of] dawn is not distant.[8]

Well might the chair-bound generals at the *Mercury* plead for "a few decisive victories." Unionists were desperate: Hooker's months of inactivity spurred a growing belief that the war had stalemated, that the time of peace was near at hand. In New Jersey (and much of the North as well) the first months of 1863 marked the apogee of Copperhead influence. The *Daily Journal*, sensing the swing of public opinion, attacked the administration at every opportunity. When the Emancipation Proclamation was officially proclaimed, Fuller called it "infamous" but "of little importance . . . if the South can maintain its position in the field." The proclamation, said the paper with obvious distaste, "takes the negroes into full fellowship, and establishes them on an equal footing with the white soldiers."[9] The Conscription Act, signed by President Lincoln on March 3, 1863, was unconstitutional, according to the *Journal*. "[I]f the people have one tithe of the virtue and manliness of their fathers, they will steadily refuse to be offered up as victims to the infernal destructive policy of the abolitionists."[10] Throwing caution to the winds, Newark Democrats (among them Editor Fuller) invited Ohio Congressman Clement L. Vallandigham to address a rally of the Union Democratic Club. A vicious opponent of Lincoln, Vallandigham would soon be arrested and deported for his treasonous activities. To the *Daily Journal*, however, Vallandigham was a "fearless champion of the people's liberties." On February 14 the Ohioan spoke at Newark's Concert Hall before a "multitudinous throng" that included Congressman Perry, Mayor Bigelow, former U. S. Senator Wright, and other leading Democrats. The crowd cheered as Vallandigham called for restoration of the Union as it was in 1860, resistance to the draft, the defeat of Lincoln in 1864, and an end to "this miserable crusade against African slavery."[11]

Newark Republicans were enraged by Vallandigham's visit. "The whole affair," snorted the *Mercury*, "needed only to have been transferred to Richmond to have been a perfect success."[12] The boldness of the Copperheads badly frightened New Jersey Unionists, who saw the state slipping toward "revolution" and "violent resistance to the United States law." Bereft of the military victories it rightly judged would still the cries for peace, the *Mercury* took comfort in the fact that the army at least could be depended upon:

Let the loyal people of the North, now so shamelessly beset by men who strive to cloak their wretched cowardice by attempting to prove the injustice of [the] war . . . , be comforted by the certainty that they have the ARMY with them. An army that will never lower the proud banner of our country to the black flag of rebellion; an army that knows the value of Constitutional Liberty, and is not yet dismayed or discouraged from the vindication of the outraged majesty of THE COUNTRY at the cannon's mouth; an army not of mercenaries, but of loyal, high-minded, intelligent citizens, who, when they gaze upon the horrid front of REBELLION still menacing them, and mark its insolent banners flaunting in their faces, and hear the voice of its defiant cannon thundering in their ears, know that it means WAR, and not "peace." And they spurn and loathe, and will some day call to bitter account the men, who, when they were in the field fighting for the life of the nation were stabbing in the back the cause for which they were willing to die.[13]

The high-water mark of Copperhead power came on March 18, 1863, when the Democratic-controlled State Legislature after weeks of heated debate passed an extraordinary resolution that protested the emancipation of the slaves, the creation of West Virginia, the suspension of the writ of habeas corpus, and a war it said was waged "for the accomplishment of unconstitutional or partisan purposes." Declaring that New Jersey's willingness to supply troops "has been occasioned by no lurking animosity to the States of the South," the so-called Peace Resolutions called for the appointment of commissioners from North and South who would "convene in some suitable place for the purpose of considering . . . what plan may be adopted, consistent with the honor and dignity of the National Government, by which the present civil war may be brought to a close."[14]

New Jersey Unionists were apoplectic. The usually imperturbable *Advertiser* heatedly denounced the "traitors at home."

While our soldiers in the field have added lustre to our name, politicians at home—the tools of demagogues of other States, have robbed us of our hard earned laurels, and for the time caused the very name of New Jersey to stink in the nostrils of patriotism. They have preached a crusade against the Government, instead of one against rebels. The Legislature of the State has insulted the nation by sending an avowed sympathizer with treason to the U. S. Senate. The copperheads have assembled in the capital of our State to inculcate treason and to advise resistance to the Government. They have invited the greatest advocate of treason, Vallandigham, to address them in the largest city in the State, and applauded him the loudest when he stabbed his country the deepest. . . . Shame where is thy blush?

Desperately, madly, have the copperheads of New Jersey attempted to rush the State into the maelstrom of secession and anarchy, but thanks to an all wise Providence, their very madness has been our salvation, and their attempts are producing a revulsion of sentiment which is destined to overwhelm these agitators and consign their names to lowest infamy. And the aroused patriotism of the sons of New Jersey will soon atone to the nation for the dishonor placed upon the State by the action of the copperheads.[15]

Infuriated by the "insignificant and contemptable faction" in the legislature that supported the peace resolutions, the *Daily Mercury* waxed eloquent, urging "the Union men of this State . . . to light the fires of patriotism on every hill-top and in every valley."

> Summon the children of the men of '76 to the redemption of their noble birth-land, and tell the world that New Jersey is not the lost and degraded creature which a miserable band of copperhead disloyalists would make her appear; but that still, as of old, her skirts are pure from taint of treason or cowardice, and her heart warm and loyal to the Union she helped to found, and which she loves with a love unsurpassed.
>
> Thirty thousand gallant sons of New Jersey are asserting this sentiment today, before the nation, and in the teeth of the foe. Let hundreds of thousands more from her iron hills to the sandy marge of her ocean-washed counties take up the cry in thunder tones—New Jersey is loyal among the loyal.[16]

The controversy at home found its echo in the Jersey regiments at the front. Most reacted angrily. The Eleventh Regiment sent a resolution to the legislature calling the introduction of the peace resolutions "wicked, weak and cowardly." The Twenty-fourth Regiment cheered as one of its officers condemned "these traitors at home . . . [who] outstrip each other in their haste to throw themselves at the feet of the slave power."[17]

First word from the Twenty-sixth Regiment gladdened the hearts of Essex County Unionists. On the eve of the grand review the field, staff, and line officers had unanimously approved a set of resolutions drafted by Lieutenant Colonel Martindale, Major Morris, Acting Adjutant Terhune, Lieutenant Beach, and Chaplain Morrill. "A Trumpet Blast from the Twenty-sixth" was the way the *Advertiser* headlined the chaplain's triumphant report:

> On the afternoon of the [grand review], the regiment formed a square and Col. Morrison introduced the subject to the men in a few neat and appropri-ate remarks. He said that [the resolutions] had been unanimously adopted at a meeting of the officers of the regiment held on the preceeding evening, and they were now brought forward for the approval or rejection of the men. He need hardly say that they were resolutions expressive of noble sentiments and firm unyielding devotion to the Union. They were presented as an offset to the proceeding of vile traitors and abettors of Jeff Davis in the State of New Jersey. He hoped that no Jersey soldier would falter in giving his approval to these resolutions. Hereafter we should all be proud of this record of pa-triotism. Let us sanction them unanimously, and the answer of the soldiers of New Jersey to the recent efforts of her cowardly and treasonable disorganis-ers will make the old State proud of her sons in the field.

According to Morrill, the resolutions were read and adopted with enthusiastic cheers, "but five dissenting votes appearing in a regiment of some eight hundred men present for duty." Foster of the *Mercury* could not have written a better statement of Republican principles:

Whereas [said the resolutions], our country is in mortal peril, and the government established by the Fathers of the Republic is engaged in a desperate struggle of life and death for its very existence, and while we are here to defend it from open foes, we learn with sorrow, shame and indignation that it is assailed by disorganizers at home, therefore

Resolved, That we are the deadly enemies of the armed traitors who have brought this calamity upon the country, and are determined to fight them until they are coerced into submission to the Constitution and all the laws of the United States.

That we are in favor of peace, but there is but one basis of peace with rebels, and that is unconditional submission to the government which their and our fathers established, and that we mean to fight for such a peace and for no other.

That compromise with armed rebels means dissolution of the Union, and would be a miserable and disgraceful death by suicide of the grandest government the world has yet beheld, and that its advocates are traitors and rebels in disguise, and in our judgment are entitled to the good offices of the military law—Short, sharp and effectual, far more than if they wore the livery of Jeff Davis openly.

That the self-styled "peace-makers," who have charged us with being demoralized or disaffected, and unable or unwilling to fight, have mistaken the temper and condition of this army and this regiment; that in our judgment, it is only their own loyalty or courage that is tainted with the leprosy of treason or cowardice, and that we advise them to wash themselves clean from the infamous infection, or else expect the sharpest remedies known in the treatment of such an unhealthy disorder.

That we are citizen soldiers, and that, as volunteers from the State of New Jersey, we warn all traitors, whether in that State or elsewhere, that we are also citizens of the United States, and will maintain the integrity and unbroken unity of the States; that our swords are as sharp and ready for secret conspirators at home, as for open foes in our front, and that they may know whom we regard as worse than open foes, we give them the following description: Those who do all they can to oppose the war, to embarrass the government, to prevent vigorous measures, to weaken credit, to magnify our defeats and glorify all the successes of our enemies, to discourage enlistments, to denounce the enrollment, to disparage and slander the officers charged with the administration of public affairs, to fill the public mind with distrust, apprehension, and a desire for a disgraceful peace; to outrage and libel the army now in the field; and leave it to perish unsupported in the struggle, or finish the contest as best it may; and in short, all who by such infamous means have justly entitled themselves to the disgraceful distinction of the sinister name of Copperhead.

That we believe the great heart of the People of this country to be sound, and that this regiment owes it to itself to denounce the "Protest and Peace Propositions" made by a traitorous fragment of our State Legislature, and to proclaim that they are an outrage upon every patriotic citizen and loyal soldier of our native State, and represent the sentiments of neither; that they are the misbegotten offspring of disaffection and cowardice, and a libel upon the patriotism and loyalty of the good old State of New Jersey, which is now, as she has always been, true and faithful to the Union, and sound and cordial in her support of the Government; that this is the work of a set of false, cowardly and traitorous demagogues, offensive to a great majority of her people, and an insult to her soldiers for which both soldiers and people will in due time call them to account.[18]

Two days after Morrill's "Trumpet Blast" appeared in the *Advertiser*, the *Daily Journal* detected a sour note.

We have received information from a member of the 26th N.J. Volunteers which authorizes us to say that the resolutions recently published in this city as the almost unanimous voice of the regiment, do not represent the views of more than one-third of its members. The non-commissioned officers and a large number of the privates were highly indignant at the imposition practiced upon them by a portion of their officers, and passed another series of resolutions repudiating the sentiments of those which were forced upon them, and protesting against such a misrepresentation of their political views. It is also reported to us that the non-commissioned officers who have given their assent to this protest are threatened with being reduced to the ranks, and that the soldiers who have had the hardihood to attempt to vindicate themselves before their friends are to be court-martialed and punished.[19]

A week later the *Journal* carried a long letter from Sergeant Major Cummings, including a set of resolutions he claimed were "passed by a majority of enlisted men."

WHEREAS, at dress parade . . . a series of resolutions were presented to the non-commissioned officers and privates of the Twenty-sixth New Jersey Volunteers, and a vote was declared to have been taken, resulting nearly unanimously in favor thereof; therefore

RESOLVED, That we, non-commissioned officers and privates of the Twenty-sixth Regiment, New Jersey Volunteers, do honestly feel it is our duty to represent to our friends and brothers at home, as well as our brave comrades in the old New Jersey regiments, that such vote was not taken in accordance with our wishes, and had the question been put fairly and squarely before the regiment the result would have been far different.

RESOLVED, That, while we are ready and willing, at all times, not only to assert, but to maintain our devotion to the Constitution as framed by our fathers, the whole Union and the dear old flag, we do heartily detest the introduction of any resolutions into the army for the purposes of a purely political effect upon the masses of the people at home. . . .

RESOLVED, That we have unbounded confidence in the Democracy of the State of New Jersey as opposed to the rabid abolition and secession disorganizers of the present day; and we hail with satisfaction and pride the recent election of Joel Parker to the Gubernatorial chair of New Jersey, as a prelude to the final advent of peace, the speedy termination of the rebellion, and the reconstruction of the Union on a firm and honorable basis.

According to Cummings, only 342 of 800 enlisted men of the regiment present for duty refused to sign the resolutions. Added Cummings:

The resolutions themselves have been framed, signed and sent forward amid considerable difficulty. The Captain of one company threatened to place under arrest every man in his company who should dare to sign them, and it is said offered a dollar for the name of every one who should place his name upon the roll. He had but lately received his commission from Governor Parker, and requited the favor by writing the words "Copperhead resolutions" above the resolution endorsing the election of the Governor. The same Captain expressed the intention of heading a mob for the destruction of a certain paper published in the city of Newark on his return home, saying that he believed he would be backed in such a course by every member of the 26th Regiment. Among the signers of the above are many Republicans; but I am sorry to say that a great many Democrats refused to sign them, fearing the future action of their officers in regard thereto. Such fears, however, were perfectly groundless, as our Colonel has always professed himself not only willing but anxious that every man in the regiment should express his true sentiments in reference to the former resolutions. Much praise is certainly due the non-commissioned officers who have boldly proclaimed their honest opinions in these resolutions, utterly regardless of the rumored reduction to the ranks therefore. They felt that if they could not wear their chevrons with honor, they would never sully them with dishonor. Truckling to power is not a prevalent characteristic of Jerseymen. We are Jerseymen—loyal Jerseymen—and we believe in the doctrine of a free press and a free expression of political opinion. We feel it a duty that we owe to the Legislature of the State of New Jersey, which has faithfully fulfilled not only its duties to the Federal Government, but also its promises to our families, to express our confidence and abiding faith in the party predominant in that council.

The resolutions passed on dress parade were regarded by us as offensively partizan in their character. . . . In Governor Parker the men all recognize a statesman, who has proved himself worthy of being the standard-bearer of the State, and one who never will prove recreant to the freemen who placed him in his position. We had heard that he was on a visit to the Army of the Potomac, and we made great calculations on his reviewing the 26th. Had he appeared among us, the way the "unterrified" would have opened their throats in cheers would have been a caution to all opposers of constitutional rights and liberty of speech at home. Some senseless persons may class us as "Copperheads," but we have always faithfully and conscientiously endeavored to do our duty to ourselves, to our State and to our Government. We are not secessionists; neither are we abolitionists; but we are Union men, and as such will labor for the preservation or reconstruction of the Union, using every means within our power for the accomplishment of such a result. We have never refused to obey an order, and are more than willing to do our whole duty whenever called on, whether before or after the expiration of our term of enlistment. Although armed with nothing but "stuffed clubs," we obeyed every order on the bloody field of Fredericksburg with alacrity and cheerfulness. We have seen a little service in the army; we have seen the military "elephant" in all his magnificent proportions, from the tip of his snout down to the last kink of his symmetrical tail, and we are willing to leave him entirely uncovered, with a special recommendation to those who think themselves more loyal than we, to step down this way and take a nine months' view of him.

Cummings closed his letter on a note of fulsome praise for a fellow Democrat.

In Colonel Morrison we recognize a man and a soldier, one from whom every member of the 26th Regiment will part with sincere regret. The highest praise that can be given him is to say that he has not an enemy among the enlisted men of the regiment. It is a favorite expression of this brigade, that "every man is up on the Jersey Colonel." In all his dealings with the regiment he has ever acted on the square, and we are proud of him. He is a true, Union-loving Democrat, and possesses the entire confidence of the regiment.[20]

An obviously reluctant *Daily Mercury* published the dissident resolutions in what it called the interest of "fair-play," setting the story in small type and burying it in the middle of a page. "We are well aware that there have been certain influences at work in the 26th which would be likely to produce just such a state of feeling as the above proceedings seem to indicate," commented the paper darkly. "We hoped, and still hope, that those influences have not been potent enough to turn the splendid 26th into a camp of copperheads."[21] More than once had Foster implied that every patriot was in uniform, every traitor at home by his cozy hearth. Indeed, less than two months earlier he had confidently predicted that the "infernal schemes" of the Copperheads would meet "their death-blow" from the army. "[T]he more a man sees of the hideousness of the rebellion," he had written, "the more sternly he fights it."[22] The news from the Twenty-sixth was unwelcome, to say the least.

The *Mercury*'s concern that the Twenty-sixth might be turned into a "camp of copperheads" was exaggerated. It should have come as no surprise to the paper that the regiment would reflect the politics of its home county. Raised in a Democratic county in a Democratic state, the Twenty-sixth was more or less evenly divided between Republicans and Democrats, with the Democrats having a slight edge. Whatever their politics may have been, however, there is no evidence the men were tainted with Copperheadism. In common with every other unit in the Northern army, the regiment was deeply discouraged at times. Fredericksburg, the Mud March, their "stuffed clubs," and the months of tiresome inactivity tested the mettle of the staunchest patriot. Understandably, the confidence of September had worn somewhat thin. Foster was too far distant from the battlefield to know that discouragement was not the equivalent of disloyalty.[23]

Foster was doubly dismayed to learn that his best correspondent in the regiment was a Parker Democrat. Cummings's earlier pieces had given no hint of his political views, although his cheery tone must have convinced Foster that the sergeant was a fellow Republican. But while Cummings was a Democrat, he was not a Copperhead. He had not sent his letters to the *Daily Journal* because he disdained the Peace Democrats as much as he did the Abolitionists. With the *Advertiser* printing the chaplain's letters, that left open only the columns of the *Mercury*. The sergeant major's role in promoting the dissident resolutions swiftly terminated his career as a *Mercury* correspondent; henceforth, despite his abhorrence of its politics, Cummings would write for the *Journal*. It was a marriage of convenience: Cummings wanted to write; the *Journal*, which prided itself as one of New Jersey's leading newspapers, needed a correspondent. The *Mercury*'s other correspondent remained true to his colors. In mid-April Private Woodruff assured his readers that the Twenty-sixth was "thoroughly drilled, and if brought under fire would make our mark."

> The army are now in better spirits than they have been before since the war commenced, and great hopes are placed in Joe Hooker as a leader. He is idolized by the men. He seems to understand the responsibilities of his position, and he performs his duty in a praiseworthy manner. We are well fed, well clothed and well drilled, and in every respect qualified to cope with the rebels.
>
> The army are strongly in favor of the draft; and the idea that has been advanced by the "copperheads" that "it couldn't be carried out," is laughed at as insane. The army unite in saying that the "Union must and shall be preserved;" and after making so many sacrifices, nothing will be listened to short of the "Union as it was and the Constitution as it is."
>
> I have heard that some malicious person in Newark charged Lieut. Sears, of Co. B. with being a "copperhead." It is false accusation. Lieut. Sears is a true patriot, and he is respected and beloved by his company. There is no better officer or more loyal citizen in the regiment than Lieut. Sears. It is shameful to use such language in speaking of a man who is risking his life and sacrificing his comfort in defense of his country.[24]

No matter how patriotic, most volunteers kept a close eye on the date their term of enlistment was to expire. Many in the Twenty-sixth counted the days, wrote Chaplain Morrill.

> A prominent topic of conversation in the Regiment, is the proper time of being mustered out of service. According to Gen. Hooker's late order on the subject it will be on the 18th of June; as that will be nine months from the 18th of September, which was the date of being mustered into the U.S. service. . . . But the Regiment was mustered in by Gen. Van Vorst on the 3d of September, and commenced duty, and has been paid from that date. Moreover, according to the Adj't General's report, the nine months volunteers were accepted in lieu of drafted men, and the time fixed for the draft was the 3d of September. On the morning of that day Adj't Gen. Stockton

telegraphed to the Adj't Gen. of the U.S., that the quota of the State was in camp ready for orders. If to remain in camp and drill is serving the country they were just as truly serving the Government during those 15 days from the 3d to the 18th of Sept., as since. The blanks furnished on which furloughs are written out, which have to be approved as high up as Corps Head Quarters, read "Enlisted at Newark on the 3d of September 1862 to serve for the period of nine months." On these grounds many maintain that in honor and equity they are entitled to be mustered out on the 3d instead of the 18th of June. The disposition to re-enlist will, it is thought, be considerably affected by the decision of the Government in regard to this question. As much as disciplined troops are needed just now it is thought that it would be "the best policy" to let the soldiers return at the expiration of the term for which they enlisted. Defending rights though they are, they are not insensible to their own rights, fancied or real.[25]

The tedium of camp life weighed heavily after nearly four months in winter quarters. Intermittent spring rainstorms found most of the men huddled in their miserable tent houses. When the sun broke through the clouds, their thoughts turned to baseball, the most popular sport in the army. On April 11, explained the chaplain,

a match game of "base ball" came off upon the drill ground of the 1st N.J. Brigade, in Virginia between the players of the 2d Regt., and the 26th, the former being the challengers. It was witnessed with much interest by the most of the Brigade and a large number of the 26th. The result was in favor of the players of the 26th, although their luck was decidedly ill until the seventh inning. Munn, catcher for the 2d, accidentally injured his hand at this time, and the game immediately turned in favor of the 26th. The 2d do not consider themselves vanquished entirely and now that the fun is started, the boys will no doubt follow it up briskly, unless called upon to indulge in games of ball more serious in their consequences. The score stood 2d Regiment . . . 12, 26th . . . 20. A challenge from the 26th is expected soon, when the 2d hope to carry off the palm.[26]

Rumors of imminent movement were widespread as the weather began to clear. "During the last few days," the chaplain wrote, "former quiet has given place to change and commotion."

Our old condemned muskets have been exchanged for new Enfield rifles, and if the Regiment does not distinguish itself on the field of battle it will not be for want of suitable arms. It has already been out once on target practice; the greatest fault in firing was that which is usual among soldiers, firing too high. . . . We had orders to be ready to move on Tuesday morning. On Monday all the wall and "A" tents were taken from the officers with the exception of three for the field and staff, and tents and extra baggage were sent to Belle Plain to be shipped to Washington. All the line officers now dwell or drench in shelter tents. On Tuesday the day set for moving, there came on a severe storm of rain which has probably delayed the move some little time. . . . The plan of the campaign no one seems able to divine. Gen. Hooker keeps his counsels well.[27]

Hooker's original plan called for a general Union movement across the Rappahannock at the upstream crossings after cavalry under General George Stoneman had softened Lee's communications and supply lines. Stoneman was scheduled to cross the river in force on April 13. On the appointed day the cavalry was poised at the crossings, and one brigade was already over the river, when the rains began. As the roads turned to quagmires and the Rappahannock began to swell to flood tide, Stoneman recalled the brigade that had crossed and settled in to wait out the weather. Hooker was furious, Lincoln, disappointed, at the delay. For nearly two weeks the much-vaunted Union advance lay stalled in its tracks as the rain-darkened skies of Virginia refused to clear.

13

My God! What Will the Country Say!

Stoneman's failure to cross the Rappahannock afforded Hooker another ten days to perfect his plan of attack. Instead of striking directly at the heavily fortified heights to the rear of Fredericksburg as Burnside had done with such disastrous results in December, Hooker now proposed a classic pincer movement: Half of his army would cross the Rappahannock River above Fredericksburg, plunge south into a densely overgrown forest known locally as "The Wilderness," then emerge at the enemy's rear, a few miles east of Chancellorsville; meanwhile, the other half of the Union forces would cross the river somewhat below Fredericksburg, diverting Lee's attention from the more powerful Union sweep toward Chancellorsville. To confuse the Rebels further, General Stoneman's cavalry would raid the countryside between Richmond and Fredericksburg, cutting Lee's lines of supply and communication. If successful, Hooker would catch the Confederate army in a vise and crush it. On paper Hooker's final plan was a masterpiece of strategy. If the plan failed, however, and much depended on close coordination of separated forces, the Union army would be divided and the road to Washington open to the enemy.

The campaign began well enough. On April 27 the Eleventh Corps, led by General Oliver O. Howard, the Twelfth Corps, under General Henry Slocum, and the Fifth Corps, General George C. Meade in command, broke camp and began their march toward the fords above Fredericksburg. Crossing the Rappahannock and the Rapidan Rivers unopposed, they pushed into The Wilderness, emerging more or less unscathed near Chancellorsville on April 30. Although burdened with eight days' rations, two blankets, a woolen overcoat, and forty pounds of ammunition, the Union soldiers were optimistic that Bobby Lee might be caught at last. As they picked their way through the heavy undergrowth with no trace of the feared enemy cavalry in sight, their spirits soared. Hooker was positively ebullient. When the Fifth, Eleventh, and Twelfth Corps reached the outskirts of Chancellorsville, the general in chief issued a congratulatory order: "The operations of the last three days have determined that our enemy must either ingloriously fly, or come out from behind his defenses and give us battle on our own ground, where certain destruction awaits him."[1]

Hooker's original plan called for a nearly equal division of his forces behind and below Fredericksburg. When it became apparent that Howard, Slocum, and Meade were having an easy time of it, Hooker altered his strategy, detaching the Second Corps under General Darius Couch and the Third Corps, commanded by General Daniel E. Sickles, from the forces opposite Fredericksburg for a rapid march northeast to Ely's Ford. After crossing the river, they were to proceed south toward Chancellorsville, there to join Hooker for a hammer blow against the rebel rear. To the Sixth Corps went the task of crossing the Rappahannock below Fredericksburg. Numbering almost 24,000 men, the Sixth was the largest corps in the Army of the Potomac. Its commander, fifty-year-old Major General John Sedgwick, was a West Point graduate and veteran of the prewar Regular Army. Known as "Uncle John" to his men, Sedgwick's jovial smile and kindly disposition belied an insistence on discipline and a fondness for drill. Somewhat of a plodder, but thoroughly reliable, Sedgwick put his troops in motion on April 28. "The quiet of camp," wrote Chaplain Morrill, "has been disturbed by receipt of orders to be ready to move on the morrow."

Among the last things done was the laying out, enclosing, and beautifying of our soldier cemetery, under the directions of Col. Morrison. It was fitting that it should be done. My heart has often been saddened to see soldier graves, in various directions, without a stick, board or stone to mark the spot. It seems hardly just that those who have died in defense of their country, should have nothing to mark the spot where their bodies repose. It is otherwise with all of our members who have died, with the exception of one who died on a march. The rest are buried where their remains will not be likely to be disturbed—each one having at the head of the grave a wooden slab, on which is carved the name, age, time of death, Co. and Regiment with which he was connected.[2]

Early the next morning the sick were removed to the hospital at Potomac Creek. Assigned to the Second Division, Second Brigade, under the command of Colonel Lewis A. Grant of Vermont, the Twenty-sixth New Jersey stepped off at dawn. "We broke camp in a rain storm," reported Sergeant Major Cummings in his first letter to the *Journal*, "and for the third time in our nine months' experience turned our faces toward the Rappahannock."

The orders against straggling were very strict. The men had grown fat and indolent during their long sojourn in camp, and the march was very fatigueing [sic] to them. The rain drizzled drearily throughout the entire afternoon, the mud waxing deeper and deeper under our feet until twilight, when we encamped for the night behind the heights crowning the northern bank of the river, and within a mile of the place of our former passage of the river. The rain fell quite heavily during the night, and the boys slept on the wet ground beneath wet tents and wet blankets, but the night's rest was very refreshing for all that.

Daylight was spreading its first flush over the sky when we were ordered to cook our breakfast and march. By 8 o'clock we were formed in division line upon the bank of the river, and on the same spot that we occupied on the 11th last December. The pontoons had been thrown across in the same old place, and the First New Jersey Brigade had already crossed. There was no firing in front of us during the day, but on our left the white smoke and occasional booming of artillery, told us that Reynolds was experiencing some difficulty. From the hill a few paces in our rear the rebel lines of battle could be distinctly seen upon the opposite plateau, their skirmishers occupying the Bowling Green turnpike. . . . The opposite ridges were crowned with yellow lines of dirt, marking out an intricate maze of batteries, earthworks, riflepits, counterscarps and ditches—a naturally strong position of defense, but rendered trebly so from the time, expense, and labor that had been lavished upon it since our former passage of the river. We momentarily awaited the orders for crossing, but darkness settled upon us in a fierce rainstorm and found us still stationary upon the muddy flat. Tents were pitched, but the continued heavy fall of rain soon found mudholes within them, and many a weary Jerseyman passed a sleepless night—island of flesh and bone, enveloped in soggy blankets.

The 3,000 men of Colonel Grant's brigade camped on the east bank of the Rappahannock until May 2. According to Cummings, April 30

dawned upon us with a cloudy sky and a foggy atmosphere, the rain dissolving itself to a dewy fineness, and still chilling the boys who were wading through the mud ankle-deep in quest of fires, with coffee-cups swinging on their fingers. Their spirits, however, were not dampened by the weather. . . . The Fourth Vermont covered a log of wood and a large stone with a rubber blanket, beneath which the toes of a brace of boots were solemnly peeping, and had the whole brigade up to see if they could recognize a man "who had just been found dead near the edge of the river." As each terrified victim approached, and raised the rubber to look at the countenance of the supposed corpse, a hearty burst of laughter would announce the finale, and the sold genius would incontinently slope, revenging himself by sending some of his comrades on the same errand of mercy. This simple incident kept the brigade in high glee until the sun appeared and cleared away the morning mists. During the afternoon the rebel battery opened upon that portion of Reynolds' Corps which were across the river, and our batteries made a spirited reply, but the affair only lasted an hour. This was on the extreme left, but in front of us all was yet peaceful, although the same ominous rebel line of battle still confronted our skirmishers on the plain. The pickets as yet, however, had not fired a single shot. The balloon "Washington" occassionally arose in the air behind us like an immense soap-bubble, as if its inmate was vainly endeavoring to fathom the rebel designs; but the rebel tents still lay, like a field of daisies, in a vast nook of the rebel ridge on the left, fronting Reynolds, and at night the lurid chain of their camp-fires was only relieved by the colors and variety of their signal lights. During the morning Colonel Morrison read a dispatch from Gen. Hooker, stating that the operation of the last three days, on the right had been entirely successful, so much so that the enemy would be forced to an inglorious retreat and an evacuation of their stronghold, or otherwise accept our gauntlet of defiance, and give us battle on ground of our own choosing. Of course the boys cheered, and loudly too; yet a great many of them doubted the accuracy of the intelligence. About twilight an immense cheer rang along the lines on the other side of the river, but I was unable to determine whether it arose from our men or the rebels. It lasted some fifteen minutes, and rolled down the somber darkness of the valley in various degrees of intensity like the shout of an army of savages. During the day heavy cannonading, on the right, proclaimed that Hooker was fiercely engaged in the furtherance of his determination to press on to Richmond with the least possible delay.[3]

Chaplain Morrill admired Hooker's strategy.

Here we are the second time on the same battle field. It is a singular fact of this war, the frequency with which the same fields have been contended for. It shows the obstinacy of the contest. The attack at this point indicates that Gen. Hooker is influenced by the magic of boldness. That he hesitates not to advance upon a stronghold from which we have been once repulsed, and which has been considered impregnable. . . . The spirit of the army is very good when the fact of its former experience is remembered.[4]

Few officers had any real confidence in the fighting abilities of the nine-month regiments, or for that matter, their utility for anything military. The Twenty-sixth at least had proven its "pontooning" skills in January and, wrote the sergeant major, at pontooning it went again:

It was probably 8 o'clock P.M., when the Twenty-sixth received orders to fall in without either equipments, arms, knapsacks, or haversack. Of course, there was any amount of speculation as to our ultimate destination, some averring that we were going over the river to labor in the trenches, while others persistently denied it. We formed in line, however, and marched through the mud to the bank of the river, where we learned that we were detailed from the brigade for the purpose of taking up one of the three pontoon bridges at that point, and transferring it to Kelly's Ford, some eleven miles distant, and the scene of future important operations. A big plump-cheeked silver moon was swung out in the centre of the heavens, and beneath its luscious smiles the boys lifted and tugged, sweated and blowed, jirked and yanked, yelled and "blub-blubbed," until all the boats were out of the river and placidly reposing on the wagons; ditto as to the planks and scantiling [sic]. The good-humored, ruby-colored countenance of General [Henry W.] Benham opened with a spicy smile at the celerity of our movements, and with dilating eyes he complimented us in tones strongly savoring of Ben Franklin's grind-stone. With a squad of men at each wagon, we commenced our march towards the Ford, passing the half-ruined city of Fredericksburg whose metallic church-spires were glittering in the mellow moonlight, and casting a softened shade toward the frowning, cannon-bristling Gibralter in their rear. At first the air was soft and balmy, the roads were good, and the men joked, chatted, and hummed "When this Cruel War is Over" (new thing in the army) alternately; but when Somnus began to draw his soft pinions over their eyes and the mud and slough-holes grew deeper—the teams sinking to the hubs therein, and requiring almost any amount of human effort to release them, the boys sometimes sinking to their waists in the slimy "sacred soil"— the novelty of the expedition quickly wore off, and we began to realize in earnest that the Twenty-sixth Regiment had unwarily fallen into another pontoon scrape—one equalling if not surpassing its predecessor on the twentieth of January.

To add to the perplexities of the movement, the night was foggy, the light of the moon became obscured, and the dew fell in globules quite large. It was midnight before we crossed the railroad. The mudholes became deeper, team after team was stuck, some were overturned, some were unladen, and two mules broke from their traces and skedaddled, falling into a spring, breaking their legs, and making a desperate but futile effort to break the head of the "dark" riding them. As the night waned and the morning advanced the boys began to straggle. Some were so exhausted that they dropped in the road, in the ditches, and behind the stumps and logs at the roadside, utterly oblivious of orders, and unmindful of either General Benham or his pontoons. Others built large fires and snoozed around them in scores, sleeping so soundly that a volcanic eruption would have failed to awaken them. About half of the regiment, however, stuck to their work bravely. Some of the drivers lost their way, and your correspondent tramped at least two miles out of the way, through mud, slush and water, on account of the ignorance of his guide. At last I fell in with the last pontoon, under charge of the energetic members of Company I, and soon brought up an old log hut, within which a bright fire was blazing, surrounded by some fifty Newark firemen, "Mohawks," Irvingtonians, etc., pale as ghosts, but laughing and chatting away with French vivacity. Daylight opened upon us while fording a brook, water above our knees, and soon afterward we were relieved by a brigade belonging to the Fifth Corps. We immediately dropped in shivering files upon the wet spring grass, and slept until the sun had climbed "heaven's bosom," when we refreshed ourselves with draughts of steaming coffee—for some had brought their haversacks despite orders to the contrary—and leisurely sauntered back to our point of starting.[5]

May 1 came and went quietly, leading the Reverend Morrill to conclude that "the main battle" would be fought elsewhere.

The morning mist has disappeared and a finer May day I do not remember to have seen. All is as quiet this morning as a country Sabbath. This morning new fortifications are disclosed, showing that the enemy have been busy during the night strengthening their defences. The day closed without any fighting on the left, not a single gun was fired. We could hear heavy though distant firing on the right. The regiment returned from the pontoon duty about noon weary with the work and walk of the night. Just before sunset the division was marched out in line of battle as if to cross under cover at night. It was intended for a feint probably. After dark we marched back and laid down to pleasant or painful dreams as it might be. The rebels lighted up more fires than any night since we have been here. Whether they have been re-enforced or wanted to make us believe they had, we of course could not tell.[6]

Added the sergeant major:

Our brigade was still quiescent, and rather anxiously awaiting orders to move. During this day (Friday) the firing was very heavy in the rear of the enemy, and everybody seemed certain that Hooker had pierced the lines of the enemy, and the heights surmounting Fredericksburg would be evacuated by them during the coming night. About sundown Reynolds brought his wagon trains across the lower pontoons, when the enemy immediately opened upon them a fierce converging fire of shot and shell, and they were forced to "take out" with a rush. The poor mules jirked [sic] the "conestogas," laden with hard tack, etc., over the bridges at a dead gallop; but even after arriving on the northern bank of the river they were not safe, and the flight was continued down the river at a 2.40 rate of speed until the wagons were released from their precarious position. That night was passed by the regiment upon the hill-side overlooking the river, and we slept—we did—slept like bricks in an oven—with clear consciences, but aching bones; pontooning the cause.[7]

Brigadier-General Albion P. Howe, commanding the Second Division, ordered his men across the river on the evening of the second, wrote Cummings.

On Saturday, May 2, the sun rose clear and beautiful, and there was but little fog upon the river. During the day Reynolds' corps was transferred to the right as a reinforcement for Hooker, but the rebs seemed to be aware of the movement, and made their dispositions to meet it accordingly. During the entire day their columns were observed proceeding in a similar direction. At one time a regiment poured over a road in direct range of one of our batteries, but they scattered in a hurry, leaving eight of their number upon the road, victims to the explosion of our shells in their ranks. About 1 o'clock P.M., the pickets commenced firing in front of us, and from that time until dark the crack of rifles was unceasing. It is said that our boys commenced the firing. During the morning a rebel officer rode along the front of his pickets several times which was in direct violation of the articles of agreement between the skirmishing lines. In case of a repetition of this offense our boys had orders to fire. The same officer tried the game in the afternoon, and our skirmishers obeyed orders, wounding the officer severely. In the desultory fire ensuing our boys got the worst of it, losing a lieutenant and several enlisted men. Night came, and with it orders to march. Across the river we went at a double quick, the pontoons vibrating violently beneath the action of our forces.[8]

With only one reinforced division of 11,000 Louisiana and Mississippi veterans to guard the Fredericksburg Heights, Major General Jubal C. Early was in no position to oppose the Union advance across the river; he posted his thin line in trenches dug at the crest of the heights and behind the same stone wall in front of which the Union soldiers had come to grief the previous December.[9]

The Twenty-sixth slept fitfully that evening, wrote Cummings:

> About 1 o'clock [A.M.] we heard the heaviest artillery firing of the war. The vibrations were tremendous. It was on the right, caused by the desperate night assault of the rebels upon Sickles' corps. The old troops were absolutely startled at the terrific intensity of the roar. It lasted nearly half an hour, and closed as suddenly as it began. From this time until daylight the armies were quiet. Early in the morning the ball was reopened. The skirmishing commenced with redoubled vigor, the shells hustled through the air like winged demons, and masses of troops were seen moving in all directions. Our regiment was moved along the Fredericksburg road until our right rested on the left of the city. Company C. moved forward, and examined an old house and barn in our front, while Lieutenant Heinisch of Company A, with half a dozen men, captured a "nigger," who was making a desperate attempt to reach the enemy's lines. After that the regiment lay in front of our batteries against the banks of the road, and experiencing a severe shelling from the enemy. Several of our men were wounded by our own shells while hissing toward the rebel batteries.[10]

Genuinely surprised by Hooker's flanking movement through The Wilderness, Lee found himself with only a single division to oppose the enemy. Gambling that Sedgwick's operations at Fredericksburg were only a feint, Lee stripped Early of most of his troops, hurrying them westward to meet the main danger, which he judged would come from his flank and rear. To Hooker it was a foregone conclusion that Lee, once his flank was turned, would fall back toward Richmond. Anticipating a quick victory, he ordered a million and a half rations placed on board ships ready to be sent up the Pamunkey River—no shortage of supplies would hinder the Union advance on the Rebel capital. Lee, however, had no intentions of flight. Intelligence reported that the Union army was now divided: If he could defeat the one half at his flank and rear, the forces under Sedgwick at his front would in all likelihood retreat. Lee and his Second Corps commander, Lieutenant General Thomas "Stonewall" Jackson, agreed to concentrate all their strength along Hooker's front.

At dawn on May 1 five Union corps rested confidently at the edge of The Wilderness near Chancellorsville. Hooker, believing the enemy was in retreat, ordered an early-morning attack. As the Union forces moved out of the thick undergrowth and onto the fields of Chancellorsville, they met fierce and unexpected resistance. At this critical juncture the odds favored the Army of the Potomac. If only its commander would put all his forces into the fight, they might overwhelm through sheer numbers an enemy now steadily being reinforced. But Hooker, fearful of Lee's intentions and unsure of the enemy's true strength, lost his nerve. With an army still twice as large as Lee's, Hooker was on the verge of the victory he so carefully planned. Yet to the astonishment of his commanders and the confusion of his troops, he ordered his men back toward Chancellorsville to prepare a defensive position. "From that time the whole situation was changed," wrote Major General Alfred Pleasanton, cavalry commander at Chancellorsville. "Without striking a blow, the army was placed on the defensive. The golden moment had been lost, and it never appeared again."[11]

Still fewer in number but led by better generals, the Confederates mounted a fearsome, almost desperate attack all along Hooker's lines on May 2. Howard's Eleventh Corps broke, the entire Union army was nearly routed, and only by superhuman effort was a defensive perimeter formed and the Rebel advance halted. It was Lee's most brilliant victory. Against long odds, he had coolly divided his forces and smashed the principal Union attack. The death of General Jackson, mortally wounded by his own men in the confusion of darkness, was the only note of sadness in the midst of Confederate triumph.

It was nearly midnight before the last Rebel attack was repulsed. In the early morning hours on May 3 the Confederates renewed their assault against the weary bluecoats. Hooker, standing on the front porch of his headquarters, was stunned when a cannonball struck the pillar he was leaning against. Turning over command to General Couch, Hooker gave orders to break off the engagement and retire to a position north of Chancellorsville close by the safety of the Rappahannock. For all intents and purposes Hooker's army was out of the fight.

To the south meanwhile, Sedgwick made ready to relieve the pressure on Hooker by an assault on the Fredericksburg Heights. Although the general in chief had already been beaten, Sedgwick knew little of the true situation around Chancellorsville. Hooker's peremptory orders to attack the heights, outdated even as they reached Sedgwick, still spoke of an enemy in retreat. In some doubt as to Hooker's plan of battle even before he crossed the river, Sedgwick now delayed, hoping for more precise instructions. Finally on May 3 he moved his forces from the river toward the heights. To General John Newton's First Division he assigned the storming of Mayre's Heights, a heavily fortified position considered the key to the Rebel defenses. Three-quarters of a mile south lay Lee's Hill, the goal of the Second Division. The assault there would be a diversionary measure intended to prevent the Confederates from concentrating their forces at Mayre's Heights. General Howe formed the Second Division into two lines. In the first he placed the Thirty-third New York, the Seventh Maine, and the Twenty-first New Jersey; the second line, commanded by

Colonel Grant, consisted of the Sixth Vermont, the Twenty-sixth New Jersey, and the Second Vermont. The Twenty-sixth held the left flank of the second line.[12]

Recuperating from a wound received at Antietam, General Sedgwick had been absent from the army in December when thousands died assaulting these same heights. But Sedgwick had studied reports of the battle, concluding that Burnside's attack failed because the Union troops halted to reload and return the Rebel fire, exposing themselves to danger longer than necessary. Sedgwick's response was sensible, though it chilled the hearts of the men in the ranks. This time the bluecoats would attack with unloaded rifles and fixed bayonets, charging across the fields and up the heights on the double.

A twenty-minute artillery barrage softened the enemy lines. Newton's division was first off, encountering severe opposition, then gaining ground rapidly. Howe's forces met equally stubborn resistance, so much so that for a time it seemed their assault might fail. Sergeant Major Cummings was in the thick of the fight:

Early in the morning Colonel Morrison had made a reconnoissance [sic] of a rebel battery on our left, and asked permission of General Howe to charge it through a ravine which led to its rear, but the General pointed to the heights as more worthy game, the capture of which would have a decisive effect upon the future movements of the enemy. The General promised to give the Twenty-sixth a chance to distinguish itself at the decisive moment, and our gallant Colonel departed satisfied. The distance between the road in which we lay and the bottom of the hills on which the rebel batteries were situated was probably three-fourths of a mile, and these flats were seamed with three ditches beside the railroad cut, which was quite deep. Another deep ditch was situated at the foot of the rebel ridge, in which were concealed the enemy's rifleman. To the 2d Vermont, 26th New Jersey, and a regiment from the Light Brigade, was assigned the arduous task of storming the enemy's position. . . . To say that I was pleased to hear that the Twenty-sixth was among the honored ones selected for the fearful work in front would be a lie. I actually turned pale, and could hardly repress a shiver at the bare thought. I never could believe it possible that we could storm those heights, fortified as they were, when the veterans of many a hard-fought field had twice been repulsed from them while in their crude state. A splendid brick house lay on the side of the hill directly in our front, and behind it a battery of bright brass pieces was belching shell and solid shot toward us continually. We were ordered to charge a battery situated on a hill a little to the right of a natural indentation on the hillside running parallel to the side of the house.

At ten o'clock A.M., Sunday, May 3d, . . . the signal for the charge was given. Our batteries were already piling the positions of the enemy with shell. "Forward, Twenty-sixth!" shouted the Colonel, and over the high bank we went at a double quick. My heart was in my mouth in an instant at the very idea of a nine months regiment on such a desperate charge, and yet I had been told that new troops were better than old ones in bayonet charges.

Hardly had we debouched upon the plain before the enemy's guns had opened upon us, and the shot and shell were already screeching above our ranks. With a yell, however, the boys pressed forward in fine style, clearing the first ditch, and still preserving a good line. Already the shrieks and heart-rending groans of the wounded were heard, but the cheers overbalanced the groans. The shells howled above us with a most fearful energy, and we could hardly hear the commands of our Colonel, but could see him in front, almost standing in his saddle and bravely waving us onward with his sword. The railroad was passed, but within its protecting banks numerous "dead beats" sought a shelter from the iron hail mercilessly bursting above us. In vain Major Morris called them cowards, and applied his sword to their backs. Fear had in a measure paralyzed them, and they lay upon their bellies like over-turned statues. Among them I noticed a color corporal, lost to all sense of shame and dishonor.

Once more the word was "Forward!" and once more the regiment raised a feeble shout, and again broke forward at a double quick. Another ditch was crossed. Half the plain was behind us. The men were out of breath, and becoming exhausted. The rebels had obtained our range, and were doing fearful execution in our ranks. The men began to scatter, and drop upon the turf. The wounded shrieked pitifully, and dead men rolled upon the ground like logs of wood. The moment was an exciting one. "Forward, boys!" shouted the Colonel, and the command was repeated by the Major. The "dead beats" were pricked forward, and again the regiment pressed to the front, first by the right and then by the left flanks, confusing the range of the enemy's guns as much as possible. The incessant roar of artillery and the pitiless explosion of shells rendered it impossible for the orders to be clearly heard, and the men scattered like a mess of chickens; but still each one pressed individually toward the heights. "Your brother is shot!" shouted one of the boys to me, and at the same moment a shell exploded so near that I absolutely thought my head was off. I had no time to think. We were going at a right-oblique past an old barn and house, behind which the cowards were breathlessly ranging themselves, and among them a First Lietuenant, upon whom one of Col. Grant's aides drew a pistol and swore he would shoot him if he refused to go onward and join his men. A shell exploded beneath the Lieutenant Colonel's horse, nearly lifting him from his saddle, but his only reply was "Forward, men—act like Jerseymen!" and toward the heights the reeling human wave again surged.

Three-quarters of the distance was passed. The regiment was much scattered, despite the gallant efforts of its field officers. Shells were exploding every second above them; the rebel riflemen had opened upon us from the ditch at the foot of the hill, and a tempest of grape and cannister was rained upon us from above. It was too much. The column of brave Jerseymen reeled like a ship in a storm, and the officer of the picket line implored our Colonel to fall back ere it was too late, as the attempt to storm the batteries must prove futile. Faster and faster fell the iron tempest; and symptoms of a break became discernable. But no; the 2d Vermont had reached the ditch on our right, and were gallantly cheering us onward. Our spirits revived, and with one last yell of determined energy the men pressed forward, drove the sharpshooters from the ditch, and mounted the hill, carrying everything before them.[13]

The force of their assault carried the Union troops far beyond the Rebel works. *Journal* readers, grown accustomed to the paper's usual glowing reports of Confederate military prowess, must have been astonished by Cummings's letter:

> The rebels were flying in dismay, and throwing away everything. Any quantity of knapsacks, blankets and equipments were strewn through the woods. The heights of Fredericksburg were ours! We chased the enemy for nearly a mile. Enthusiasm got the best of me, for I discarded the sword, picked up a musket, and joined the skirmish line. Mistaking a rebel regiment for the 5th Vermont, I came very near being captured. At one time four sergeants, two corporals and three privates, besides myself, lay within thirty yards of the rebel cannon, behind some white oak stumps, and these alone saved us from the effect of their double dose of grape and cannister.[14]

Mayre's Heights were taken and Newton's command had advanced nearly half a mile before General Howe's men dislodged the enemy from Lee's Hill. General Sedgwick, standing beside General Newton when Howe made his final attack, "expressed himself highly displeased at the attempt, as the enemy was already virtually dislodged, and a short time would have brought Gen. Newton upon the enemy's rear and flank." Sedgwick "stigmatized the attack as useless, and as an unnecessary effusion of blood," added George Stevens, a surgeon attached to the Sixth Corps. "The enemy must have fled in a few moments in any event." Howe's men knew nothing of Sedgwick's annoyance, only that they had taken the heights that had daunted Burnside only six months earlier. It was a great triumph, made sweeter by the capture of two stands of colors, several batteries, some 200 prisoners, and all of the enemy's camp equippage.[15]

With Early's troops in full flight and the entire ridge in Union hands, Lee's rear was now in terrible danger. A vigorous push westward along the Turnpike Road might yet redeem the fortunes of the Union army and catch the wily Lee in a mortal trap. But it was not to be. Exhausted by the heat, fatigue, and excitement of battle, Sedgwick's men halted in the litter-strewn Rebel works for a victory celebration. For the men of the Twenty-sixth the storming of Lee's Hill had been their first taste of battle. "We were," wrote one of the soldiers, "wild with delight."

> The terrible Fredericksburg heights had been captured, and we now stood victors on those dreaded hills which we had so often gazed upon from the other side. The Twenty-sixth had fought its first battle, and had done well and courageously. We could now go home proudly, with an honorably-scarred flag. Our loss had been light in spite of the fire to which we had been exposed and we hardly gave it a thought as yet. Such were our feelings as we

marched back to the place where we had left our knapsacks. In the road we made our coffee and ate a few hard tack, which was about all the refreshments we had that day.[16]

Drinking their coffee by the side of the road, the Jerseyman talked for the first time of the fate of their colonel, who, soon after the charge up the heights began, had been ordered to the rear. A Republican with little use for the flamboyant colonel, Sergeant Dodd claimed that his commander had blundered "[f]rom the very first," leading the men "wildly in a wrong direction under the very guns of one of our own batteries."[17] The rapid pace of the assault and frequent, often contradictory commands of the colonel threw the line into "considerable disorder," added an officer.

> Colonel Morrison, riding far ahead of us on his white-footed charger, urged us forward, but Lieutenant-Colonel Martindale with better judgment, begged him, "For God's sake, Colonel, halt your regiment and dress it up"; and then himself gave the order and posted the guides. No old regiment could have been cooler. There we were, half way across the field from the hills, on one side of which a perfect storm of shell and shrapnel was sweeping, but at the command the men halted and dressed up the line, not as accurately, perhaps, as we would have done on the parade ground, but still, well.[18]

The men had not especially taken to the mustachioed lieutenant colonel when he first joined the staff in early January 1863. Where Morrison had been lax, Martindale was strict. To the discomfort of many, he was a firm disciplinarian who played no political favorites. But once Martindale assumed command on Lee's Hill, the Twenty-sixth at last found what it long needed—a true leader. Colonel Grant spoke of Martindale's crucial role in his official report of the storming of the heights: "Soon after passing the railroad, the Twenty-sixth New Jersey broke, and, in some confusion, bore to the left and in front of the Second Vermont. . . . I am happy to report that Lieutenant-Colonel Martindale, assisted by Major Morris, rallied a portion of the regiment, formed a line, and gallantly engaged the enemy."[19]

Two hours after taking the Fredericksburg Heights, Sedgwick's corps was on the march again. An urgent message had come from Hooker: "You will hurry up your column. . . . You will attack at once."[20] There was no time for further delay. The dead were buried, the wounded sent to the river crossings, regiments reformed, and by two in the afternoon the Sixth Corps was on the road toward Salem Church, an unpretentious village midway between Chancellorsville and Fredericksburg. The First Division ran into opposition almost immediately. A series of sharp skirmishes broke out as the advancing bluecoats clashed with the enemy, now slowly retreating toward Lee's main body. The Rebels, writes one officer, delayed the Sixth Corps "by frequent stands, retiring successfully from hill to hill, and opening with artillery. Ravines running at right angles to the main road and the rolling character of the country were favorable for impeding the pursuit."[21] Howe's Division was posted at the rear of the Federal column.

At nightfall on May 3 the Jerseymen camped in a gully alongside the turnpike. "We slept on our arms," said Sergeant Cummings, "and without our coffee that night." Sedgwick's capture of the Fredericksburg Heights placed Lee's entire army in jeopardy. Only two days before, Hooker had been the aggressor, Sedgwick, only a nuisance. Now Hooker was penned in along the Rappahannock while Sedgwick threatened. Less than half a day's march separated the Union forces. If Sedgwick resumed his advance along the turnpike, Lee's lines of communication would surely be cut. Worse, if the Union commander pushed forward vigorously, he might fall upon the Confederate rear and roll it up. Once again Lee gambled. Dividing his outnumbered forces, leaving a thin line to contain Hooker, he sent three full-strength brigades south toward Howe's position. General Early spent the night regrouping his scattered forces, successfully reoccupying Mayre's Heights soon after dawn on May 4. By sunrise the tables had been turned. Cut off from the Rappahannock, with strong Rebel forces at its front and rear, the Sixth Corps was trapped.[22]

The men in the ranks saw the danger, wrote Cummings:

> We were in a precarious position. The enemy was in strong force on either flank, and the countenance of General Howe betokened a fearful uncertainty. The city was again in the possession of the rebels, and the probabilities were that we were nearly if not entirely surrounded. Our line of battle was quickly changed, the enemy then lying both in our front and rear. We were then moved some distance to the left of the plank road amid a severe shelling, taking up a strong position in a dense pine woods. The boys commenced tearing up their letters for fear of an engagement, when the loving words of the ones at home might fall into the possession of the "Johnnies."[23]

After a hasty conference with his staff, General Sedgwick ordered Howe to extend his lines northerly toward Bank's Ford, six miles above Fredericksburg. Howe's rear now became his front, one end of which he anchored on the Rappahannock. The movement was accomplished rapidly despite an early morning attack by the Fifty-eighth Virginia that threatened the lines briefly.[24] Explained Sergeant Cummings:

> Hardly had we formed this new line of battle before the enemy charged upon us in two strong lines, and with fierce yells, but our batteries opened upon them such an infernal fire that they fell back, still, however, preserving their lines intact. Soon afterward our brigade fell back from the woods, and formed in an open grassy field to the rear. There we lay until sundown, listening to the roaring of artillery, the sharp musketry of our skirmishers, and occasionally dodging the shells of the enemy, which howled around us with a vengeance. General Howe rode along the line frequently, but his face still bore an anxious expression.[25]

Not until dusk was Lee able to position his troops for the main attack. By then General Howe had formed two lines, the first along a crest overlooking a ravine, the second to the rear and behind a second ravine masked by a thin skirt of forest. The Twenty-sixth was posted near a wooded area on the left of the second line, protected only by a slight swell of ground. Soon after five-o'clock the Rebel signal guns sounded along the lines. A moment later the Confederates struck Howe's right with great fury, the shock of their attack throwing the Union line into disorder. As the Rebels gained ground, they bore toward the woods at Howe's left where the Twenty-sixth waited.[26] Sergeant Cummings told of the desperate fighting near Salem Church:

About 5 P.M. the enemy opened upon us with all his artillery, the shells came more frequently and exploded about us nearly every second. It was evident that they were about to make a desperate charge upon our lines, with the hope of breaking through them, and driving us into the river. Had they succeeded, it would have insured the total destruction of the entire Sixth Army Corps. Our regiment moved by the right flank, forming on the right of the glorious 6th Vermont. We crossed a narrow ditch, and were ordered to lie down behind a small ridge, and await the approach of the foe. Hardly had this been done before the woods on our left and the ridges in our front were covered with the "butternuts," who were gallantly surging upon us like an immense wave, exciting each other with wild shouts and firing very rapidly.

Our boys opened a severe firing upon them, but it had only a slight effect upon their progress. Bullets flew through the air like hail. The smoke of the conflict enveloped both lines of battle like a thick strip of fog. The dead were rolling on the ground to our right and left, and the wounded were shrieking piteously. Our boys still held their position bravely, and the shells from a battery in our rear were bursting momentarily within the enthusiastic files of the still advancing enemy. We could hear their shouts, and see them still advancing through the smoke of the battle. Now they are within fifty feet of us, and still pressing forward, but on our left they filled the woods like hornets, and were gradually flanking us, pouring a most destructive fire upon our prostrate files. Observing this movement, Lt. Col. Martindale, who is the coolest and bravest man I ever saw, gave the order to the regiment "Left half wheel," for the purpose of presenting another firm front to the demons flanking us in the woods. In the confusion attendant upon the execution of this maneuver, the order was misconstrued, and the right of the regiment gave way, causing the centre and the left to fall back on confusion. Captains Fordham and Pierson made desperate attempts to rally the right wing, while Major Morris, Captains Rogers, McIntee, Sears and Hunkele reformed the left in the road fronting our battery, and once more the men lay down in a line with the Sixth Vermont, and poured another destructive fire into the enemy's line, which was still advancing, though with a broken front. The battery behind us was doing fearful execution, and lying within thirty feet of the mouth of its guns, I could distinctly hear its commandant giving his orders in regard to the length of his fuses. "Second and a half," "one second," "half second," "Canister—give it to them." At this moment the brigade to our right gave way, and our right followed its example. The men were dropping like leaves under the tremendous blaze of the enemy, and the whole regiment began to fall back. In vain did Captain Fordham draw his sword upon the fugitives; in vain did the Lt. Col. and Major Morris entreat them; in vain did Captain Rogers with tears in his eyes implore them to rally around the colors if it were only a dozen; in vain did the gallant McIntee shout until he was hoarse; the men had started in a panic, and for a moment nothing could stop them. "Quick, quick, pioneer, down with that fence!" shouted the Captain of the battery to Corporal Divine, and three roads were cut through the brush fence in an instant. The battery limbered up with the exception of one piece, and the cannon whirled through the openings like chariots of fire. One gun was still left upon the field, and our boys were wildly flying past it despite the maledictions of its Lieutenant, who wildly shouted "You damned cowardly villains, would you leave my gun to the enemy?" Capts. Rogers, Pierson and McIntee, together with Lieut. Thomson, Sergt. Tucker, the Sergt.-Major and several other "non-coms." and privates, seized the gun, and endeavored to roll it off, but this was impossible until the rope was unwound from its carriage. At that instant the rebs pressed forward, and one of them laid his hand upon the hot muzzle of the gun, cooly saying, "Hold on, hold on, boys, you are too late," but a blow from the butt of a musket punished him for his temerity, and the piece was rolled within the fence, where it was limbered and carried off in safety.

In the meantime, the rebel line had approached the 6th Vermont, which was lying in line on our left. They reserved their fire until the enemy were within thirty yards of them, then each one picked his man and fired. The ground was strewn with rebel corpses in an instant, nearly every one of whom were shot through the head. "Charge, boys, charge!" shouted Col. Burney, and charge they did. The rebel lines reeled and were broken in an instant. The gallant 6th swept them from the woods like chaff, and the ground was covered with one commingled mass of rebel knapsacks, haversacks, canteens, muskets and equipments, beside the dead and dying.

But to return to the 26th. The boys rallied immediately, formed behind the fence, and opened another vigorous fire upon the rebs. Corporal Drake of Co. C, ran out to the road and wildly called upon the men to follow him. Color-Sergeant Taylor, wounded at Fair Oaks, clambered the fence, waving the flag, and the boys rushed to its support in scores. The gallant Fordham, Pierson, McIntee, Linen and Thomson, again took their men to the front, and a new line of battle was formed. The cowards had been weeded out, and the men then on hand were to be depended upon. Many of our officers, however, were missing, some of whom, I am sorry to say, had ingloriously skedaddled from the field of battle, while others were wasting their energies in Vermont regiments. Sergeant Sheridan was placed in command of Co. C, Sergeant Stager bearing the colors, and the Sergeant Major of the regiment was placed in command of a division. Lieut. Col. Martindale coolly cantered along the lines, encouraging the boys, and exhorting them to stand fast. And thus in five minutes after the break a new line of battle was formed—one to be depended on—and that in advance of the former.[27]

The fight at Salem Church began badly for the Twenty-sixth. According to the official records, it was the only regiment in the brigade to run in the face of the enemy. The Vermont regiments, strengthened by elements of the Twenty-sixth New Jersey, broke the enemy's attack. "In the meantime," wrote Colonel Grant, "Lieutenant-Colonel Martindale, with great gallantry and perseverance, rallied the Twenty-sixth New Jersey, and then charged down on the right of the Sixth Vermont."

> The enemy was utterly routed. The masses (there seemed to be no distinction of the enemy's lines at this time) gave way in great confusion, and many of them were taken prisoners. The ground in front of the Second and Third Vermont, and the ravine through which the Sixth Vermont and Twenty-sixth New Jersey charged, were literally covered with the rebel dead and wounded. So far as this point was concerned, a complete victory was gained, and the opposing force was almost entirely killed, wounded, or taken prisoners. . . . The Twenty-sixth New Jersey redeemed itself. It charged gallantly down with the Sixth Vermont, and left the conflict a victorious and compact regiment. When it marched up to take its position in the new line formed in the road, it marched in good order, and its ranks were well closed.[28]

The fighting at Salem Church ended as darkness fell and a dense fog settled over the battlefield. At Howe's order Colonel Grant reformed his lines in anticipation of another attack, but none came. Severely mauled, the Confederates had no stomach for any more work that night.

All this day Hooker lay unaccountably inactive. With an army considerably larger than Lee's, Hooker could easily have broken through the thin enemy lines facing him and fallen upon the Confederate rear. Acting in concert with Sedgwick, Hooker might yet have won the battle. Instead, he did nothing. After an early-evening conference with his corps commanders, Hooker decided to abandon battle and withdraw his entire force to the other side of the Rappahannock. Elated by his success at Salem Church, Sedgwick was eager to counterattack, obeying Hooker's order to retreat only reluctantly. During the early morning hours the Sixth Corps marched to Bank's Ford, crossing the river to safety between 2:00 and 3:00 A.M. on May 5. Less than an hour after the main elements of the corps reached the river crossing, the enemy opened a heavy fire from their batteries on the heights. One pontoon bridge was shattered, the other "barely saved from destruction long enough to allow the troops hurriedly to pass over."[29] With Sedgwick safely beyond his reach across the river, General Lee shifted the bulk of his soldiers once again to Hooker's front. When on May 6 the Confederates prepared for battle they found that Hooker too had escaped to the other side of the Rappahannock.

The week-long Battle of Chancellorsville ranks as "the most brilliant victory" of Lee's career.[30] An army twice the size of his own had been soundly whipped and chased back to its former position. Confederate losses in the battle were 12,754 killed, wounded, and captured. The Army of the Potomac lost 16,792 men, fourteen pieces of artillery, and 20,000 stands of arms. But although it was one of the finest feats of Confederate arms, Chancellorsville was essentially a standoff. The Northern army had been beaten but not destroyed. The South had lost thousands of irreplaceable soldiers without gaining any strategic advantage. And Stonewall Jackson, Lee's strong right arm, would never humble the Union again.

Early reports of the engagement reaching the North were confusing at best. On May 1, while the Twenty-sixth Regiment was still safely camped on the northern bank of the river, the *Daily Journal* carried a frightening article:

> A private letter was received here this morning from the Rappahannock, containing a report that the 26th N. J. Regiment was terribly cut up in crossing the river on Wednesday morning. Although the information is not confirmed, it has created an intense excitement in the city. . . . We hope to have some definite intelligence from the Rappahannock before the JOUR-NAL goes to press. The absence of all official information keeps up the public excitement, and leads to the belief that events are progressing unfavorably in the army.[31]

The *Daily Advertiser* was more optimistic, reporting as late as May 6 that a Union victory seemed likely.

> From the confused and in some respects conflicting accounts which reach us from the main scene of battle, near Chancellorsville, it is difficult to arrive at a correct judgment as to the results of the desperate fighting of Saturday, Sunday and Monday, though they are generally considered to have been favorable to our army. On both sides the carnage was frightful; the enemy, nerved to desperation by their critical position, being hurled upon our entrenched works and vast parks of artillery, to be mowed down by thousands.[32]

In its issue of the same date the *Daily Mercury*, confessing it had "no definite intelligence," called upon all patriots to pray "that God will give us the victory."

> There can be no doubt that the carnage on both sides has been frightful: probably exceeding any battle of the war, although it is certain that the rebel loss far exceeds our own, as they seem to have dashed their columns against our death-dealing batteries with a perfectly frantic gallantry, having themselves no artillery worth mentioning, while our army is abundantly supplied.
> On the whole, the aspect of affairs, though still doubtful, is by no means discouraging. The superb generalship which General Hooker has shown, inspires every confidence in his ability, when reinforced by two fresh corps, to hold his own where he is, which is equivalent to a great victory, as it must result in the retreat of the enemy to a new line, or, if we succeed in cutting his lines of communication, in his ultimate destruction.[33]

Government officials in the national capital were the first to receive accurate reports of Hooker's failure, and Washington fairly staggered under the blow. Hurrying to Secretary of War Gideon Wells with the news, Massachusetts Senator Charles Sumner cried out, "Lost, lost, all is lost!"[34] Many panicked. rumors abounded: Hooker had been arrested; Lee was advancing on the capital; McClellan would be returned to command. For a time it appeared the war was lost, the Confederates, invincible. Lincoln took the news hardest of all. Noah Brooks, a newspaper correspondent and the president's friend, was at the White House when word of Hooker's retreat arrived. "[A]bout 3 o'clock in the afternoon the door opened and Lincoln came into the room," wrote Brooks. "He held a telegram in his hand, and as he closed the door and came toward us I mechanically noticed that his face, usually sallow, was ashen in hue. . . . He gave me the telegram, and in a voice trembling with emotion, said 'Read it— news from the army.' The despatch was from . . . Hooker's chief of staff . . . and was to the effect that the army had been withdrawn from the south side of the Rappahannock. The appearance of the President, as I read aloud these fateful words, was piteous . . . broken . . . and so ghostlike. Clasping his hands behind his back, he walked up and down the room, saying 'My God! my God! What will the country say! What will the country say!' "[35] Some months after it was all over, General Hooker would admit privately where the fault lay. "I was not hurt by a shell, and I was not drunk," he told a friend. "For once I lost confidence in Joe Hooker, and that is all there is to it."[36]

Reaction to the Chancellorsville debacle was milder than might have been expected. Though appalled that yet another mighty attack had been repulsed with heavy loss, the North was not plunged into that same despondency which had followed earlier defeats. Some saw in the nation's curious mood a reflection of indifference spawned by two years of fruitless warfare. Others suggested the presence of a new resolve among the people.

Newark newspaper reaction was predictable. The *Mercury* put the best face possible on the events at Chancellorsville, asserting that only "one of the most tremendous storms of the season" had prevented Hooker's success. "There certainly was no defeat in the matter," contended the paper. "It is the very height of injustice to say that the gallant Hooker was forced to retire, by the enemy." Having placed so much faith in the army, Foster had no choice but to excuse its defeat:

Much, therefore, as we must deplore the unfortunate events which have stayed our victorious progress, we have no reason for anything but the utmost pride in the achievements of our glorious army, and its commander; and we do that army, and that commander an injury, and injustice, when we fail to award them the liveliest gratitude and praise.

With regard to the army, no praise surely can be extravagent, for no army ever evinced more unflinching heroism, or more superb enthusiasm. The country honors its magnificent army of the Potomac, ready to-day, we believe, as ever, to meet and best the enemy. . . .

Gen. Hooker, it is not too soon to say, has proved himself the general of the war. He could not subdue the elements; but for that he cannot be blamed. Every military movement he has made has tended more clearly to prove his ability as a commander. . . . But aside from this he has this last campaign shown himself to possess a scope and comprehensiveness of military skill, combined with the rarest strategical ability, which place him among the great captains of the age.[37]

The *Mercury*'s view, so preposterously wide of the mark, reflected the administration's official position. Dispatches from Washington labeled Hooker's advance a mere "demonstration," his retreat, "no disaster" but simply "a failure, owing to the impracticality of the position which the army had gained with so much skill and energy." Fuller would have none of it: Chancellorsville, said the *Journal* bluntly, was a "disaster." The official dispatches, charged the paper, amounted to "a wanton trifling with the great people whose kindred still lie suffering and dying upon the bloody battlefields."

Every man has read and heard enough for the past week of the terrible destruction of our brave soldiers before the most resistless army of modern times. . . . It is a fresh insult to the intelligence and common sense of an afflicted and deceived people, who are sick and disgusted with the resort of the Administration to petty falsehoods and equivocation, at an hour when the gravest events which can happen to any nation are agitating millions of hearts to their profoundest depths. Have we, as a people, fallen to that state of shame and degradation, when we cannot afford to know and appreciate the naked truth of our situation? . . . If so, the situation is indeed desperate, and the government, which is obligated to resort to such tricks and the people who can only find comfort in deliberate lying, deserve to be blotted from the face of the earth or become the abject tools of the weakest and silliest tyrants whom God ever suffered to afflict a people.[38]

Blaming Hooker's defeat on the "desperate energy and overpowering force of the enemy, combined with the unfavorable elements," the *Daily Advertiser* frankly acknowledged the truth in its May 8 editorial:

Every loyal American bosom will throb with painful emotions over the sad intelligence that we have received of the retreat of the magnificent army, which a few days since crossed the Rappahannock flushed with hopes of a decisive victory over the foes of the Republic. After a week of uninterrupted fighting, in which our troops manifested the most conspicuous courage, those from this State signalizing themselves in a peculiar manner, the attempt to destroy the rebel army has failed, and our own army, weakened by successive battles, has been forced to give way before the overwhelming columns of the enemy. It has now crossed, we trust in safety, the swollen waters of the

Rappahannock and lies nearly upon its old camps—still a noble and powerful army, sufficient to repel the further advance of the rebels, but yet its heroic columns sadly depleted and defaced by the ravages of relentless war.

Much like its field correspondent, Chaplain Morrill, the *Advertiser*'s spirits had revived with the coming of spring, and the paper urged its readers to take heart:

> This is a sore and unexpected calamity; but while it cannot fail most painfully to affect our countrymen, and to promise a prolongation of the war which we had flattered ourselves was approaching its conclusion, we trust it will not unduly depress them. While a favorable issue to our arms in the dread conflicts that have just been fought would have been almost necessarily fatal to the enemy, it is not so with us. We have vast physical and other resources that are yet intact. Our country is blessed with every element of prosperity, and the blight of war has not been felt in all our borders. Let us then rise with the exigency and prove to the world that we are worthy of the precious trusts that are reposed in us. Let there be no unmanly repinings, no invidious fault-finding; but let our whole people join in a generous offer of sympathy and support to those in whose hands are placed the destinies of our nation in this hour of supreme trial.[39]

It would be several days more until Essex County learned of the losses suffered by the Twenty-sixth Regiment. In a letter dated May 7 and published on May 11, Chaplain Morrill listed the casualties.

> To-day the regiment is resting some two or three miles in the rear of the ford where they recrossed. The most of the army, with the exception of the Sixth Corps, has returned to its former position. We have received a fresh stock of ammunition and are waiting for orders. I append a revised list of the killed, wounded and missing, as known up to this time. The wounded are doing very well. Those that were wounded and taken prisoners, of course we know nothing about. The army is disappointed, but not so dispirited as when repulsed at Fredericksburg before.[40]

Total regimental losses were 5 killed, 48 wounded and 71 missing. Accurate intelligence regarding casualties was hard to come by even in Washington. Three days after the fighting ended, General John H. Martindale, military governor of the District of Columbia, having read a newspaper account that his brother, Lieutenant Colonel Martindale, had been killed in battle on May 4, sent a stiffly formal letter to General Hooker:

> I am anxious to obtain accurate intelligence, and if it be true that my brother is killed to recover his body. For that purpose I have sent down Capt. Montgomery, a member of my staff. Such action as Capt. Montgomery may desire to take to accomplish the object for which I have sent him, I hope you may find it expedient to approve.[41]

On May 9, wrote the chaplain, the Twenty-sixth New Jersey marched back
to Stafford Heights, transformed by its baptism by fire.

> Here we are again, encamped within a mile of the place from whence we
> marched forth eleven days ago. These have been exciting and eventful days.
> We have come back to rest and recuperate and prepare for something else. . . .
>   I began by saying: "here we are again." But we are not all here. Some died
> on the field amid the din of battle; others lingered a few hours in the hospital
> and then died; others were left wounded on the field to be cared for by rebel
> hands. As the regiment falls in line for dress parade, it is manifest that the line
> has been considerably shortened by the casualties of the last few days; but
> this is part and parcel of the soldier's life. The effective fighting force of the
> Regiment I supposed to be greater to-day than before. This baptism of fire
> and blood is essential to the highest development of true soldierly spirit. . . .
> There is better fellowship between this Regiment and the other Regiments of
> the Brigade than before, produced by the joint sufferings and successes of the
> last few days.

Morrill, declaring he had "not the heart nor the head to criticize this campaign," had a few words of criticism nevertheless.

> For some reason we failed to connect and co-operate at the critical moment.
> Some corps were not called into action while others were pressed beyond
> endurance. We did in this instance, as in some others, err in underrating the
> force of the enemy. I do not think that the enemy numerically outnumbered
> us, but his superior facilities for moving and massing his troops enabled him
> practically and effectively to outnumber us.

But the chaplain was not at all disheartened by events. Unconsciously (for he
could not have yet seen the *Advertiser's* May 8 editorial), Morrill echoed Kinney's call for renewed determination.

> If we had had more force, if one or two hundred thousand conscripts were
> ready now to take the field, the prospect of [a] short war would be better than
> it is. We do not rise, we are only driven by the logic of defeat to apprehend
> the magnitude of the contest, and the force that is requisite to put down this
> rebellion. The face of the country here gives the enemy an almost impregna-
> ble position, acting as he is on the defensive. The intense earnestness of the
> rebels magnifies his work. Take an illustration. When they shelled one of our
> hospitals on this side of the river as they inhumanly did, there were two or
> three rebels there exposed to the same fire and they said, "That's it, give it to
> 'em Jack" don't spare on our account." And we did not find evidences that
> "Gen. Starvation" was like to vanquish them very soon. The prisoners and
> knapsacks taken show that they are still pretty well fed and for all practical
> purposes for summer service better clothed than we are; their clothing is
> lighter and of a color that makes their position and movements less visible.

Gen. Fighting Force is the only General that I know that can conquer a peace. The sooner we understand that as a nation the shorter the war will be.

All the wounded not able to do duty have been sent away, some to Potomac Creek and others to Washington, from whence I suppose some of them will be transferred to Newark hospitals. A few of those whose names I have forwarded have returned to the regiment. . . . The men are in very good spirits, though much fatigued.[42]

Morrill forwarded a revised list of casualties a week later, including the names of men recuperating at Potomac Creek Hospital. There were twenty-seven in all, several with legs and arms amputated.

All our wounded whom we were compelled to leave behind us have been paroled and brought over, and are at Potomac Creek Hospital doing very well, with a fair prospect of recovery except in one or two instances. They say that the Rebels seemed disposed to do the best they could for them with the limited medical stores they had. A word or two in regard to the anxiety which is felt at home amid the conflicting rumors that are current in time of battle. I told my friends never to bewail me as dead until it was seen in print. For rumor is a great falsifier at all times, and especially so amid the confusion of battle and retreat. But one may be reported as dead by reliable correspondents and still not be injured in the least, as was the case with Lt. Col. Martindale. I have tried to send you the earliest and most reliable information that could be obtained, and yet some mistakes have occurred. Robert H. Boyden, whom several said they saw killed, has since been seen carried off as a prisoner. Sergt. J. M. Wheeler, Co. F, who was reported as wounded, has since died and was buried in the enemy's lines. Having had several inquiries on this point, let me say that at present, until we gain the ground again, the remains of none of those who were buried over the river can be obtained. Several who were reported as slightly wounded have since returned to the Regiment.[43]

Chaplain Morrill's gentle critique of the Chancellorsville campaign and the mention in one of his letters of the "courage and coolness" of several officers did not pass unnoticed. Another officer, possibly Captain Peter F. Rogers of Co. K. scolded the chaplain's partiality:

I see in the *Advertiser* of the 9th a letter from our chaplain, in which he mentions a number of our officers as being so brave, &c. Now, it is a fact, that a number of these same officers could not be found on the field. I think the chaplain should not mention some to the disparagement of others. Why not name all who deserve honorable mention? Lieut. Heinisch, myself, and many others, were with the boys all the time, and in front, while some, at least, of those he mentioned, "took out," in double-quick time. At one time the regiment broke, and one half of the officers mentioned by the chaplain "took out" early, while Heinisch, myself, and a few others rallied the rest of the boys, made a stand, and fought them well. The fact is, the chaplain knew but little more of what was going on than you do; he was on this side of the river during the fight. I would not allude to the matter but I think our chaplain has inadvertently or otherwise disparaged those who did their whole duty by giving them no mention, while others, more favored it may be by his friendship, have been held up to the gaze of Jerseymen as distinguished for courage and bravery who were really undeserving any mention at all.

The "gentleman of this city" to whom the letter was addressed, equally vexed by the chaplain, offered it to the *Advertiser* for publication but was refused because, said the *Mercury*, "it would reflect upon their correspondent." The *Mercury* printed it "cheerfully," merely, it said piously, for the sake of "correction."

> [T]he chaplain referred to seldom appears to us to be fair in his statements, or speculations. He seems quite disposed to croak and criticise unfavorably the policy of the Government, the conduct of the war, and everything in fact that looks to the aid of the administration, or the honor of the Government in suppressing this most iniquitous rebellion.[44]

Morrill read the officer's letter when the *Mercury* arrived in camp, but he thought it best to turn the other cheek:

> I deem it but just and right to rectify any seeming injustice that I may have thought to have done in my correspondence to any officers or men in the Regiment. It may not have been best to have mentioned any names. . . .
> I have no doubt that some whose names were not mentioned bore themselves as well and bravely as some of those whose names were mentioned. . . . It is true that I knew very little of the battles from immediate personal observation. I was on both sides of the river both Sunday and Monday, but my time and attention were mainly concerned with the wounded, dying and dead. I regret that any have inferred that through inadvertence or any other cause I would disparage any who did their whole duty. . . .
> In regard to your contemporary's remarks respecting the unfairness of your Correspondent's "criticisms and peculations," concerning the policy of the Government and the conduct of the war, I have little to say. I wish these things could always be spoken of favorably, and fairly and truthfully at the same time, but if they cannot I am not at a loss as to my duty.[45]

Morrill was no doubt unaware of the growing movement at home to obtain his dismissal.

The Army of the Potomac spent the remainder of May in its cantonments, wrote Morrill.

> "All is still quiet on the Rappahannock" save the excitement that is caused by the reported victories of Gen. Grant and his armies in the West. These reports are taken with some allowance, the army has so frequently had re-

ports of victories that were never realized. During the late battles, when the encouraging and somewhat boastful order of Gen. Hooker was read, our Regiment cheered most enthusiastically, while the Vermont veterans uttered hardly a cheer. When asked for the reasons, they replied that they had been sold in that way too often during the war by almost every General in Command.

There is some drilling now, but the main effort is directed to the comfort and health of the army. This is absolutely essential if this position is to be held, for nothing but the very best sanitary measures, with the blessing of God, will save this region from being visited with pestilence. Offal, carrion and excrement have rendered the air in many places almost intolerably offensive to olfactories that are not very acute.

Most of those who were reported missing have reached Camp Parole at Annapolis, Md. They say that they had a rough time in going to Richmond. I regret that I am not able to give a complete list of their names. One of the wounded, Henry H. Hoffman, of Co. F, has since died of secondary hemmorage at the hospital. His body was embalmed and sent on home.[46]

Colonel Morrison meantime remained under arrest, impatient for the results of his court martial. Rumors of the colonel's disgrace reached Newark at midmonth: some said he was drunk on the field of battle, others claimed he had pressed higher authorities too hard regarding the date of the regiment's discharge. Home in Bloomfield on a brief leave, First Lieutenant Henry C. Terhune decided to set the record straight in a letter to the *Daily Journal*.

My attention has been called to an article in your issue of the 12th inst., stating that Col. Morrison, of the 26th N.J. Vols, was under arrest by order of Gen. Hooker and intimating the cause of the arrest to be his (Morrison's) "determined attitude" upon the point in relation to the date of the expiration of the term of service of the regiment. Being conversant with the facts, let me correct your statement. There is a question as to the expiration of the term of service of our regiment, but I presume military law is understood by all well informed officers sufficiently to deter them from assuming an attitude upon any such point of dispute.

The facts are these. Col. Morrison was put on arrest by Col. Grant, the commandant of our Brigade, for drunkenness on the field of battle. It was done upon representations made by myself at the request of the line officers. Colonel Morrison was, to my knowledge, drunk on the 3d and 4th of May, while the regiment was engaged in battle; likewise at the battle of Fredericksburg, in December last. Upon such representations being made to Colonel Grant, he informed me that he was aware of Morrison's inebriety, and immediately placed him in arrest. Charges have been preferred and the proof is abundant. Your information, doubtless, came through sources interested— the object being to create sympathy. Other reports of like character are being circulated for the same purpose, and thus for truth's sake I feel called upon to make known the fact. It is but right that the public should know the officer who, for rum's sake, seeks to sacrifice so many lives. There has been and is too much of this in the army. How long shall it continue?

Let me add that it seems but just that the regiment should be discharged on the 3d of June next, as by that time it will have been in service nine months.

But the Secretary of War has decided that the term of service shall commence on the day of the mustering in of the last company. In this case the companies were mustered in the United States service simultaneously, the date being Sept. 18, 1862. The men were in camp, however, and mustered in the State service on the third day of Sept. This is a matter of great interest to the men, and in case of a battle during the interim, might be one of serious moment to the government. I trust, for the sake of all concerned, it will be equitably adjusted.[47]

Colonel Morrison's friends in the regiment jumped to his defense. A dozen wounded enlisted men of the Twenty-sixth recuperating at Mount Pleasant Hospital in Washington penned a joint reply to Terhune's letter, their spokesman none other than Corporal Charles W. Cummings, the sergeant major's brother:

We feel it not only a duty we owe to Colonel Morrison, but to the public, to disavow the charges made against him, and to denounce them as utterly false; and we believe they were got up for the purpose of giving a few other officers a chance to satisfy their own military aspirations. We were in the fight, and certainly had a better chance to observe whether Colonel Morrison was drunk than Lieutenant T., who skulked out of the battle. "Honor to whom honor is due!" is our motto. On the morning we charged up the heights of Fredericksburg, Lieutenant T., up to half an hour previous, had been riding a horse belonging to the Chaplain. It was a general remark in the regiment, that, notwithstanding appearances indicated different, he (T) would not go into battle when the time comes; but would suddenly be taken with a feigned sickness of some sort, which would be a pass for his remaining behind. As far as the remaining behind was concerned, the boys were right in their supposition, but [it] was upon the plea that he had no horse to ride (which was there at his service); so he got the consent of the Colonel to remain behind and guard the knapsacks! (Mark you! each company left men to guard their knapsacks.)

Now, should this man's evidence be entitled to weight? We leave it with the public to judge. We hate a coward! and honor and will always cheer bravery; but, since we have been in the army, we have never seen Terhune show the least spark of the latter. Col. Morrison has always exerted himself in behalf of his regiment; and the hearts of the Twenty-sixth will always beat for him. The boys, while charging on Sunday, filled the sky with cheers to see his noble form flit through the smoke far ahead of his regiment, while the shot and shell were dropping around him like hail, and to see his hat swinging to the breeze, waving us on to victory! Even the Vermonters are proud of him, and all unite in saying they never saw a braver man in battle. We had an opportunity of hearing him converse, and part of us conversed with him a few moments before the charge; and, to our certain knowledge, he was not drunk.

The fact is, a good many were astonished to see him so brave; and we presume Terhune came to the conclusion that a man could not act as brave as Morrison without being drunk. T. must bear in mind that men can be brave as well as cowardly. That Lieut. T. was lingering around the hospital on Monday during the battle, we can testify.

Now, then, we have never had any personal disfavor to Terhune; but when we see an article in the *Journal* preferring false charges against Col. Morrison, from the pen of a man who was not in the fight, we claim the privilege, as wounded soldiers of the 26th N.J. Regiment, to say a word or two in defense of our noble Col. Morrison.

There are a great many who have left the hospital within a few days, who would cheerfully subscribe to the above, had they the privilege. All belonging to the 26th who remain in this hospital have approved of the above. Were we able to walk around, we could procure many more who are scattered in the different hospitals in this city. The wounded are all doing very well, and we hope to be able to go home with the regiment when it passes through this city, with Col. Morrison at its head.[48]

Sergeant Major Cummings's own furious response to Terhune's letter must have gladdened the heart of every *Journal* reader:

This communication is signed by "H.C. Terhune, Acting Adjutant 26th N.J.V.," who is sailing under false colors, in wearing staff straps and buttons, when nothing but a simple Lieutenant of Company E. At the time expressed in the date of that letter Lieutenant Albert Allen, of Company I, was the Acting Adjutant of this regiment, and not "H.C. Terhune," who is now reported "absent without leave," an offense for which a private would be severely punished. Lieut. Terhune may be under the impression that no one is capable of filling the Adjutant's position but himself—from my acquaintance with him I have no doubt but what he really does labor under that impression—yet that does not alter the "Morning Report Book" of the regiment.

He says that Colonel Morrison was put under arrest "upon representations made by myself at the request of the line officers." You can judge of the truth of this statement when you are informed that over two-thirds of the line officers of the regiment have drafted, signed, and forwarded a petition to Colonel Grant, asking that Col. Morrison should be immediately restored to his command, which is tantamount to expressing their disbelief in the charges preferred against him.

But this misstatement was not sufficient for this bogus "Acting Adjutant," and he follows it with one, if possible, still more enormous. He says: "Colonel Morrison was, to my own knowledge . . . drunk on the 3d and 4th of May, while the regiment was engaged in battle," thus adroitly creating the impression among those personally unacquainted with him that he participated in those engagements. Even had this statement been true, would it become a soldier and a gentlemen to basely endeavor to forestall public opinion in reference to an officer under arrest on such a charge, whose position precluded a reply, and who was making energetic but futile attempts to have his case brought to a trial with the least possible delay? But, sir, what will your readers think when they learn that this same "Acting Bombastos Furioso," on the plea that he had no horse to ride, (something he never has had since he joined the regiment—Major Morris was on foot,) besought Colonel Morrison to leave him in the road in charge of the knapsack guard, while our brave boys followed their idolized Colonel, who volunteered to lead the desperate charge on the steep heights to the left of the Fredericksburg plank road? It was afterward ascertained that the chaplain's horse was at his service, a fact which was entirely overlooked by the "Acting Adjutant" while making his skin-saving request of Colonel Morrison. Let these facts be remembered—that while Colonel Morrison was bravely leading his troops into action the com-missionless "Adjutant" who caused his arrest for drunkenness on the field of battle from a personal knowledge thereof, was snugly ensconced in the road-side near the bank of the Rappahannock, making a desperate effort to pre-serve his precious carcase from the perforations of the rebel bullets, under the plausible pretence of guarding knapsacks unslung by men whom he should have led on to the charge! But perhaps the most remarkable thing of all was his eyesight. Although a full mile from the battle-field, he plainly discovered Colonel Morrison's inebriety, something entirely unperceived by the officers and men who were actually in the engagement. . . .

During the morning of the 4th Col. Morrison led his troops through a severe shelling to a place of comparative safety. It was 12 M. before he was placed under arrest—the rebels charging our lines about 5 P.M., at which time the battle of the 4th began, the Lieut. Colonel in command of the regiment. Now where was "Acting Adjutant" Terhune at that time? Was he in the fight, and doing his duty? If so, how did he notice the condition of Colonel Morrison, who did not participate in that battle, although nervously pacing to and from within close ear-shot of the fight . . . ? If "Acting Adjutant" Terhune was not in the fight, how is it that Lt. Colonel Martindale praises him for his gallantry? Which horn of this dilemma will he take? For what specific act of bravery did he receive the tribute of an official mention from the officer in command? Was it because the red flag of the Division field hospital had a peculiar attraction for him, or was it on account of his pedes-trian achievements after the regiment rallied and made their final advance upon the wavering rebel lines? Did any enlisted man see "Acting Adjutant" Terhune with the regiment after it fell back and rallied? If so, let the "Acting Adjutant" show that man up, and for every man saying he saw him, I will produce a dozen who will swear before a magistrate that he was greatly demoralized (not D. Morrill-ized, as the *Advertiser* on a recent date certainly shows,) and making most extraordinary speed in the direction of the river. And is it this spiritless Iago in military swaddling-clothes who asserts from personal knowledge that Colonel Morrison was intoxicated during the action of May 4? Heaven save the mark!

Once more this valiant "Acting Adjutant" remarks: "Charges have been preferred, and the proof is abundant." For God's sake, is he a witness? Is this "proof" of a nature corresponding with his letter?

Colonel Morrison is too well known in this army and in Newark to have his reputation tarnished except by the strongest kind of evidence—the evidence of brave men who were with him on the field of battle, and not the evidence of envious and cowardly officers whose shame is the subject of open remark among the privates of the regiment. I do not believe that a single line officer in this regiment will swear that Colonel Morrison was drunk on the 3d and 4th inst.

It seems that the "Acting Adjutant" was afraid of an expression of sympathy at home in favor of Colonel Morrison. Why was this? Was it because the truth in the matter was leaking out through the letters of the men to their friends? Was it to tinge the facts in the case with the essence of falsehood under the garb of truth that "Acting Adjutant" Terhune procured a pass, on the plea of "official business connected with the War and Adjutant General's Department," to visit Newark, (!) or was it for the purpose of poisoning the public against Col. Morrison, squelching him by hook or crook, guilty or not guilty, and raising himself from a brave man's military ruin—losing his honor for the sake of placing a paltry brass leaf on his shoulder? It is but right that the public should know the officer who, for personal motives, seeks the sacrifice of a brave soldier's reputation. This same officer refused to furnish the official report of Col. Morrison on Sunday's fight for publication with that of the Lieut. Col., and this same officer has been tainted with sickness whenever there were prospects of an engagement with the enemy.

Colonel Morrison possesses the heart of this regiment, and their sympathies are with him in his affliction. The non-commissioned officers recently surrounded his tent with a beautiful bower of pines, as a tribute of their respect and sympathy with him. I have also several letters now in my possession from our wounded boys in Washington, and they all speak very bitterly of what they term the conspiracy against Col. Morrison. His friends are content to wait, confident that time will expose the proceedings of this moral military leper, and Col. Morrison will arise from the cloud of calumny now enshrouding him like a phoenix from the ashes—all the brighter for the trials through which he has passed.[49]

Colonel Morrison was never vindicated, if indeed he was innocent of the charges brought against him. On June 11 he was sentenced by general court martial to be cashiered for drunkenness on duty and dismissed from the service of the United States. Whether Morrison was actually drunk or had simply "fortified" his courage as did so many soldiers or was as sober as the chaplain was of little account to Cummings or his brother or, for that matter, to Terhune or the *Daily Journal*. Ever since that day of the grand review, the regiment had become increasingly politicized. Without question, the dissident resolutions had angered the unit's Republicans, and doubtless an effort had been made to suppress them. The men who broke and ran at Chancellorsville were suspect and, in the eyes of some, disloyal. Morrill's "croaking and criticizing" annoyed a good many of his charges. When Colonel Morrison, a Democrat, was unceremoniously relieved of command and replaced by Lieutenant Colonel Martindale, the Republican brother of a well-known Republican politician, many in the regiment (and at home) saw the evil hand of partisanship at work. Morrison had unwittingly become a symbol of the contest for New Jersey's allegiance.

14

Row, Damn You, or
I'll Cut Your Head Off!

Lee's superb victory at Chancellorsville was in sharp contrast to the gloomy Southern military picture elsewhere. In Tennessee the Army of the Cumberland under General William S. Rosecrans threatened Chattanooga, gateway to all Georgia and Alabama. Vicksburg, the last remaining bastion of the Confederacy on the Mississippi, was under siege by 54,000 Union troops commanded by General U. S. Grant. If Rosecrans took Chattanooga, the Southern heartland would be in jeopardy. Should Vicksburg fall, and there was precious little hope that it would not, the western Confederate states of Louisiana, Arkansas, and Texas would be lost. Meanwhile, the Union naval blockade of the Southern coastline grew ever tighter. Only two major ports, Mobile and Charleston, remained in Rebel hands, and both of these were closely patrolled by Union warships.

The end of May found President Jefferson Davis, his cabinet and generals sharply divided. General Pierre Beauregard spoke of sending Lee and a portion of his army to Tennessee, there to crush Rosecrans and frighten Grant from Vicksburg. General James Longstreet lobbied for a similar but less ambitious plan for the relief of the beleaguered city. Postmaster General James Reagan pleaded for a direct assault on Grant, whom he considered the Confederacy's main threat. Lee disagreed. His own Army of Northern Virginia must be strengthened, he said, so that it might advance against Hooker. Were his army to cross the Potomac and invade the North, argued Lee, the Lincoln administration would have little choice but to rush reinforcements from Vicksburg and Tennessee, relieving pressure at both places to insure the safety of Baltimore and Washington. Davis and his cabinet adopted Lee's proposal after two days of intensive discussion.[1]

Between June 3 and 5 the whole of Lee's army, excepting three divisions under General A. P. Hill, started north from Fredericksburg toward Maryland. Lee hoped to withdraw from Fredericksburg in secrecy. Hooker's reconnaissance balloons were up, however, and the activity in the enemy's camp was detected. "The indications for a day or two had been that the enemy were moving," wrote the war correspondent of the New York *Times*, "but the smoky, dusty state of the atmosphere, and the absence of any offensive demonstrations against any portion of our lines, left the direction of their march in much doubt. On Thursday a number of camps heretofore in sight suddenly disappeared, and Thursday night the line of pickets along the river was doubled."[2]

On June 5 Sedgwick received orders to make a reconnaissance in force across the Rappahannock at Franklin's Crossing to probe the enemy lines. The Twenty-sixth New Jersey and Fifth Vermont, supported by the Fifteenth and Fiftieth New York Engineers, drew the assignment. The order to move, according to one of the soldiers, caught the Jerseymen by surprise.

Our term of service was all but ended. The men who had been detailed as clerks at headquarters, teamsters, ambulance drivers, etc., had been sent back to their companies in anticipation of our speedy mustering out; everything seemed quiet along the Rappahannock; we reckoned our battles all fought and dared at last to believe that home-going for those who were left of us was actually a possibility. "Home again!"—it was all we talked of by day, it coloured our dreams by night as we slept in our pleasant camp under the summer moon.

When . . . the command came to strike tents and prepare to move, a thrill of expectation went with it through the regiment. But our vision of home quickly melted as we saw the stir of preparation spreading like an advancing wave into all the regiments about us, and its last pathetic remnants were rudely blotted out by the distribution of the ominous twenty extra rounds of cartridge. . . .

Late in the afternoon a short march brought our division to the hills above the fateful river; for the third time we beheld sleepy old Fredericksburg away at our right, and directly before us the familiar amphitheatre of fields shut in by distant hills. It seemed incredible that twice within six months trampling armies had here been locked in the bloody embrace of mighty battle; no more peaceful sight could be imagined than those gently rolling, grassy plains with their crown of wooded, leafy upland all bathed in the slanting rays of sweet June afternoon sunshine.

A single suspicious blot marred the landscape. Opposite where we stood, at the farther side of the river guarding our old crossing place, the yellow mound of a freshly dug earthwork loomed up; yet for all we could see it might have been a great grave, so silent, so apparently lifeless was it.

But there was no lingering for the view. Down the hill we went, out over the level ground beneath, and from every side we could see the dark lines pouring over the slopes until, with swift and silent precision the division was formed in battle array. In a few moments as if by magic the northern side of the river valley had become alive with the presence of a sternly-marshalled host. . . .

The feeling in our ranks was picturesquely expressed by a stuttering little fellow in our company when, as we halted for a few moments on the hills above and watched the silent river and apparently-deserted plain and hills, some one ventured the rash opinion that the enemy had decamped. The stammerer quickly replied:

"You j-just g-g-go ov-ver and s-stir up the hive, and the b-b-bees will c-come out f-fast enough!"[3]

General Howe planned to hurry his infantry across the river as soon as the New York engineers had assembled the pontoon bridge. But when the engineers set to work, it quickly became apparent that the Rebels had not abandoned the opposite bank, as expected.

Just as we got everything ready and had commenced pushing our boats into the river, the rebels came out of the woods, on a run and started for their rifle pits, directly in front of us, on the opposite bank of the river.

Between the river and the woods where they came from was a large open plain of nearly a hundred acres, which they were obliged to cross before reaching their pits. They had reached a point about half way between the woods and pits, and were coming on in double quick, when our batteries opened upon them. Our entire line of artillery opened at once. For a moment I held my breath expecting to see every man of them fall, as our cannon ball and grape went sweeping through their ranks. But only a few were killed, though most of them dropped to the ground, so sudden and unexpected was the shock. They were quickly rallied by their officers, and again started on a dead run, nor did they stop again until they reached the pits, except those who ran against a cannon ball on their way. For two hours our artillery shelled them while they were pouring their bullets down upon our boys with fearful profusion. At length it became evident that we could not drive them from the rifle-pits with our artillery, and the old method of pushing men across the river in boats was resorted to.[4]

With less than three weeks left of their enlistment, the men of the Twenty-sixth now unexpectedly found themselves obliged to make a river crossing in the face of enemy rifle fire, a task even experienced troops dreaded. Wrote Sergeant Dodd:

Our attention had been riveted upon the scene before us and we failed to notice that our colonel had been called away by a message from the commander of the brigade, but as he galloped back one look onto his grave determined face was enough. We knew what was coming before the sharp command rang out. "Attention, battalion! Forward, double quick, march!" . . . Before we could fairly ask ourselves what it all meant, we were swiftly moving toward the river by the road over which the pontoons had passed. We had travelled that road before, we knew it well. At the edge of the plateau it turns sharply and descends by a dug way in the steep bank parallel with the stream to a small piece of open level ground close by the water; and when we reached the turn of the road where we could look down, a glance showed what the din of the cannonade had concealed. The earthwork was but part of the defence of the crossing. Below the line of our battery fire, out of reach of its shells, was a row of rifle-pits manned by sharpshooters who were doing deadly work. A few of the pontoon boats were on the ground close to the water, but none of them were launched; the train was in disorder, the engineers were being shot down at every attempt to handle their boats and our task was clearly before us. With another regiment from the brigade which was coming down by a different route through a little ravine, we must force the passage of the river. . . .

When we reached the boat-landing the ground was absolutely bare; there was not a bush, or tree, or rock; the only possible shelter from the leaden hail was a spring, a mere mud hole, perhaps three feet in diameter. By lying down and curling himself up in the mud and water a man might fit into it. If the desirability of land is the measure of its value, then that mud hole was priceless, for it was occupied every minute and each occupant was envied by other would-be tenants. As I came down the hill I saw one of the fellows who had just been routed out. A bullet had pierced his arm as he arose from his muddy bed, and he was dancing with pain, clasping his wounded arm with his unhurt hand and muttering angry curses upon the officer who had disturbed his repose.

Crowded along the naked riverbank, the Jerseymen were easy targets for enemy sharpshooters a hundred yards away. Three or four boats were hastily shoved into the water.

There was a moment of desperate confusion; no one responded to the frantic but unfamiliar orders of officers to "Get into those boats!" when out of the crowd one man sprang forth, leaped to the gunwale of one of the boats and waving his gun high in the air cried, "Come on, boys!" . . . Instantly the boat was filled, pushed off from the bank, and the engineers with their big oars began to row out into the stream. Another boat quickly followed, and soon a flotilla of seven of these great scows, deeply laden, bristling with bayonets, was making such speed as is possible for such awkward craft toward the opposite shore.

When we were half way across the stream a bullet struck the oar of one of our rowers, close to his hand with sharp ping and shock. For an instant the man seemed paralysed; he stopped rowing and our boat's head swung around, threatening collision with the craft beside us. In that other boat was a red-haired captain, a fiery little Irish gamecock. Quick as thought he grasped the situation, and leaning far over the gunwale with uplifted sword, he hissed at the frightened oarsman: "Row, damn you, or I'll cut your head off!"[5]

Captain Samuel U. Dodd commanded the lead boat. As officer of the day, he wore "a large red sash, which he did not discard when ordered to cross the river."[6]

When we went down to the river that day, Captain Dodd's company led the line and filled the first boat. The enemy's fire was at its hottest when they were shoved off. Caring always for others more than for himself, he commanded his men to lie down and shelter themselves, but his perilous duty was to direct the rowers and guide the course of the fleet. He stood up to do it better. The risk was fatal; his commanding figure became the mark for many rifles, and he fell before we were half way across.

The enemy's bullets pattered "like hail upon the water."

A few struck the boats or the men in them, but the fire slackened as we neared the bank. Our opposers were too few to resist us when once we landed, and they began to scatter. Some ran from the rifle-pits toward the earthwork, others disappeared through the bushes. Before the shore was fairly reached our men sprang out into the water and waded to the land, the boats were emptied quicker than they had been filled; no one paused to fire; there was a pell-mell rush of bayonet charge up the river bank straight at the earthwork.

It was, wrote Sergeant Dodd, "all quickly over."

The cannonade, which ceased only when our charge began, had half buried and almost wholly paralysed the defenders of the little fort, only a few feeble shots met us and we took nearly eighty prisoners—all who were left alive when we entered.

There were some ghastly sights inside that yellow mound. A Confederate officer, torn by one of our shells, lay dying; the captain of our company sprang to his side, raised him tenderly, gave him a drink from his canteen and tried to soothe his passing moments. But it was surprising how few of the defenders had been killed. The worst complaint of those brave men was that they thought our batteries meant to bury them alive![7]

The Twenty-sixth lost two men killed and seventeen wounded at Franklin's Crossing, nearly one casualty for each minute they were engaged. In a brief letter that appeared in the *Advertiser* four days after the crossing, Chaplain Morrill congratulated the men. "Their conduct," he wrote, "is everywhere spoken of in high terms. When it is remembered that their time (in equity) though not in law—had expired, it is still more creditable." At the command to cross, added Morrill, the soldiers "jumped into the boats with as much eagerness as men would start for a race."[8] The *Advertiser* itself lavished the regiment with praise, calling the charge "brilliant" and "deserving of the highest praise," fully sustaining "the high reputation [the regiment] had gained in the terrible fight" at Chancellorsville.[9] The *Mercury* too praised the "gallant conduct" of the Twenty-sixth, but, without a correspondent in the field after Woodruff took a Rebel minié ball on May 4, it had to rely on a letter from a member of the New York Engineers. Although the men of the Fiftieth New York and Twenty-sixth New Jersey were "within a few days of the expiration of their terms of service," wrote the New Yorker, "neither [regiment] faltered in the least in going forward. . . , and they deserve and should receive honor from all men."[10] Even the *Journal*, ever careful while condemning the war not to disparage the conduct of local soldiers, hailed the "brilliant charge of the Twenty-Sixth Regiment." In a hastily written note, Sergeant Major Cummings said the "regiment acted splendidly," charging "gallantly" across the river.[11]

Soon after the rifle pits were secured and skirmishers deployed, the Twenty-sixth New Jersey and Fifth Vermont advanced in the direction of the Bowling Green Road. Another sixty or seventy prisoners, chiefly of the Second Florida, were captured. On June 6 the Jerseymen camped on the plain, "wondering what was to be done."

There were the frowning batteries of the enemy on the hills in front, apparently able to blow the whole division into the air, and we could, with our glasses, discover great numbers of infantry at the base of the hills, half hidden by the low growth of pines. The main body of our army still remained in camp; only our Sixth corps had moved. Evidently the enemy concluded that the advance was rather one of observation than attack, and quietly awaited our movements. Some firing was for a time kept up on the skirmish line, and now and then a shell would come crashing through some of the houses at the right, where our pickets were concealed; but at length, by mutual consent, the pickets of each army watched the movements of their opponents without molesting them. During this quasi-truce, a spirit of sociability manifested itself, and our boys soon struck up an acquaintance with their dangerous neighbors. At length an exchange of papers was proposed, and upon mutual agreement of temporary amity, a Yankee and a Johnnie would step into the open space between the two lines, shake hands, inquire [of] each other's regiment, trade papers and retire.

Copies of hometown newspapers and religious tracts were among the items exchanged.

The trade was not kept wholly within the limits of literary exchange, but sugar and coffee passed into the rebels' hands in return for plugs of tobacco. At length an order came from division head-quarters, stopping this illicit practice. Our boys declared that they were acting the part of colporteurs to the barbarian rebels, and, if they had been allowed to continue the distribution of religious papers among them, they would soon be convinced of the error of their ways, and desist from further fighting.[12]

After sundown on June 7, Howe's division was relieved by other elements of the Sixth Corps and withdrawn to their bivouacs on the north side of the river. "It was a welcome relief to recross and be where we were beyond the easy reach of shot and shell," wrote the chaplain.[13] Information from the captured Rebels as well as the stiff opposition that greeted the river crossing convinced Hooker that the bulk of Lee's army still lay in the vicinity of Fredericksburg. Not until several days later did it become apparent that a major Confederate movement was under way, probably in the direction of the Shenandoah Valley. On June 13, prompted by instructions from Lincoln to keep his army between the Confederates and Washington, Hooker began shifting his troops to the right, up the Rappahannock in a line parallel with Lee's force.

The Twenty-sixth New Jersey's role in what one war correspondent called "the boldest reconnaissance of the war"[14] was marked by both heroism and cowardice, a fact Chaplain Morrill and the sergeant major failed to mention. The order to cross the river, coming nine months and two days after the Twenty-sixth had been sworn into service at Camp Frelinghuysen, was received by the regiment "with a great deal of grumbling and even some talk of 'stacking arms.' "[15] At least thirty-nine men, possibly more, "fell behind, not through cowardice or inability to keep up, but deliberately, because they thought that there was no obligation on them to fight after the 3d of June."[16] On June 15 the Sixth Corps camped for the night at Dumfries, Virginia. "Here the Vermont brigade was drawn up in line," wrote a physician assigned to the corps, "and some twenty-six men, skulkers, principally from the 26th N.J., were drummed out of camp, the bands of the brigade playing 'The Rogues March.' "[17]

Lee's invasion of Maryland threw the North into a mighty panic. News of his advance north through the Shenandoah Valley overshadowed all else in the daily press. His destination, whether Harrisburg, Philadelphia, Baltimore, Washington, or all of these, was unknown. It made little difference: the prowess of his army, proven but recently on the Chancellorsville battlefield, was cause for the deepest anxiety. On June 15 Lincoln issued an urgent call for 100,000 six-month militia to put down "the armed insurrectionary combinations . . . threatening to make inroads" into the North.[18] The governor of Pennsylvania and the mayor of Philadelphia appealed for immediate aid. Fear spread over the lush spring countryside of Pennsylvania while in Washington and Baltimore there were rumors of barricades in the streets.

As the days passed with no word from the Army of the Potomac, it seemed that the defense of the Union must be entrusted to the state militia, some 50,000 of them, now pouring into Pennsylvania from New England, New York, New Jersey, and Ohio. In mid-June the enlistments of the nine-month regiments raised in the summer of 1862 expired. Despite the emergency, fifty-eight regiments numbering 25,000 men took their discharges from the Army of the Potomac. On June 17 Governor Joel Parker appealed to those New Jersey regiments not yet disbanded to come to the aid of Pennsylvania:

> Soldiers! The Governor of Pennsylvania has requested your services to assist in repelling an invasion of that State. Your term of service has expired. You have performed your duty, and your gallant conduct has reflected honor on yourselves and the State that sent you forth.
> It will take time to organize and send other troops to the aid of Pennsylva-

nia. You are already organized and drilled. The hard service you have seen in Virginia has made you veterans—far more efficient than new troops can possibly be.

I regret any necessity that may detain you from your homes, but can this appeal from a sister State, in her hour of danger, be disregarded?

Your State and United States pay will be continued. You will not be required to go out of the State of Pennsylvania, and will return as soon as the emergency will admit. Your response to this appeal will add to the fame you have already achieved.[19]

The governor's proclamation was virtually ignored. Of the eleven nine-month units from New Jersey, all but two reached the safety of home before the Battle of Gettysburg began. The Twenty-sixth New Jersey, enroute from Washington to Philadelphia when Parker issued his appeal, continued its journey.

Consternation swept New Jersey as Lee's vaunted army marched northward. From mid-June the overshadowing news in the press, and the only important subject of conversation, was the Confederate invasion. Not until July 5, when word of Lee's defeat at Gettysburg reached the state during morning church services, was the tension broken. Up to that moment, every patriot held his breath, expecting the worst, praying that the Rebel host—said to number more than 100,000 men and 250 cannon—could be stopped. On June 15, the same day Lincoln called for volunteers to meet the new emergency, the advance guard of the Confederate army crossed the Potomac. Each day that followed brought further news of Lee's seemingly inexorable progress. The city's emotions were running high when the Twenty-sixth Regiment returned to Newark on June 19. Under any circumstances the unit's arrival would have been a cause for celebration; the Rebel invasion transformed the city's welcome into an extravaganza of patriotism the like of which Newark would not see again until war's end. It was a hero's welcome, as much for the regiment (which had performed less than heroically) as for the cause the faded and dusty uniforms represented. Newark's three major newspapers covered the story in detail, the *Advertiser* alone lavishing a column and a half on the "Grand Ovation." It was an "imposing and enthusiastic welcome," said the paper, one calculated to "inspire the populace with renewed sentiments of patriotic devotion to the country which these fatigued and war-worn veterans have just served so well." The *Mercury*, fairly bursting with pride, claimed that it was a day "long to be remembered in the history of our city, one which in anxiety and excitement has been surpassed by few days since the breaking out of the rebellion." So intense were emotions that the *Daily Journal*'s story—but for one conspicuous omission—could easily have appeared in the pages of its rivals. The arrival of "these noble sons of New Jersey," said the *Journal*, "called forth the most exciting and enthusiastic demonstration that has ever been witnessed in this city."[20]

The *Daily Advertiser* carried the fullest account of the day's events:

The weather, which had been damp and lowering throughout the day, cleared off beautifully as the afternoon advanced, and the glorious sun dispelled the dismal clouds and shed his genial smiles over all as the train of cars, with its precious freight, came thundering along from the South into the immense crowd of expectant people, who swarmed about the southern borders of our city.

During the whole afternoon indeed, the streets were enlivened by the arrival of carriages from the surrounding towns, innumerable flags were streaming in the fitful breeze from every pole and house top which could bear one, the people of all ages and conditions gathered in the public places, and the military, and firemen, with the brilliant equipments, and brightly burnished apparatus, flitted about in quest of their companies, while the clangor of signal bells announced the progress of the train, and the spirit-stirring music of the bands broke forth in strains of welcome amid which the favorite air "home sweet home" was grandly conspicuous. . . .

The announcement, on our bulletin, that the regiment had left Philadelphia caused a great sensation in the city, and at an early hour our people began to turn out, and the street corners were soon crowded with knots of people, discussing the probable hour of arrival.

The progress of the train, as it reached the various stations on the route, was placed upon our bulletin, and at each new announcement the excitement increased. . . .

About 4 o'clock in the afternoon the military and firemen assembled on Military Park. The carriages containing the aldermen of this city and Orange were soon on the ground, and at half-past four the cortege, headed by a file of policemen and Rubsam's brass band, marched down Broad street to its junction with Railroad avenue. . . .

On reaching the lower end of South Broad street the proper disposition was made of the military and all was in readiness to receive the veterans. The scene here was an animated one; the streets and vacant lots were filled with people. Mothers, wives, sweethearts, sisters and brothers were there with eager faces, beaming eyes, and nervous with excitement; some, too, there were who had heavy hearts and tearful eyes, for they knew the coming train would fail to bring back loved ones, who went away with the regiment, full of strength, to lose it, aye, and life also, on the bloody fields of Virginia. To them the coming train brought sorrowful emotions and opened afresh wounds that had been partially healed.

The roads near the junction were crowded with vehicles of every description—large numbers of them being from adjacent towns—filled with ladies and gentlemen all eager to do honor to "our Regiment."

The booming of a cannon and the shrill shrieking of a locomotive whistle in the distance, at last gave intimation of the approach of the train, and at 5 o'clock and 20 minutes the cars came sweeping up, when the immense crowd surged to and fro in uncontrollable emotion, loud cheers filled the air, and the excitement was at its height.

Owing to some misunderstanding the train did not stop at the junction, but kept on to Chestnut street depot. Men, women and children started at a run on the back track, and some good time was made by the crowd in its anxiety to reach the train in season to see the regiment disembark. The military, firemen and carriages executed a flank movement and proceeded to the depot, which they found encircled by an almost impenetrable crowd. After some little delay the members of the regiment filed out of the cars, and, as they did so, were greeted with cheer after cheer from the enthusiastic multitude which rushed forward, and soon every man of the 26th was surrounded and taken captive, by relatives and friends; hands were shaken, eager enquiries made, kisses exchanged, and congratulations freely bestowed.

As soon as the tumult of individual welcome was over, and when it became possible to do so, the Regiment was formed into line and marched up to Broad street, passing through a hollow square formed by the firemen and military, who stood uncovered in honor of the brave men; and the sick and wounded were placed in carriages that had been provided for them.

The line on Broad street was soon formed and the column, headed by the 1st Regiment, took up the march toward the Park. The ovation, as witnessed on Broad street, was grand; the housetops, sidewalks and streets, as far as the eye could reach, were crowded with people; every balcony and window along the route was a living mass of humanity; flags were flying from almost every building, and many were suspended across the street, while the waving of handkerchiefs was like the "white-caps" of the sea in a storm.

The steamers of the Fire Department were run out to the curb, with steam up, and as the Regiment passed by they saluted it with shrill whistles.

Some of the members brought home with them dogs, muskets, swords, and other trophies from the battle field, and one of them was followed by a live "contraband." The darkey, who was very black, had no hat and was attired in a long coat and the usual singular costume of the race in Dixie. He kept close behind his protector, notwithstanding the laughter and jeers of many of the crowd.[21]

At the City Hotel the procession halted for speeches by General Theodore Runyon and Lieutenant Colonel Martindale. Runyon welcomed the men with eloquence, complimenting their "soldierly devotion and fortitude and death-defying courage." Martindale replied, thanking God for "bringing the Regiment safely home" and the mayor, Common Council, and the people for "this cordial welcome and magnificent reception." Then Martindale turned to the question on everyone's lips—"the intention of the Regiment in the new and pressing emergency which has just arisen." In the only part of his speech not printed by the *Daily Journal*, Martindale echoed a favorite theme of the *Mercury*, promising the crowd that he for one was ready "to be used and spent in the sacred cause of the country until every danger from treason and rebellion was dissipated."

And he believed [according to the *Advertiser's* paraphrase] the same could be said for the large majority of the officers of the Regiment—and as for the men. . . , he would say he believed the ready answer "here" would be heard from them should the roll be called to-morrow. They had gone out as volunteers, actuated by patriotic principles and a determination to do all in their

power to subdue the rebellion. . . , and they had brought back these principles with them strengthened and confirmed by their experience of the dread-
ful realities of war.[22]

The speech-making over, the Twenty-sixth reformed its lines and continued
the march toward Military Park. Passing the McGregor House, the men recognized Colonel Morrison standing on the balcony. When someone called for
three cheers, the men responded "with a will," reported the *Advertiser*, hurrah-
ing loudly (although not loudly enough for the *Mercury*'s reporter, who failed to
hear them). Colonel Morrison, explained the *Advertiser* obliquely, "was and is a
great favorite with the regiment, and it was no fault of theirs that he was not in
command on their return home." The *Advertiser* continued:

> The march through Broad street was a prolonged ovation, and it was with
> the greatest difficulty the regiment could keep its ranks and get along, so
> immense was the crowd, and so frequent the interruptions caused by relatives
> and friends rushing forward to grasp some loved and recognized one by the
> hand. The crowd was not all smiles however, for there were many who
> looked in vain for the expected ones. We noticed standing on the corner of
> Broad and Market streets supported by a gentleman, a young lady, who
> seemed convulsed with emotion and distress. She, poor girl, had no doubt
> lost a brother, or mayhap, one closer than a brother, from the regiment, and
> her agonized sobs and streaming eyes bore witness to her sorrow, and yet the
> nervous waving of her tear-bedewed handkerchief, now and then, as the
> regiment passed by her, was testimony that she felt that those who had
> returned should be honored and welcomed even by her.
> As the procession reached the Park—which wore its neatest and greenest
> dress for the occasion—the gates were thrown open and the column passed
> in. The escorting military companies and firemen were then posted around
> the entire Park; the 26th was drawn up in line and ordered to stack arms.[23]

The scene at Military Park was soon one of general confusion. Said the
Mercury:

> The collation consisting of sandwiches and lager beer, was now taken
> round by the firemen, and homely as it was, ample justice was done it, and
> the soldiers sat down on the cool grass and enjoyed it as they had not prob-
> ably done for many a day. After a while persons began to quietly climb over
> the fence, and the police not being in sufficient force to guard the whole park,
> it was soon filled with people, rushing hither and thither.[24]

Added the *Daily Advertiser:*

> It was at first intended to march the Regiment to Camp Frelinghuysen, and
> quarter them there until mustered out of the service, but it was found almost
> impossible to keep the men together; so they were dismissed with orders to

report at the camp at 9:30 A.M. next Monday, and in a few moments the ranks were broken, and the members proceeded homeward.[25]

Thoughts of Lee's army marching north through Maryland could not be put out of mind, no matter how grand the welcome. Lieutenant Colonel Martindale and his officers were ready to answer the governor's call, or so Martindale said. But the rank and file seemed less eager, a fact alluded to by the *Mercury* in the only note of criticism heard that day:

> Many of our people were disappointed that the regiment had not volunteered for service in Pennsylvania, but we are informed that the subject was not broached to the men at all. There is no doubt that had they so volunteered the satisfaction in their conduct would have been far greater, and the reception would if possible, have been still more enthusiastic.[26]

On June 22 the regiment gathered for the next to last time at Camp Frelinghuysen, said the *Advertiser:*

> The men . . . assembled . . . at half-past 9 o'clock this morning; when the baggage of the regiment, which came on a freight, was opened and the overcoats, &c., distributed. Most of the men of the regiment reported, and the camp presented quite an animated appearance. After roll-call the regiment was ordered to assemble at 1 o'clock P.M., for the purpose of proceeding to Orange to participate in the funeral obsequies of Captain S. U. Dodd.
>
> Several of the members of the 26th Regiment who are detained at Washington under sentence to the Rip Raps, have families in this city, who, we learn, are entirely destitute and dependent upon the charity of their neighbors. Their pay having been forfeited, and the State pay ceasing renders their pecunniary condition extremely pitiful. One of these is a woman, whose case has been brought to our notice, resides in Walnut street, and has 5 young children, 2 of whom are twins. She was assisted by her neighbors on Saturday night. Other cases of a similar character have been related to us, and call loudly for the benevolence of the community.[27]

Captain Dodd's funeral was, said the Orange *Journal*, "of the most imposing character." After a sermon by Chaplain Morrill and prayers by the congregation, the men of the Twenty-sixth "took a last look upon the countenance of him who had been their loved commander."

> The coffin was draped in the stars and stripes, and surrounded with beautiful roses placed in the form of a cross; when the last look had been taken, the beloved features were covered up, and the precious casket was placed in the hearse, and the procession was formed.
>
> The beautiful hearse was ornamented with plumes of black and white; the horses were covered with black robes, upon which were inscribed in silver letters "Capt. S. U. Dodd, Co. H, 26th Regiment, N.J.V." They also bore nodding black and white plumes. . . .

The procession, comprising the Mayor and Common Council of Orange, and many of the citizens in carriages, and the hearse, escorted by Co. H, of the 26th, with arms reversed, moved slowly on to the sweetly mournful music of the funeral dirge, furnished by a brass band. Nothing that could be done to add emphasis to the expression of their grief at the loss of their noble fellow citizen was omitted by the people of Orange, and as the procession moved mournfully along, in all the "gorgeous pomp and circumstance" of a military funeral, the stores were closed, the flags were drooped at half mast, and the people bared their heads in respect to the memory of the dead warrior.[28]

Essex County paid its final tribute to the men of the Twenty-sixth in the picnic groves and parks of Bloomfield, Orange, Newark, and Irvington. Members of Companies G and H and their families were feted at Freemen's Woods in Orange. Over 300 people gathered at Satterwaite's grove in Belleville to honor the men of Company C. Company E gathered at Baldwin's Woods near Irvington, reported the *Advertiser:*

The day was fine, the groves were in their early summer livery, the soldiers were happy, and their friends had the satisfaction of rendering a tribute of respect and esteem to the battle-scarred boys that they will not soon forget. A suitable band was in attendance, and discoursed pleasantly at intervals to the merry dancers who filled the circle made by the crowd.

At 2 P.M. the order of "Company fall in" for dinner was given, and such celerity of movement in falling in as the braves exhibited on that occasion has never been witnessed in any army, either on advance or retreat.

Afterward the guests being comfortably disposed of in groups upon the grass, or enjoying a quiet after dinner quadrille with their sweethearts, the families and friends of the company sat down to the seeming inexhaustible bounty. There was a great variety and a sufficient number of kindly hands to distribute all, so that not even the ugliest urchin—whose only possible claim to dinner could be that he lived next door to a volunteer—departed unfed.

During the afternoon the Chaplain of the Regiment, Rev. Mr. Morrill, rallied the little band about him and recounted the "sieges, battles, fortunes they had passed." He wished to express their gratitude to Providence for the kindly care that had brought them back unharmed, and their thanks to the ladies for the entertainment and bountiful repast. . . .

Tea was served to the soldiers at 7 o'clock, after which a part of the company withdrew, but many a Yankee boy and blooming girl, and many a German volunteer and "gutc frow" tripped upon the elastic turf till the moon went down.[29]

Conclusion
A Higher Appreciation

News of Lee's surrender at Appomattox came nearly two years after the men of the Twenty-sixth Regiment stacked arms for the last time at Camp Frelinghuysen. Newark (along with every village and crossroads hamlet in the state) erupted in a cacophony of jubilation. Reported the *Advertiser:*

> From five to six o'clock yesterday afternoon the whole city rang as if with a cheery, triumphal tumult in honor of recent victories and the prospect of Peace. Church and factory, and all other kinds of bells, were rung; steam whistles sounded, guns of every calibre were fired, and the streets were alive with happy multitudes. One man in Broad street hung out a large bar of steel in front of a store, and made it ring with the regular strokes of the hammer. Such a day of excitement and good feeling has not been witnessed here for a long period.[1]

Only five days later, on the eve of Easter Sunday, came the report of Lincoln's assassination. "The flags that but yesterday floated in honor of our great triumph are to-day at half-mast, in token of the general sorrow over a calamity without parallel in our history," said the *Daily Advertiser*. Within hours public buildings, churches, and private homes were draped in black and white bunting. General Runyon, now mayor of Newark, ordered all city offices closed "in token of public grief." The *Advertiser* printed full details of "the monstrous infamy," adding: "Never in all our eventful history was a people so startled, bewildered, and almost dumb-founded as they were by the news of the unparalleled and unspeakable atrocity perpetrated in Washington last night."[2] The *Daily Journal*, one of Lincoln's harshest critics while he lived, spoke for many at his death: "We have no heart to contemplate the event. . . . For whatever objections we may have editorially expressed in times past in reference to the President's policy, recent important events have led us . . . to a higher appreciation of the man than we had ever before held." Newark, wrote one newsman, was literally hung in black. "The grief of the people at the death of Mr. Lincoln is deep and intense," reported the *Journal*. "The evidences of public mourning are all around us; in the streets, in the churches, at places of private business and on the apparel of our citizens."[3]

On April 20 the people of Newark held funeral exercises for the fallen president, with Major Morris of the Twenty-sixth New Jersey as grand marshal. Hundreds of veterans of the major's old regiment joined nearly 5,000 of their fellow citizens in a mournful procession along Broad Street to Military Park. To the veterans went the honor of guarding the empty hearse, swathed for the occasion in red, white, and blue, capped with black plumes and drawn by six horses covered with heavy black palls. Said the *Daily Advertiser:*

> During the march, the tolling of the bells, the booming of the minute guns, the steady tramp of the mourning multitude, the melancholy flapping of the muffled flags, the sombre appearance of the buildings, and the sad faces of the immense and quiet throngs which filled the streets, the balconies, the windows, and clustered even upon the house tops, all assisted in composing a scene of such real and extensive woe and mourning as this city has never witnessed.[4]

Four days later the president's funeral train passed slowly through the Newark station on its mournful journey westward. Shortly after dawn thousands of people began to gather along Railroad Avenue, the *Advertiser* reported, "and soon not only covered the entire street, but all the adjoining house-tops, sheds and windows."

> A feeling of deep sorrow appeared to pervade the entire mass, while the fluttering of the black trimming from the neighboring buildings, the mourning badges upon the coat or mantle, and the other tokens of grief gave an unusually sombre cast to the scene.
>
> Shortly after 9 o'clock the members of the Common Council, city officers, clergy, a detachment of the Veterans Reserve Corps, and the city Police took possession of the Market street depot, and after removing the crowd, awaited the arrival of the train, whose approach had been announced by the arrival of the pilot locomotive, heavily draped in mourning. Its appearance was heralded by the tolling of bells and the firing of minute guns, and as the train with the remains passed along the avenue, heads were uncovered and bowed with reverence, many persons shedding tears.[5]

All across New Jersey the voices of partisanship were stilled for a brief moment as the people wept for their martyred president. And they wept, too, for the 6,300 men of New Jersey who lay in their graves, all martyrs to the cause of Union—and victims, some would claim, of a war that "in part originated in a partisan press" that was, in the words of Chaplain Morrill, "fed and fanned by public misrepresentation."

Notes

CHAPTER 1

1. Maurice Tandler, "The Political Front in Civil War New Jersey," *Proceedings of the New Jersey Historical Society* 83, no. 4 (October 1965): 223 (hereinafter cited as Tandler).

2. Ibid.

3. Ibid.

4. Thomas Fleming, *New Jersey, A Bicentennial History*, (New York, 1977), p. 116.

5. John T. Cunningham, *New Jersey, America's Main Road* (New York, 1966), p. 172 (hereinafter cited as Cunningham, *New Jersey*).

6. John T. Cunningham, *Newark* (Newark, N.J., 1966), p. 151 (hereinafter cited as Cunningham, *Newark*).

7. Newark *Daily Mercury*, November 6, 1860 (hereinafter cited as *Mercury*).

8. Ibid., November 9, 1860.

9. Newark *Daily Journal*, November 9, 1860 (hereinafter cited as *Journal*).

10. Cunningham, *New Jersey*, p. 175.

11. *Journal*, December 19, 1860.

12. Ibid.

13. The Somerset *Messenger*, January 3, 1861.

14. Philadelphia *Inquirer*, February 22, 1861, quoted in Earl Schenck Miers, *New Jersey and the Civil War* (Princeton, N.J., 1964) p. 7 (hereinafter cited as *Inquirer*).

15. Newark *Sentinel of Freedom*, February 26, 1861 (hereinafter cited as *Sentinel*).

16. *Inquirer*, pp. 5–6.

17. Trenton *Daily State Gazette and Republican*, March 1, 1861 (hereinafter cited as *State Gazette*).

18. The *Sommerset Messenger*, February 21, 1861.

19. Newark *Daily Advertiser*, April 5, 1861 (hereinafter cited as *Advertiser*).

20. Ibid., April 6, 1861.

21. Princeton *Standard*, April 12, 1861.

22. *State Gazette*, February 8, 1861.

23. Princeton *Standard*, February 8, 1861.

24. John T. Cunningham, *New Jersey: A Mirror on America* (Florham Park, N.J., 1979), p. 179 (hereinafter cited as Cunningham, *America*).

25. *Advertiser*, April 15, 1861.

26. The *Somerset Messenger*, May 9, 1861.

27. *The New-Jersey Journal*, April 23, 1861.

28. *Advertiser*, April 13, 1861.

29. Cunningham, *America*, p. 179.

30. *The New-Jersey Journal*, April 23, 1861.

31. Cunningham, *New Jersey*, p. 179.

32. *State Gazette*, July 26, 1861.

33. *Journal*, July 2, 1861.

34. *State Gazette*, July 26, 1861.

CHAPTER 2

1. James I. Robertson, Jr., ed., *The Civil War Letters of Robert McAllister* (New Brunswick, N.J., 1965), p. 106 (hereinafter cited as *McAllister*).

2. John Y. Foster, *New Jersey and the Rebellion* (Newark, N.J., 1868), p. 211 (hereinafter cited as Foster).

3. *Advertiser*, May 11, 1861.

4. Charles M. Knapp, *New Jersey Politics during the Period of the Civil War and Reconstruction* (Geneva, N.Y., 1924), p. 59 (hereinafter cited as Knapp).

5. Herman K. Platt, ed., *Charles Perrin Smith: New Jersey Political Reminiscences, 1828–1882* (New Brunswick, N.J., 1965), p. 139.

6. William C. Wright, "New Jersey's Military Role in the Civil War Reconsidered," *New Jersey History (Proceedings of the New Jersey Historical Society)* 92, no. 4 (Winter 1974): 198.

7. Tandler, p. 233.

8. Knapp, p. 134.

9. Tandler, p. 230.

10. Knapp, p. 129.

11. F. J. Urquhart, *A History of the City of Newark, New Jersey* (New York, 1913, 2:1076) (hereinafter cited as Urquhart); Tandler, p. 231.

12. Knapp, passim.

13. Tandler, p. 225.

14. Knapp, pp. 82–83.

15. *Advertiser*, June 11, 1864.

16. Tandler, p. 225.

17. *Journal*, January 1, 1864.

18. Ibid., June 25, 1864.

19. Tandler, p. 223.

20. Ibid., pp. 223–24.

21. Larry A. Greene, "The Emancipation Proclamation in New Jersey and the Paranoid Style," *New Jersey History (Proceedings of the New Jersey Historical Society)* 91, no. 2 (Summer 1973): 122–23 (hereinafter cited as Greene).

22. Bernard A. Weisberger, *Reporters for the Union* (Boston, 1953), p. 10 (hereinafter cited as Weisberger).

23. Frank L. Mott, *American Journalism, A History: 1690–1960*, 3rd ed. (New York, 1962), p. 253.

24. Weisberger, p. 227.

25. Ibid., p. 220.

26. Joseph J. Mathews, *Reporting the Wars* (Minneapolis, Minn., 1957), p. 81 (hereinafter cited as Mathews).

27. John Tebbel, *The Compact History of the American Newspaper* (New York, 1963), p. 121. And see Mott, *American Journalism*, p. 253.

28. Frederic Hudson, *Journalism in the United States from 1690 to 1872* (New York, 1873), p. 187.

29. Knapp, pp. 62–63.

30. Ibid., p. 119; *Journal*, July 21, 1864.

31. New York *Daily News*, August 12, 1861; *Journal*, passim.

32. William Warren Rogers, "C. Chauncey Burr and The Old Guard," *Proceedings of the New Jersey Historical Society*, 93, no. 2 (July 1955): p. 168 (hereinafter cited as Rogers).

33. Carl E. Hatch, "Negro Migration and New Jersey—1863," *New Jersey History (Proceedings of the*

New Jersey Historical Society) 87, no. 4 (Winter 1969): p. 242 (hereinafter cited as Hatch, "Migration"); *State Gazette*, January 10, 1863.

34. *Journal*, November 30, 1863.
35. Rogers, p. 171.
36. Ibid., p. 173.
37. Ibid., p. 172.
38. Ibid., p. 175.
39. Carl E. Hatch, "Editor David Naar of Trenton: Profile of the Anti-Negro Mind," *New Jersey History (Proceedings of the New Jersey Historical Society)* 86, no. 2 (Summer 1968): 73.
40. Ibid., passim.
41. Knapp, p. 95.
42. Ibid., p. 62.
43. *State Gazette*, July 26, 1861.
44. *Mercury*, August 2, 1862, quoting the *True Democratic Banner* of Morristown.
45. *McAllister*, p. 543.
46. *State Gazette*, July 10, 1861.
47. *Mercury*, February 23, 1863.
48. Mathews, p. 81.
49. New York *Evening Post*, May 30, 1863.
50. Cunningham, *New Jersey*, p. 173.

CHAPTER 3

1. William H. Shaw, *History of Essex and Hudson Counties, New Jersey* (Philadelphia, 1884), 1: 562–63 (hereinafter cited as Shaw).
2. New Jersey Civil War Centennial Commission. Fourth Annual American History Workshop, Trenton, New Jersey 1965 (hereinafter cited as Fourth Annual Workshop), p. 11: *The American Annual Cyclopaedia . . . of the year 1861* (New York, 1865), p. 514.
3. Joseph Atkinson, *The History of Newark, New Jersey* (Newark, N. J., 1878), p. 239 (hereinafter cited as Atkinson).
4. Cunningham, *Newark*, p. 151.
5. *Mercury*, November 10, 1860.
6. Shaw, 1: 563.
7. Fourth Annual Workshop, pp. 10–12.
8. Cunningham, *Newark*, p. 152.
9. Shaw, 2: 698.
10. Shaw, 1: 516; Urquhart, p. 678.
11. Shaw, 1: 518–20.
12. Hatch, *Migration*, p. 233; *Journal*, November 6, 1862.
13. Hatch, *Migration*, passim.
14. *Journal*, January 18, 1864.
15. Greene, passim.
16. Shaw, 1: 563.
17. Fourth Annual Workshop, pp. 11–12.
18. Ibid., p. 12
19. *Journal*, January 18, 1864.
20. Postelection issues of the *Advertiser* and the *Journal*. Beyond the corporate limits of Newark, the county seat, lay Orange, an industrial center three miles to the west, and the villages of rural Essex County. Nearly three-quarters of the county's population lived in Newark. Orange, with some 8,900 people, was the county's second city. Another 18,000 earned a comfortable living from the truck farms and orchards that characterized suburban Essex. During the war Orange, Caldwell,

Clinton, West Orange, and South Orange generally voted Democratic. Belleville, Bloomfield, Livingston, Millburn, and East Orange, after it was formed in 1863, usually voted Republican. Republican candidates tended to carry suburban Essex by one or two hundred votes. Democratic margins of 1,500 to 1,600 in Newark, where fully 70 percent of the voters in the county lived, rendered those Republican victories meaningless.

21. Shaw, 1: 59.

21. Urquhart, p. 688.

23. Shaw, 1: 59–61.

24. *Advertiser*, July 22 and 24, 1861; *Journal*, July 22 and 23, 1861; *Mercury*, July 23 and 24, 1861.

25. Shaw, 1: 219–26; William C. Wright and Paul A. Stellhorn, *Directory of New Jersey Newspapers 1765–1970*. (Trenton, N. J., 1977), pp. 149–171 (hereinafter cited as Wright and Stellhorn).

26. Shaw, 1: 223–24.

27. Atkinson, p. 326; Urquhart, 3: 362–63.

28. Atkinson, p. 323.

29. William S. Myers, ed., *The Story of New Jersey* (New York, 1945), p. 125.

30. Atkinson, p. 327.

31. *Mercury*, March 8, 1860.

32. Shaw, 1: 283; Knapp, p. 44; Maurice Tandler, "H. N. Congar's Letters from Hong Kong," *Proceedings of the New Jersey Historical Society* 84, no. 2 (April 1966): 76–78.

33. Daniel Porter to Horace N. Congar, September 21, 1861. Manuscript Collections of the New Jersey Historical Society, Manuscript Group 408 (hereinafter cited as Congar Papers).

34. *Newark Evening News*, November 13, 1896; *Proceedings of the New Jersey Historical Society*, Third Series, 2, no. 1 (January 1897): 7–8.

35. Congar Papers, Daniel Porter to Horace N. Congar, September 21, 1861.

36. *Journal*, June 18, 1864.

37. *Advertiser*, December 6, 1860.

38. Congar Papers, Daniel Porter to Horace N. Congar, September 21, 1861.

39. *Journal*, June 18, 1864.

40. Congar Papers, Daniel Porter to Horace N. Congar, January 12, 1862.

41. Ibid., March 19, 1862.

42. Ibid., June 16, 1862.

43. *Advertiser*, October 2, 1885.

44. *Mercury*, August 2, 1862.

45. *Sentinel*, July 21, 1863.

46. *Advertiser*, January 2, 1864.

47. *Journal*, January 2, 1864.

48. *Journal*, November 1, 1866; New Jersey Historical Society Biographical Files; Congar Papers, Daniel Porter to Horace N. Congar, January 12, 1862; Atkinson, pp. 323–24.

49. Atkinson, p. 323.

50. Ibid.; *Journal*, April 15, 1865.

51. *Mercury*, February 27, 1863.

52. Atkinson, p. 323.

53. *Journal*, June 1, 1864.

54. Ibid., January 18, 1864.

55. *Mercury*, August 2, 1862; *Journal*, August 6 and 8, 1862.

56. *Advertiser*, July 30, 1862; *Journal*, August 1, 1862.

57. *Journal*, June 25, 1864.

58. Ibid., July 19, 1864.

59. Ibid., July 21, 1864.

60. Knapp, pp. 119–21.

61. *Journal*, April 15, 1865.

62. *Mercury*, February 23, 1863.

63. *Journal*, June 18, 1864.

64. Morris Schonbach, *Radicals and Visionaries: A History of Dissent in New Jersey* (Princeton, N.J., 1964), pp. 29–32; Knapp, passim; *Proceedings of the New Jersey Historical Society*, Third Series, 6, no. 2 (1908): 93.

65. Knapp, pp. 41–42.

66. *Journal*, June 18, 1864.

67. Ibid.

68. Ibid.

69. Daniel Dodd, Jr., and others to Thomas T. Kinney, June 8, 1864. Manuscript Collections, New Jersey Historical Society, Manuscript Group 785, Box VII.

70. Thomas T. Kinney to Messrs. Dodd, et al., June 10, 1864, ibid.

71. *Journal*, June 18, 1864.

72. Newark *Evening News*, November 13, 1896.

73. *Journal*, June 18, 1864.

74. *Advertiser*, June 20, 1864.

75. Congar Papers, Monroe Porter to Horace N. Congar, October 1, 1864.

76. *Advertiser*, November 7, 1864.

77. Wright and Stellhorn, p. 160; Newark *Evening News*, November 13, 1896.

CHAPTER 4

1. Mathews, pp. 81, 86.

2. Roy P. Basler, ed., *The Collected Works of Abraham Lincoln* (New Brunswick, N.J., 1953), 5: 292. (hereinafter cited as Basler).

3. Shelby Foote, *The Civil War, A Narrative* (New York, 1958), 1: 516 (hereinafter cited as Foote).

4. Ibid., p. 524.

5. Basler, 5: 297.

6. Ibid., p. 296.

7. Foote, 1: 524–26; Bruce Catton, *Terrible Swift Sword* (New York, 1963), pp. 403–4.

8. Quoted in *Sentinel*, August 8, 1862.

9. Bruce Catton, *Terrible Swift Sword* (New York, 1963), pp. 404–5.

10. *Advertiser*, August 11, 1862.

11. Quoted in *Sentinel*, August 5, 1862.

12. *Journal*, August 21, 1862.

13. Ibid., August 5, 1862.

14. Bell Irvin Wiley, *The Life of Billy Yank* (Indianapolis, Ind., 1952), pp. 37–40.

15. Ira Seymour Dodd, *The Song of the Rappahannock* (New York, 1898), pp. 42–44 (hereinafter cited as Dodd).

16. Alan A. Siegel, *Out of Our Past: A History of Irvington, New Jersey* (Irvington, N.J., 1974), p. 125.

17. Lynn G. Lockward, *A Puritan Heritage* (Privately printed, 1955), p. 181.

18. *Advertiser*, August 25, 1862.

19. Ibid., August 26, 1862. At the outbreak of the war an infantry private earned $11 a month. Congress raised it to $13 in August 1861.

20. Orange *Journal*, September 6, 1862.

21. *Advertiser*, August 16, 1862.

22. Orange *Journal*, September 6, 1862.

23. *Mercury*, August 11, 1862.

24. Ibid., August 12, 1862.

25. Ibid., August 8, 1862.

26. *Advertiser*, August 20, 1862.

27. Ibid.

28. Ibid., August 25, 1862.

29. Ibid., August 30, 1862.

30. Ibid., August 26, 1862.

31. Ibid., September 4, 1862.

32. Ibid., September 9, 1862. Both Foster and Stryker assert that the drawing for the draft was to begin on September 3, but that by then New Jersey's quota had been met. The Newark newspapers, however, reported the deadline as September 5.

CHAPTER 5

1. David L. Pierson, *Narratives of Newark* (Newark, N.J., 1917), p. 292; David L. Pierson, *History of the Oranges to 1921* (New York, 1922), 2: 334.

2. Orange *Journal*, September 6, 1862.

3. *Advertiser*, September 2, 1862.

4. Pierson, *Narratives of Newark*, p. 293.

5. *Advertiser*, September 11, 1862.

6. Ibid., September 16, 1862.

7. Dodd, pp. 45–47. By the time Morrison was commissioned colonel of the Twenty-sixth New Jersey, he had already seen action in the Mexican War, marched with William Walker through the jungles of Nicaragua, nearly lost his life in a harebrained expedition to Cuba, and fought in the Italian wars of liberation under Garibaldi. He had shown great personal courage in the opening months of the war, suffering a painful wound at Oak Grove, the first of the Seven Days' Battles. A strapping six footer, with blue eyes and brown hair, Morrison cut a dashing figure about camp. At heart a cavalryman with no experience in leading untrained infantrymen, Morrison had at least seen war firsthand, something few other members of the unit could boast. The men in the ranks took to their new commander immediately; despite his later fall from grace at Mayre's Heights, most never lost confidence in him.

Morrison's father, Andrew, a native of Ireland, had been an officer in the American army during the War of 1812. His namesake, born in Argyle, Washington County, New York, on October 3, 1831, longed to follow in his father's footsteps. His opportunity came when war with Mexico broke out. In 1847, at the age of sixteen, he enlisted in a regiment mustering at Albany for duty in California. Young Morrison, a private in Captain Frisbee's company, reached only as far as New York City before his irate father caught up with him, promptly arranging his discharge. Determined to enlist, Morrison escaped from his father, took the train to Philadelphia, and there joined the First United States Dragoons under Captain John Butler, who was raising troops for service in Mexico. Shortly before the company was to depart, however, Morrison's boyish face betrayed him. Once again discharged, but undeterred by army regulations, Morrison wrangled permission to accompany the troops to Mexico as Captain Butler's aide, serving on his staff until the captain was killed in action near Mexico City.

Returning to New Orleans after the war, Morrison fell under the spell of General Narciso Lopez, a high Cuban military official who had fled to the United States in 1848 after he was sentenced to death for his role in a plot against Spanish domination. With Cuban independence his mission and annexation to America the goal of his Southern backers, Lopez led three ineptly organized filibustering expeditions to Cuba. His third, the largest of them all, proved the most disastrous. With 500 adventurers recruited from the streets of New Orleans, Lopez landed near Havana in August 1851. Instead of the anticipated native uprising, Lopez was met by a strong force of Spanish regulars who forced his quick surrender. Fifty-one of the invaders, including Lopez himself, were executed, while many others were sentenced to penal servitude. Morrison escaped a like fate by the slimmest of margins. Ordered to assist with the embarkation of the landing force, he was on the last boat to head for shore. Morrison's ship turned tail for New Orleans as soon as it became obvious the invasion had failed.

When Spanish authorities in Havana seized and confiscated the cargo of an American steamer in February 1854, many Americans cried for war with Spain. Then in Albany, Morrison helped organize the Worth Guards, a volunteer outfit that proclaimed its readiness to free Cuba from Spanish domination should hostilities break out. After cooler heads smoothed over the trouble with Spain, the Worth Guards disbanded. Little more than a year later Morrison, now twenty-four, set out on his next adventure, this one to Central America. In May of 1855 William Walker, Tennessee-born physician, lawyer, journalist, and adventurer, sailed with fifty-six followers to join a civil war in Nicaragua. Within six months Walker and his ragtag army, dubbed "the Immortals," had seized virtual control of the country. Walker's success stirred the nation; hundreds of young men, anxious for glory, shipped out of San Francisco, New Orleans, and New York to join the general. Walker's agents painted a glowing tale of the opportunities awaiting Americans in Nicaragua now that a civilized government was in place. Cornelius Vanderbilt's Accessory Transit Company, formed to carry California-bound passengers across the Nicaraguan isthmus, offered free passage to "emigrants," most of them single men more interested in fighting than colonizing. The federal government, which had long ignored such blantant violations of the neutrality laws, finally acted in December of 1855. On Christmas eve, U.S. marshals seized the *Northern Light*, an Accessory Transit steamer, as she was about to depart the port of New York for Nicaragua with 170 "emigrants" on board. Among those arrested was Morrison, who had given up his post with the U.S. Customs House to join Walker. Federal officers boarded the ship, seized its crew and forced the filibusters to disembark, arresting eleven of them. Captain Faunce of the U.S. revenue cutter *Washington* persuaded most of the would-be "Immortals" to depart the ship peacefully, reported the New York *Times:*

Some, too drunk to articulate their ideas strait forward, hiccuped out their opposition or willingness to go, according as the caprice took them. By ingeniously chiming in with the various whim of the divers parties he had to deal with, at one time joking and at another showing decisive earnestness, Captain Faunce at length succeeded in removing to the steam tug the entire party, in all 170, with the exception of two. These—John Creighton and [A.] J. Morrison, both of New-York, and formerly attached to the Custom-House, persisted that they would not be put ashore anyhow. Captain Faunce accordingly ordered that they be placed in irons. They were fastened to the wheel of the wheel-house, and, from their uncomfortable position, having to stand up, speedily regretted that they had not yielded to the commands of the Captain. The residue, who were placed aboard the steamtug, were landed at the foot of Pier No. 4. It was nearly 8 o'clock when the steam-tug bore the party away. Their yells and songs bordered on the terrific, and must have been heard at a great distance.

Detained in Ludlow Street Jail as material witnesses, Morrison and Creighton were soon released. In mid-1856, after Walker had been elected president of Nicaragua and his government accorded United States recognition, Morrison joined another group of volunteers, who left New York aboard the *Star of the West*. Morrison served in Walker's army until May of 1857, when the filibuster's regime collapsed and his forces fled the country, receiving a hero's welcome upon their return to the United States.

Three years later Morrison, who had met the Italian patriot Giuseppe Garibaldi when he visited New York City in 1850–51, joined some 10,000 foreign volunteers, chiefly French and Hungarian, who fought under the banner of Italian unification. A cavalry major in Garibaldi's army, Morrison saw action in Sicily and southern Italy and was present when King Victor Emmanuel made his triumphal entry into Naples in November 1860.

Morrison boarded a steamer for America as soon as news of the attack on Fort Sumter reached Italy. Arriving in Troy, New York, he offered his services to New York Governor Edwin Morgan, who appointed him on October 2, 1861, "to take command of the volunteers for a Cavalry Regiment to be quartered at Troy." Known as the Black Horse Regiment, the Seventh New York Cavalry was mustered in on November 6, 1861, for three years. Morrison was commissioned colonel. In the confusion of the first months of the war, the Seventh New York never received its horses and on March 31, 1862, after less than four months, was mustered out "by direction of the Secretary of

War, in consequence of the excess of cavalry." Although without command or commission, Morrison remained at the front as a volunteer aide-de-camp to Brigadier General Innes N. Palmer, commander, Third Brigade, Third Division, and later, First Brigade, First Division, Third Corps, throughout the Peninsular Campaign. One of Palmer's two aides from the early part of May to mid-September 1862, Morrison rendered yeoman service, bearing all his own expenses and losing his horse at the Battle of Fair Oaks. Morrison, who received no army pay as a volunteer, was wounded at the Battle of Oak Grove on June 25, 1862, by a piece of shell that carried away the second and third fingers and metacarpal bones of his left hand. So severe was the damage that Morrison's left hand was totally useless for the remainder of his life. As Innes's aid, Morrison participated in the battles of Williamsburg, Seven Pines, Fair Oaks, the Seven Days', and Malvern Hill.

Following the Peninsula Campaign, General Innes was ordered to organize and forward the nine-month New Jersey regiments that began arriving in Washington in the early fall of 1862. Morrison's outstanding service as the general's aide-de-camp, together with his proven courage, helped secure the colonelcy of the Twenty-sixth New Jersey. Morrison's record with the regiment is not easy to judge: Sergeant Major Cummings, a fellow adventurer in Nicaragua, could not praise him too highly; others, who may have resented his flamboyance or distrusted his politics, were far less enthusiastic. On balance, the rank and file, who cheered him even after he was removed from command, found little fault with their amiable colonel. Morrison's fondness for the bottle, a not uncommon weakness among Civil War soldiers, proved to be his undoing at Mayre's Heights. Relieved from duty, he was sentenced by general court martial to be "cashiered for Drunkeness on duty and dismissed [from the] service" on June 11, 1863.

Morrison, who led the Twenty-sixth New Jersey as if it were a troop of cavalry, found a command more to his liking when the governor of New Jersey authorized him on November 4, 1863, to raise a cavalry unit at Camp Bayard, Trenton. The First United States Hussars, later known as the Third New Jersey Cavalry, was recruited during the winter of 1863–64 and mustered into federal service in February 1864. Relieved from "the disability incurred by the sentence of a General Court Martial" on February 6, Morrison was commissioned colonel on February 10. A reporter for *Frank Leslie's Illustrated Newspaper* who visited Camp Bayard in late December 1863 wrote that the regimental uniform "is a showy and attractive one, being based on that of the Austrian hussars. The pantaloon is the usual cavalry one, with a yellow stripe; and the jacket is trimmed with yellow cord. The baldrick and agrete are worn over the shoulder, across the breast. Instead of an overcoat they wear a talma, with tassel over the left shoulder. The cap is very neat and comfortable. The hussars carry a very fine carbine. . . , sabre and pistol." The regiment, added the reporter, would soon be ready "for real service in the country."

The Third Cavalry, which soon discarded both its original name and showy hussar uniform, left Trenton for Annapolis, Maryland, on March 29, 1864, 1,200 men strong. After nearly four months of routine scouting and patrol duty along the Orange and Alexandria Railroad and at Germania Ford, Chancellorsville and City Point, it was transferred in early August from its position in front of Petersburg to Winchester, Virginia, in the Shenandoah Valley. Numbering less than 500 effectives, the regiment was placed under the command of General Philip Sheridan who was then moving to block a Confederate thrust toward Washington. Before his men could see any real action, Colonel Morrison's weakness for whiskey, attributable in some measure perhaps to his painful wound, caught up with him a second time. On August 12, 1864, a general court martial that convened to hear charges of conduct "unbecoming an Officer and a Gentlemen" and "prejudicial to good order and military discipline" acquitted him of both offenses. As part of the bargain, Morrison submitted his resignation from the service on August 25, 1864, citing "reasons referring to the interests of the service and myself." On August 29 he was honorably discharged. John Y. Foster, author of the first complete account of New Jersey's role in the Civil War, judged Morrison harshly. The Third Cavalry, wrote Foster in 1868, "deserved a far higher place in the estimation of the people of the State than it enjoyed while in the field. Unfortunate in its commandant, when first entering the service, it was ever after, with singular injustice, judged in the light of this fact; no adequate allowance being made for its subsequent improvement in efficiency and discipline. No regiment was ever more efficiently officiered than this after the suspension of the original Colonel."

Returning to West Troy, New York, Colonel Morrison spent the next several years writing of his experiences in Mexico, Cuba, Nicaragua, Italy, and the Civil War, publishing his memoirs under the title *Fighting Under Three Flags*. In 1870 he received an appointment as United States railway postal agent between Rutland, Vermont, and Troy, a position he held until shortly before his death. Morrison, who studied art during his Italian sojourn, took up the brush and palette again after the Civil War. "His paintings of Italian scenes," wrote one observer, "showed a great degree of talent." By special act of Congress, Morrison was awarded a pension of twenty dollars a month in 1879. A member of Griswold Post, GAR, and Trinity Episcopal Church, both of Troy, Morrison was seventy-five when he died at the home of his nephew on January 28, 1907. "In the death of Colonel Andrew Jackson Morrison," said the Troy *Record*, "a gallant soldier, a genial spirit, and a fine type of the old cavalier passed from the field of the world's fortune, leaving a brilliant record and a personal history full of romance and stirring adventure." He was, said the newspaper, "a soldier of fortune, but not in the mercenary meaning of the term. He fought for what he believed to be the cause of the weak against the oppressor, and in his own land he fought against treason. That he died unburdened by wealth. . . , furnish[es] the best proof that he did not draw his sword in the many causes he fought for through desire for gain. And he died as he lived, bravely meeting what fortune brought him." *Frank Leslie's Illustrated Newspaper*, January 9, 1864; New York *Times*, December 25, 1855; Troy (New York) *Times*, January 29, 1907; Troy (New York) *Record*, January 29, 1907; Foster, pp. 661–69; Military and Pension Records, National Archives.

8. New York *Times*, September 22, 1862.

9. Pierson, *History of the Oranges, 2: 335.*

10. *New York Times*, September 22, 1862.

11. New York *Evening Express*, September 22, 1862.

12. *Advertiser*, September 20, 1862.

13. Pierson, *History of the Oranges*, 2: 335.

14. *Advertiser*, September 22, 1862. Skedaddling was nothing new at Camp Frelinghuysen, which may explain both Colonel Van Vorst's and the *Daily's* remarkably calm attitude. On August 31, 1862, the Thirteenth Regiment, a three-year outfit and the first to be assembled at Camp Frelinghuysen, took French leave under nearly identical circumstances. Members of the guard posted by nervous officers anticipating a skedaddle decamped along with the rest, jamming their bayonet-tipped rifles into the ground before departing for home.

15. Ibid., September 23, 1862.

16. *Journal*, September 23, 1862.

17. *Mercury*, September 23, 1862.

18. *Journal*, September 26, 1862.

19. *Mercury*, September 26, 1862.

20. *Journal*, September 26, 1862.

21. *Advertiser*, September 26, 1862.

22. Ibid.

23. Pierson, *History of the Oranges*, 2: 336; *Advertiser*, September 26, 1862.

25. *Mercury* and *Advertiser*, September 26, 1862. Organized at Camp Frelinghuysen, Newark, New Jersey, the regiment was mustered into United States services for nine months on September 18, 1862. Officers, 38; noncommissioned officers and privates, 960. Total strength, 998. The regiment was organized into ten companies: A, B, I, and K from Newark; C, Newark and Belleville; E, Newark and Irvington; D, Livingston and Caldwell; F, Bloomfield; and G and H, the Oranges.

The Twenty-sixth Regiment departed New Jersey for Washington, D.C., on September 26, 1862. Upon arrival, it went into bivouac on Capitol Hill and was assigned to General Briggs' brigade, Second Army Corps, remaining in Washington until October 1. The regiment moved to Frederick, Maryland, on October 1, thence to Hagerstown, Maryland, October 11. It remained at Hagerstown until October 31, then marched to camp at Falmouth, Virginia.

In August 1862, the Second, Third, Fourth, Fifth and Sixth regiments of Vermont infantry were combined into the Second Brigade, Second Division, Sixth Corps, Army of the Potomac, Colonel Henry Whiting and later, Colonel Lewis A. Grant, commanding. At Hagerstown the Twenty-sixth Regiment was attached to the "Vermont Brigade."

The Twenty-sixth New Jersey participated in the Battle of Fredericksburg, December 12–15, 1862; Mud March, January 20–24, 1863; Chancellorsville campaign, April 27–May 6, 1863; and Franklin's Crossing, June 5–7, 1863. The unit's time having expired, it reached Washington, D.C., on June 17, 1863, and Newark, New Jersey, on June 19, 1863. It was mustered out of service at Camp Frelinghuysen on June 27, 1863.

Official reports list 36 men killed in action or died of wounds or disease; 27 discharged on account of wounds, disease or debility; 26, deserted, most of them before the unit left Newark; 40, court-martialed for various offenses; and 2, final record unknown.

CHAPTER 6

1. Foster, p. 539.
2. *Advertiser*, October 2, 1862.
3. Margaret Leech, *Reveille in Washington, 1860–1865*(New York, 1941), p. 207.
4. Dodd, pp. 50–51.
5. *Advertiser*, October 14, 1862.
6. Ibid., October 20, 1862.
7. Dodd, p. 52. Thirty-three years after the Twenty-sixth Regiment stacked arms, Sergeant Ira S. Dodd, then a Presbyterian minister in New York, wrote several articles about his wartime experiences for *McClure's Magazine*. Later gathered into a slim volume by the family publishing firm, Dodd's articles are the only published reminiscences by a member of the unit.

Ira Seymour Dodd was born in Bloomfield, New Jersey, on March 2, 1842. His father, Moses, an elder in the Presbyterian Church, was a founder of Dodd, Mead and Company. Rachel Hoe, his mother, was the sister of the inventor of the Hoe printing press. Dodd, twenty years old when he enlisted in Company F, held the rank of sergeant until June 7, 1863, when he was promoted to first sergeant. Following his discharge, Dodd entered Yale College, obtained his degree in 1867, then studied theology at Union Theological Seminary and Princeton, where he was graduated in 1870. On May 11, 1870, Dodd was ordained by the Presbytery of Newark.

Dodd left New Jersey in mid-1870 for what was then the frontier, serving for two years at the Presbyterian Church in Garnett, Kansas. After marrying, he went West again to the Presbyterian Church at Winnebago City, Minnesota, remaining there nine years. The Reverend Dodd returned east in 1882 to become minister of the Riverdale, New York, Presbyterian Church, a post he held until 1916, when he was named pastor emeritus. While at Riverdale, Dodd was instrumental in establishing the Edgehill Community Church in nearby Spuyten Duyvil. Although the Reverend Dodd preached at both Riverdale and Edgehill for many years, neither was a large congregation and his was a quiet, contemplative life. Dodd was "a man of scholarly tastes and wide reading" whose published works include two volumes of his sermons, *The Upper Room* and *The Brother and the Brotherhood*. An authority on hymnology, he was the editor of the *Riverdale Hymn Book*. Between 1896 and 1898 the Reverend Dodd penned his reminiscences for *McClure's Magazine;* in 1898 they were published by Dodd, Mead and Company as *The Song of the Rappahannock: Sketches of the Civil War*. The volume was reprinted in 1918. Dodd passed away at the age of eighty on August 3, 1922, at Matunuck, near Wakefield, Rhode Island. New York Presbytery, Supplemental Reports and Biographical Sketches, 1920–1922, Presbyterian Historical Society; New York *Times*, August 4, 1922.

8. Bell Irvin Wiley, *The Life of Billy Yank* (Indianapolis, Ind., 1952), pp. 263–64.
9. *Advertiser*, October 24, 1862 The most prolific of the regimental scriveners was the chaplain, the Reverend David T. Morrill, who wrote nearly forty letters for the *Daily Advertiser*. Morrill's growing concern over the seeming futility of the war and the scandalously inept leadership of the

Army of the Potomac generated considerable anger among Newark Republicans, so much in fact that they complained privately to the administration in Washington. By Special Order no. 268, dated June 17, 1863, the War Department dismissed Morrill "from the service of the United States, for writing for publication, a highly unbecoming and disloyal letter, or series of letters." Whether by accident or design, the War Department's order reached Newark only after Morrill had been honorably discharged with his regiment on June 27. Years later, when the Reverend Morrill applied for a pension, the War Department concluded that Special Order no. 268 was "inoperative and void for the reason that he failed to receive notice of such dismissal prior to his said muster out and honorable discharge." Morrill qualified for the pension.

The regimental chaplain was born in Danville, Vermont, on October 24, 1825, spent his childhood on the family farm, taught school for several years, then attended Union College, where he received his B.A. in 1849. An 1853 graduate of Rochester Seminary, Morrill was ordained a Baptist minister at Rahway, New Jersey, on March 5, 1854. Three weeks later he accepted a call as pastor of the Fifth Baptist Church, a fledgling mission in what is now Newark's East Ward. After a year of struggle the church was formally incorporated in March 1855 and within five months a building fund was established. In 1858 a "very commodious edifice" in the Greek Revival style was completed at a cost of over $10,000.

The Reverend Morrill resigned his pastorate in October 1862, rejoining Fifth Baptist when the Twenty-sixth New Jersey returned to Newark. He resigned again in April 1869 after a ministry of fifteen years to accept a new post in Missouri.

There is evidence that the Reverend Morrill was active in recruiting the Twenty-sixth Regiment: members of his congregation enlisted and several war meetings were held at the church. On October 1, 1862, the field officers and company commanders unanimously elected Morrill regimental chaplain. Certifying to the War Department their colleague's fitness for the post, five of Morrill's brother Baptist pastors affirmed that his "appointment to the office of Chaplain in the Army was unsought by him in any sense whatever, but greatly desired by his numerous friends." Morrill enlisted at Trenton, New Jersey, on October 17, 1862.

Morrill's duties as chaplain were many and varied, as his correspondence records. One important task required his return to Newark. On April 15, 1863, Colonel Morrison requested that the assistant adjutant of the Sixth Corps order Morrill "to report at Newark, N.J., immediately as he has in his possession some $30,000 deposited by the men of the Regiment, it having just been paid." A voluntary system of allotments enabled many soldiers to send home a portion of their monthly pay, and the chaplain was the trusted courier.

After leaving Fifth Baptist, the Reverend Morrill served as pastor of Fourth Street Baptist Church (1869–74) and Park Avenue Church (1874–76), both in Saint Louis, Missouri. The next ten years were spent in Illinois at the Upper Alton (1876–83) and Virden (1883–86) Baptist Churches. Morrill returned to Missouri in 1886, serving at the LaGrange Baptist Church until 1892. In 1876 Morrill was district secretary of the American Baptist Publication Society and in 1892 received an honorary D.D. from Shurtleff College.

Morrill suffered a disabling stroke in 1889 that left him paralyzed on the right side. Retiring from the active ministry, he lived in Fargo, Missouri, and Belvidere, Illinois, where he passed away on October 9, 1893, at the age of seventy-two. One of Morrill's longtime friends eulogized him as "one of the best known men of the church" who had lived "a life of remarkable usefulness." Added the friend: "It is told of him that he never missed an appointment and was never late but once when his watch happened to be five minutes slow." Thomas S. Griffiths, *A History of the Baptists in New Jersey* (Highstown, 1904), pp. 310–11; *Illinois Baptist Annual*, 1898, pp. 25–26; Military and Pension Records, National Archives; miscellaneous information furnished by the American Baptist Historical Society, Rochester New York.

10. *Advertiser*, October 24, 1862.
11. *Mercury*, October 27, 1862.
12. Foote, 1: 751–53.
13. Basler, 5: 474.

14. *Mercury*, October 25, 1862. In 1862 the *Mercury* reported that it had lost nearly half of its staff to the military. Among them was Charles S. Woodruff, eighteen, single and a printer by trade when he joined the Twenty-sixth. A private in Company B, Woodruff was severely wounded at Chancellorsville, applying for an invalid pension after he returned home in October 1863. In a statement dated May 13, 1864, Woodruff explained that he "was wounded in both hips by [a] minnie ball at [the] battle of Chancellorsville, May 4th [18]63; was a prisoner six days; was then paroled; was sent to Potomac Creek Hosp[ital] on the 9th of May; was removed thence to Finley Hosp[ital], Washington, about the 20th [of] June; about the 26th of June was removed to Chestnut Hill Hosp[ital], Phila[delphia]; received an order for discharge . . . on the 14th of October and on the same day was removed to Trenton, N.J., where he received his discharge papers."

Woodruff was treated for his injuries by Jonathan R. Sweet, a Newark physician. When Woodruff first came to his office in late October or early November 1863, wrote Dr. Sweet, he "was greatly debilitated and unable to work by reason of a gunshot wound in the left thygh which had been superficially healed. When he came to me his knee was stiffened and inflamed. I treated him for such injury until the last of May 1864 when he was able to go about with the help of his cane."

Born in Newark on March 20, 1844, Woodruff moved to New Brunswick, New Jersey, in 1867, then to Minneapolis, Minnesota. In 1880 he returned to New Brunswick, went to Seneca Falls, New York, in 1881, then moved again to Minneapolis in 1883. Woodruff was in the real estate business in his later years. He was commander of Bryant Post, G.A.R., in Minneapolis when he died on May 16, 1921, at age seventy-seven. Minneapolis *Journal*, May 18, 1921; Pension Records, National Archives.

15. *Advertiser*, November 3, 1863

16. Ibid.

17. Foster, p. 540. The officer exaggerates somewhat the inexperience of his colleagues. Major William W. Morris and Captain John Hunkele of Company E had previously served in the State Militia. Other officers had enlisted in the First New Jersey Regiment, a three-month unit mustered into federal service on April 30, 1861. Among these were Captains Mark Sears of Company B, Stephen C. Fordham of Company A and John McIntee of Company I, all of whom served as ensigns; Captain Samuel H. Pemberton of Company C, who was a sergeant; Captain John H. Higginson of Company I, a captain; and Captain Henry M. Bush of Company D, a private. Colonel Morrison had also seen previous service as colonel of the Seventh New York Cavalry.

CHAPTER 7

1. Dodd, pp. 58–59.

2. Catton, *Terrible Swift Sword*, pp. 477–78.

3. Foote, 1: 766.

4. *Mercury*, November 7, 1862.

5. Ibid., November 17, 1862. Sergeant-Major Amos Jay Cummings, who was to enjoy perhaps the most distinguished postwar career of any of his fellow volunteers, was also the only member of his regiment to be decorated for bravery in battle. On March 28, 1894, Cummings received the Medal of Honor for rendering "great assistance in the heat of action in rescuing a part of the field batteries from an extremely dangerous and exposed position" at the Battle of Salem Heights, May 4, 1863.

Cummmings was born in Conkling, New York, on May 15, 1838, the son and grandson of clergymen of the Christian sect. His father, Moses Cummings, was a traveling evangelist, jeweler, dentist, and printer who settled in Irvington in 1855, Two years later Moses Cummings became editor of the *Christian Palladium*, a bimonthly newspaper issued by the Christian Publishing Association. In the columns of the *Palladium* and from the pulpit of Irvington's First Christian Church, where he often preached, Cummings, a fervent abolitionist, thundered denunciation of human slavery in all its forms. The paper was published in a small shop on the first floor of the Cummings home.

Although Moses Cummings had given strict orders that his son was not to enter the *Palladium* composing room, young Amos bribed the printer, Sylvester Bailey, "with tears and tobacco" to let him in through the window. For nearly a year Amos set type for the *Palladium*. Once he learned the trade, he went to New York City, where he earned a meager living as a journeyman printer. By the time he was eighteen he was "restless of spirit," so he said in later years, and left New York to work his way across much of the eastern and southern United States as a tramp printer.

In the fall of 1857 he happened to be in Mobile, Alabama, where William Walker, the famous filibuster, was recruiting men for yet another assault on Central America. Joining the forces of "the gray-eyed man of destiny" Cummings and a hundred others sailed south for glory only to surrender to the United States Navy the following spring.

At the outbreak of the Civil War Cummings was setting type for the New York *Tribune* with Sylvester Bailey. A year later Bailey, Amos Cummings and his younger brother, Charles, enlisted as privates in the Twenty-sixth Regiment. When his tour was finished Amos returned to the *Tribune* in time for another kind of warfare. On July 13, 1863, a howling mob of antidraft rioters stormed the *Tribune* building, intent on burning it to the ground. While soldiers and policemen fired on the rioters from City Hall Park, Cummings and three others barricaded the composing-room doors, saving it from the mob. The *Tribune*'s great editor, Horace Greeley, first took notice of Cummings one morning in 1865 when he returned to the composing room and without a line of copy put the story of a fire in type for the early edition. Later that year Cummings became editor of the *Weekly Tribune*, and then in rapid succession night editor, city and political editor of the daily edition. Cummings resigned from the *Tribune* in the fall of 1868.

In December of the same year Cummings became night editor and later managing editor of the New York *Sun*, infusing the paper with new vigor. Twenty-five years after his death Cummings was remembered in New York newspaper circles as the best all-around newsman of his day. According to Frank O'Brien in his history of the *Sun*,

He had the executive ability and the knowledge of men that make a good managing editor. He knew that the newspapers had yet to touch public sympathy and imagination in the news columns as well as in editorial articles; and he knew how to do it, how to teach men to do it, how to cram the moving picture of a living city into the four pages of the *Sun*. He advised desk men, complimented or corrected reporters, edited local articles, and when a story appealed to him strongly, he went out and got it and wrote it himself. Among the oldest generation of newspapermen Cummings is revered as a great reporter. He was the first real human-interest reporter. He knew the news value of the steer loose in the streets, the lost child in the police station, the Italian murder that was really a case of vendetta. The *Sun* men of the time followed his lead . . . but he was the pioneer of modern journalism.

Cummings was the first to assign men regularly to the police stations, filling column after column with their lively stories. Readers were so delighted that in two years the paper's daily circulation shot up to 100,000. There were so many mysterious murders in the *Sun* that competitors were said to harbor the thought that Cummings went out at night and committed them for art's sake. When men and women stopped murdering each other, Cummings turned to politics. It was during Cummings's years as editor that the *Sun* established its reputation as the finest source of political news in New York City.

The pace was so terrific that after five years Cummings was exhausted, resigning as managing editor in 1872. He toured the South and West for the next three years, writing a series of travel articles for the *Sun* under the pen name "Ziska." When he returned to New York in 1876 he became managing editor of the *Evening Express*. But after building its circulation, he suddenly resigned when the publisher attacked Samuel Tilden's candidacy for the Democratic presidential nomination.

Cummings rejoined the *Sun* as editor of the weekly edition in 1876. Given free reign by the owners, he improved the paper in every department, from time to time contributing feature articles on political events and reporting firsthand a number of notorious murder trials. President of the New York Press Club for two years, Cummings was a polished writer and storyteller who was in constant demand as an after-dinner speaker. In 1880 Cummings published his only book, *Sayings of Uncle Rufus*, a small volume of humorous anecdotes.

Cummings turned to politics in 1886. Elected as a Democrat to the House of Representatives from the Wall Street district, he still maintained his connection with the *Sun* and in 1887 became editor of the *Evening Sun*, a new venture. Within two years its circulation was above 100,000. Cummings declined renomination in 1888, claiming he was too poor to be a congressman, but in September of 1889, following the death of S. S. Cox, he was elected to the vacancy. Cummings was reelected in 1890 and 1892 but defeated by a Republican two years later. Appointed commissioner of New York City subways, he was displaced by a change of administration and in 1895 was again elected to Congress, where he served until his death. In 1892 and 1896 he was a delegate to the Democratic national convention. Cummings spent fifteen years in the House of Representatives, earning a record as a great labor advocate and friend of postal workers, printers, navy-yard employees, and musicians. He was a staunch ally of the United States Life-Saving Service and a champion of a strong American navy. Extremely popular with his colleagues, Republican and Democratic alike, Cummings remained at heart a newspaperman. His "Washington Letters," written for a newspaper syndicate, were widely published.

Cummings died at age sixty-four on May 2, 1902. On May 6 his body was laid to rest in the family plot in Irvington's Clinton Cemetery. Forty-two carriages conveyed the mourners, including senators, congressmen, labor officials, and newspapermen, from New York City to the grave site. Siegel, *Out of Our Past*, pp. 124–28; U.S. Government Printing Office, The Medal of Honor of the United States Army, Washington, D.C., 1948; Newark *Evening News*, May 7, 1902.

. 6. *Advertiser*, November 7, 1862.

7. Ibid.

8. *Mercury*, November 17, 1862.

9. Ibid.

10. *Advertiser*, November 13, 1862.

11. Ibid.

12. Ibid.

13. *Mercury*, November 17, 1862.

14. Ibid.

15. *Advertiser*, November 17, 1862.

16. *Mercury*, November 17, 1862.

17. Dodd, pp. 69–72.

18. *Mercury*, November 17, 1862.

19. *Advertiser*, November 17, 1862.

20. Ibid., November 24, 1862.

21. Dodd, p. 67.

22. *Mercury*, November 28, 1862.

23. Major William W. Morris was the unofficial postwar commander of the Twenty-sixth New Jersey Volunteers. With both Colonel Morrison and Lieutenant Colonel Martindale living out of state, Major Morris represented the unit for nearly four decades at local parades, reunions, and funerals. Fittingly, he was president of the Twenty-sixth Regiment Veterans Association at his death in 1905.

Descended from soldiers of the Revolution and the War of 1812, Morris, who was born in New York City on February 18, 1830, came to Newark with his parents when he was two. Educated in the city's public and private schools, he was apprenticed to the coach, harness, and saddlery business. At the outbreak of war he was superintendent of a large saddlery-hardware factory in Newark.

As a young man, Morris had joined the Lafayette Guards, a unit of the state militia commanded by General Theodore Runyon, rising in rank from private to ensign. When the guards were disbanded, he joined the city battalion. In 1861 Morris was in the process of raising a company of volunteers when "a severe family affliction" forced him to remain at home. Lincoln's July 1862 call for volunteers prompted him to raise another company, which enlisted in the Twenty-sixth as

Company A. Morris served as captain of Company A until his promotion to major on November 19, 1862.

Before Lieutenant Colonel Martindale was assigned to the regiment in early January 1863, Morris was frequently in virtual command of the Twenty-sixth. Morrison's fondness for the bottle made Morris an indispensable man; the colonel's December illness left the major as senior officer of the regiment during the Battle of Fredericksburg. All in all, Morris was an exceptional soldier. Colonel Grant singled him out for praise in his official report of the assault on the Fredericksburg Heights. Lieutenant Colonel Martindale's account of the reconnaissance at Franklin's Crossing commends the "fidelity and good conduct of Major Morris in every requirement of duty in the crossing and in forming upon the opposite bank and particularly upon the exhausting and trying duty of the skirmish line." On another occasion Martindale wrote "in terms of high commendation" of the major's "unflinching and faithful performance of duty."

In common with many Civil War veterans, Morris suffered the ill-effects of exposure and lack of proper shelter long after he returned to civilian life. While on a three-day picket near White Oak Church in late December 1862, the major was thoroughly drenched. He developed bronchitis, sciatic rheumatism, and pneumonia, spending four days in Potomac Creek Hospital on orders of the regimental surgeon. After the war Morris qualified for a pension. According to one supporting affidavit, his sciatica was so severe that "a great deal of the time he was lame and would limp about, and at other times, he would have to dispense with his buggy, being unable to get into it." A friend declared that "shortly after his return from the army [Morris] was dangerously ill from an attack of sciatica. The attack was so severe that his life was despaired of, he was confined to his home for some four weeks. The pains were of the most excruciating character, so violent were they that the slightest movement would almost take away his breath."

A lifelong Republican, Morris was a delegate to the national convention that nominated Lincoln; when the president-elect visited Newark in February 1861, he was one of his military escorts. During the 1860s and 1870s, he was an active member of the Republican "Wide-Awakes." After the war the major was elected to the Newark Board of Excise and was twice appointed street commissioner. Somewhat later he joined the city clerk's office as document clerk, a position he held until his death. During the railroad riots of 1877, Newark Mayor Henry J. Yates commissioned Morris to organize a contingent of veterans "to secure arms, ammunition and cannon, and protect the public buildings from the mob."

Morris was a member of the New Jersey Historical Society, the Sons of the Revolution, the Odd Fellows, and was past commander of Garfield Post, GAR. Morris was struck by a delivery wagon on the corner of Broad and Market Streets in Newark, suffered a fractured rib, and died at home on August 8, 1905. Samuel Toombs, *New Jersey Troops in the Gettysburg Campaign* (Orange, N.J., 1888), pp. 398–99; Newark *Evening News*, August 8, 1905; Pension Records, National Archives.

24. *Advertiser*, November 24, 1862.
25. Basler, 5: 497–98.
26. *Advertiser*, November 28, 1862.
27. *Mercury*, November 28, 1862.
28. *Advertiser*, November 28, 1862.
29. Ibid.
30. *Advertiser*, December 5, 1862.
31. Ibid., December 8, 1862.
32. Stevens, p. 164.
33. *Advertiser*, December 8, 1862.

CHAPTER 8

1. Bruce Catton, *Never Call Retreat* (New York, 1965), pp. 14–16.
2. *Mercury*, December 15, 1862.
3. *Advertiser*, December 12, 1862.

4. *Mercury*, December 15, 1862.

5. Ibid. General Vinton, actually twenty-seven, was severely wounded at Fredericksburg and resigned from the army in May 1863.

6. Ibid. The men called their old muskets "stuffed clubs," and they were about as effective. In all probability, the regiment carried the Model 1842 percussion musket, caliber .69, which was accurate at about 100 yards. It could be fired at a rate slightly better than two shots per minute.

7. *Advertiser*, December 18, 1862.

8. Joseph Cullen, "The Battle of Fredericksburg," *American History Illustrated* 13, no. 3 (June 1978): 40.

9. Foote, 2: 24–29.

10. *Mercury*, December 18, 1862.

11. Foster, p. 541.

12. *Mercury*, December 22, 1862.

13. Ibid.

14. Foote, 2: 33–39.

15. *Mercury*, December 22, 1862.

16. Foster, p. 542.

17. *Mercury*, December 27, 1862.

18. *Advertiser*, December 30, 1862.

19. *Mercury*, December 27, 1862.

20. *Advertiser*, December 22, 1862.

21. Foote, 2: 42.

22. *Advertiser*, December 15, 1862.

23. Ibid, December 17, 1862.

24. *Mercury*, December 17, 1862.

25. *Journal*, December 16, 1862.

26. Ibid., December 17, 1862.

27. Foote, 2: 108–9.

28. Joseph Cullen, "The Battle of Fredericksburg," *American History Illustrated* 13, no. 3 (June 1978): 47.

29. *Mercury*, December 27, 1862.

30. Stevens, p. 169.

31. Quoted in *Sentinel*, December 30, 1862.

32. *Advertiser*, December 30, 1862.

33. Quoted in *Sentinel*, December 30, 1862.

34. *Advertiser*, December 30, 1862.

35. Ibid.

36. *Mercury*, December 27, 1862.

37. Ibid.

38. *Advertiser*, January 6, 1863.

CHAPTER 9

1. Foote, 2: 113.

2. *Advertiser*, January 13, 1863.

3. Ibid.

4. *Mercury*, January 26, 1863.

5. *Advertiser*, January 21, 1863.

6. Foote, 2: 129.

7. Foster, p. 543.

8. *Mercury*, January 26, 1863.

9. Foster, pp. 543–44.

10. *Mercury*, January 26, 1863.

11. Foster, p. 544.

12. *Mercury*, January 26, 1863.

13. Foster, p. 544.

14. *Advertiser*, January 28, 1863.

15. *Mercury*, January 26, 1863.

16. Foote, 2: 130.

17. David S. Sparks, ed., *Inside Lincoln's Army: The Diary of Marsena Rudolph Patrick, Provost Marshal General, Army of the Potomac* (New York, 1964), p. 206.

18. *Mercury*, January 31, 1863.

CHAPTER 10

1. Bruce Catton, *Glory Road* (New York, 1952), pp. 140–45.

2. Ibid., p. 145.

3. *Advertiser*, February 16,1863.

4. Foote, 2: 262.

5. *Advertiser*, February 24, 1863.

6. *Journal*, February 17, 1863.

7. *Mercury*, March 3, 1863.

8. Ibid., March 7, 1863.

9. Stevens, p. 183.

10. *Advertiser*, February 24, 1863.

11. *Mercury*, March 3, 1863.

12. *Mercury*, February 12, 1863.

13. *Advertiser*, February 16, 1863.

14. *Journal*, February 17, 1863.

15. *Advertiser*, February 16, 1863.

16. *Journal*, February 17, 1863.

17. Ibid.

18. *Mercury*, March 3, 1863.

19. Ibid., February 28, 1863.

20. *Mercury*, March 12, 1863.

21. *Advertiser*, February 24, 1863.

22. Ibid., March 7, 1863.

23. Stevens, p. 183; Bell Irvin Wiley, *The Life of Billy Yank* (Indianapolis, Ind., 1952), p. 170.

24. *Mercury*, March 7, 1863.

25. Ibid.

CHAPTER 11

1. *Mercury*, March 12, 1863.

2. *Advertiser*, March 7, 1863.

3. Ibid., April 6, 1863.

4. Ibid., March 23, 1863.

5. *Mercury*, March 12, 1863. Liberty No. 1 was a Newark fire company, many of whose members had enlisted in the Twenty-sixth.

6. *Advertiser*, March 16, 1863.

7. Ibid., March 23, 1863.

8. Ibid., April 6, 1863. "Yellow covered leaves" alludes to the cheap, paper-bound novels of the period.

9. Ibid., March 7, 1863. In February Congress passed the Conscription Act, directing that the country be divided into districts with provost marshals and enrollment boards authorized to draft all able-bodied men between the ages of twenty and forty-five.

10. *Mercury*, March 7, 1863.

11. Foote, 2: 262.

CHAPTER 12

1. Carl Sandburg, *Abraham Lincoln: The Prairie Years and the War Years* (New York, 1954), pp. 357–59 (hereinafter cited as Sandburg).

2. *Mercury*, April 7, 1863.

3. Sandburg, pp. 357–59.

4. *Mercury*, April 13, 1863.

5. *Advertiser*, April 14, 1863.

6. Ibid.

7. *Journal*, May 1, 1863. The *Journal's* account is contrary to the weight of historical evidence. According to most observers, Lincoln was well received and his visit a success. Sandburg, p. 360; Leech, p. 230.

8. *Mercury*, February 14, 1863.

9. *Journal*, January 2, 1863.

10. Ibid., March 2, 1863.

11. *Journal*, February 16, 1863.

12. *Mercury*, February 16, 1863.

13. Ibid., February 17, 1863.

14. Earl Schenck Miers, *New Jersey and the Civil War* (Princeton, N. J., 1964), pp. 103–5.

15. Quoted in the *Sentinel*, March 24, 1863.

16. *Mercury*, March 21, 1863.

17. Cunningham, *New Jersey*, p. 183.

18. *Advertiser*, April 15, 1863.

19. *Journal*, April 17, 1863.

20. Ibid., April 25, 1863.

21. *Mercury*, April 27, 1863.

22. Ibid., February 17, 1863.

23. The political complexion of the unit is difficult but not impossible to gauge. New Jersey politicians of the period believed, intuitively at least, that the soldier vote was Union Republican. Charles Perrin Smith, a mainstay of the Union Republican party, declared that Joel Parker had been elected mainly through the absence of a large proportion of the Union party in the ranks of the army. In 1863 and again in 1864 the Copperheads prevented passage of a bill that would have permitted soldiers to vote in the field, clearly because they felt the soldier vote would have damaged their cause. Marcus Ward's election as governor in November 1865 by a margin of 2789 votes was, wrote Professor Knapp, "probably due, largely, to the returned soldiers."

The voting habits of the Twenty-sixth would have disappointed the Union Republican leaders of the state. Most probably, its political views reflected the Democratic voting pattern of wartime Essex County. In the fall 1862 elections, for example, the Democratic candidates for governor, Congress, and the State Assembly received an average of 6,301 votes in Newark and 2,087 in the balance of the county, while the Union Republican nominees tallied 4,754 and 2,133, respectively. The Democratic city margin of nearly 1,600 votes overwhelmed the narrow Republican victory in the suburbs and Orange. In the municipal elections of April 1863, Democrats prevailed in Caldwell, Clinton, and South Orange, Unionists in Belleville and Millburn. Bloomfield elected two Republicans and two Democrats. The regiment's response to the Peace Resolutions is revealing. Chaplain Morrill's assertion that the Unionist resolution was adopted with but five dissenting votes may be factually correct, but that vote could hardly have been a true reflection of regimental sentiment. The official resolution, it will be remembered, was adopted by voice vote at dress parade in the presence of the very officers who framed it. Sergeant Major Cummings's claim that 458 noncommissioned officers and men signed the Democratic resolution is more plausible. Interestingly, the 57 percent of the regiment Cummings says signed the Democratic resolution closely matches the 55 percent of Essex County's vote won by the Democrats in the 1862 elections. Knapp, p. 153; postelection issues of the *Advertiser* and *Journal.*

24. *Mercury*, April 6, 1863.

25. *Advertiser*, April 28, 1863.

26. Ibid., April 15, 1863.

27. Ibid., April 20, 1863.

CHAPTER 13

1. Foote, 2: 271.

2. *Advertiser*, May 4, 1863.

3. *Journal*, May 13, 1863.

4. *Advertiser*, May 4, 1863.

5. *Journal*, May 13, 1863.

6. *Advertiser*, May 6, 1863.

7. *Journal*, May 13, 1863.

8. Ibid.

9. Jubal A. Early, *War Memoirs* (Bloomington, Ind., 1960), p. 169.

10. *Journal*, May 13, 1863.

11. Robert Underwood Johnson and Clarence Clough Buel, eds., *Battles and Leaders of the Civil War* (New York, 1888), 3: 176 (hereinafter cited as *Battles and Leaders*).

12. Stevens, p. 448; p. 194.

13. *Journal*, May 14, 1863.

14. Ibid.

15. Stevens, pp. 448–49.

16. Foster, p. 546.

17. Dodd, pp. 96–97.

18. Foster, p. 545.

19. *The War of the Rebellion: A Compilation of the Official Records of the Union and Confederate Armies*, Series 1, vol. 25, Part 1, Washington, D.C., 1889, pp. 602–3. (hereinafter cited as *O.R.*).

In the opening months of the Civil War the Union army was officered by men chosen largely "on the good old rule of political patronage—he's a good fellow and he needs the job, and he's got backing!" As the war dragged on, many an incompetent officer retired or was transferred to a backwater command out of harm's way. While too many "good fellows" remained in uniform, the North was fortunate that gradually an officer corps emerged whose overall efficiency and resolute gallantry would ultimately prove the salvation of the country. Lieutenant Colonel Edward Martindale was typical of the breed. From September 1861 to August 1865, as captain, lieutenant colonel, and colonel, he defended the Union cause with great courage and high ability. A quarter of a century after the war his biographer would write of the "[f]our years of his life he gave to the service of his country" He was, he added, "a brave and faithful soldier."

Martindale was born at Sandy Hill, Washington County, New York, on February 4, 1817. His father, Henry C. Martindale, an attorney who served five terms in Congress during the administrations of Monroe, Adams, and Jackson, was an influential member of New York's Whig Party for many years. Congressman Martindale's oldest son, John H., attended the United States Military Academy at West Point, graduating in 1835 third in a class that included George G. Meade.

Resigning from the army within a year, John Martindale turned to law, serving as district attorney of Genesee County for nine years. His younger brother, Edward, graduated from Union College in Schenectady, studied law with his father, and gained admission to the bar in 1839. The following year he moved to New York City, where he practiced successfully until 1883.

When war came, John H. Martindale gave up a flourishing law practice in Rochester, New York, for a commission as brigadier general of volunteers. His son, Lieutenant Edward H. Martindale, and the general's two brothers, Brevet Major F. E. Martindale and Colonel Edward Martindale, also entered service at the same time. Commissioned captain and commissary of subsistence, U.S. Volunteers, on September 19, 1861, Colonel Martindale was attached to the staff of Brigadier General William F. Smith, then in command of a division of the Army of the Potomac and later commander of the Second Division, Fourth Corps, and Second Division, Sixth Corps. As a member of "Baldy" Smith's staff, Martindale saw action at Yorktown, Lee's Hill, Williamsburg, Fair Oaks, Savage's Station, Glendale, Malvern Hill, and Antietam. "He participated in all the principal engagements of the Peninsular campaign in 1862," wrote one historian, "and was always found with his command at the front, encouraging his men by his daring spirit and bravery."

Tiring of staff duty, Martindale enlisted the aid of his brother, General Martindale, then recuperating in Washington from a severe bout of typhoid fever, to secure a command of his own. In late December of 1862 Martindale obtained a leave of absence from Smith's staff and on January 6, 1863, was commissioned lieutenant colonel of the Twenty-sixth New Jersey Volunteers.

When the Twenty-sixth was mustered out, Martindale reverted to his former rank of captain. Again, he sought an active command. Now military governor of the District of Columbia, General Martindale no doubt played a role in securing his brother's appointment on January 18, 1864, as colonel, United States Colored Infantry. By the end of the war some 300,000 blacks in 166 regiments had enrolled in the Union army. For the most part the black regiments, about sixty of which saw duty in the field, were led by white officers. Ordered to report to Major General Nathaniel P. Banks, then commanding the Department of the Gulf, Martindale was commissioned colonel of the Elevenh Regiment (later known as the Eighty-third), Corps d'Afrique. After several weeks in New Orleans, Martindale's regiment was ordered to Baton Rouge, Louisiana, where he was placed in charge of the commissary department. Later the regiment was posted to Port Hudson and Morganzia.

Wearying of garrison duty and hungry for action, Martindale sought a return to the Eastern theater of operations. Again his brother, now leading the Eighteenth Corps before Petersburg, proved invaluable. By special order dated July 25, 1864, Martindale was detached from the Department of the Gulf and directed to report "without delay" to Major General Benjamin F. Butler, commander of the Army of the James, at Fortress Monroe, Virginia. The department of the Gulf was, however, slow to release him. As late as August 15, 1864, he was in New Orleans for an interview with a three-man board of examiners appointed to assess the qualifications of all field officers assigned to the Colored Infantry.

Upon reaching Virginia in late October 1864, Martindale was placed in command of the 118th Regiment, U.S. Colored Infantry, a newly organized unit that was then ordered into the breastworks in front of Bermuda Hundred, south of Richmond. The following month Martindale was given command of the Provisional Brigade, Third Division, Twenty-fifth Corps. The brigade, consisting of the Ninth and Forty-first U.S. Colored Infantry and the Twenty-ninth Connecticut Colored Infantry Regiments, was immediately sent to the trenches before Petersburg.

Martindale remained in Virginia on detached duty despite his assignment on September 28, 1864, to command of the Eighty-first U.S. Colored Infantry at Brazos Santiago, Texas. The Eighty-first was fated never to see its absent colonel. On December 29, 1864, Brigadier General George L. Andrews of the U.S. Colored Infantry "earnestly recommended that Col. Martindale be relieved from his present command and ordered to rejoin his regiment," a request that was refused on the ground that Martindale's assignment to the Army of the James was sanctioned by the War Department. Two months later Martindale was again pressured to return to his command, this time by Brigadier General William Birney, commander of the Second Division, Twenty-fifth Corps, who requested that Martindale be relieved and sent to his regiment at Brazos Santiago. Said Birney: "While I am ready to admit the merits of Colonel Martindale, there are colonels in this division who rank him and who, by merit, are as well entitled to command brigades." To avoid imminent banishment to Texas, Martindale petitioned the War Department for a transfer "to a new Regiment to be raised and assigned to active duty in the Field in the 25th Army Corps, and that I may be authorised to raise such Regiment at and near Norfolk, Va." Brigadier General Godfrey Weitzel, then chief engineer of the Army of the James, endorsed Martindale's request: "Col. Martindale's regiment is at Brazos Santiaga. He was ordered up here, so that he could get into active service. He has commanded a brigade in this corps efficiently and I can recommend him and do so cheerfully for authority to raise even a full brigade." While Martindale's request to raise a regiment was disapproved, he was relieved from duty with the Twenty-fifth Corps on March 24, 1865, and ordered to Norfolk, where he served for a time as judge advocate of the Department of Eastern Virginia.

At war's end Colonel Martindale was reassigned to the Twenty-fifth Corps, an all Black unit, for duty as chief drill instructor of the Second Division, then at Petersburg. Read his orders: "He will superintend all drills and render weekly reports of the progress made in each Brigade. Colonel Martindale is also especially charged with the general supervision of the educational interests of this command." Martindale remained behind after the corps was sent to Texas to serve as military governor of Petersburg during May and June 1865, under Major General George L. Hartsuff. On June 27, 1865, Martindale was relieved of further duty with the Department of Virginia and ordered to report to the Eight-first Regiment, U.S. Colored Infantry, then still in Texas. Rather than comply with the order, Martindale obtained a thirty-day leave of absence, then tendered his resignation on August 1, 1865. "I entered [service] with the single purpose of aiding in putting down the rebellion," he wrote, "and that this purpose accomplished, it is of the utmost importance to my private interests that I may be permitted to retire from the Service."

Martindale returned to New York City to resume his long-neglected law practice. In 1883, two years after his brother, General Martindale, died, he moved to Des Moines, Iowa, where he conducted a specialized practice for many years. A Republican and an Episcopalian, he served as chancellor of the diocese of Iowa, was a member of Crocker Post no. 12, GAR, in Des Moines, and of the Loyal Legion of the Commandery of Iowa. About 1900 Martindale moved to San Diego, California, where he died on July 14, 1904, at the age of eighty-seven. Writing in 1890, an Iowa historian described Martindale as a "gentlemen of liberal culture [who] possesses a large fund of information, acquired by reading and experience. His conversational powers are far in advance of the average, and he is an entertaining and instructive talker. . . . He possesses in a high degree the esteem of all who know him." R. Ernest Dupuy, *The Compact History of the United States Army* (New York, 1961), p. 120; Francis B. Heitman, *Historical Register and Dictionary of the United States Army* (Washington, D.C., 1903), 1: passim; *Annals of Iowa, 1903–1905*, 6: 639; *Portrait and Biographical Album of Polk County, Iowa* (Chicago, 1890), pp. 684–86; Department of Iowa, Grand Army of the Republic, Records, Iowa Historical Library, Des Moines, Iowa; *The Republican Advocate*, Batavia, N.Y., September 24, 1874; *Progressive Batavian*, Batavia, N.Y., September 25, 1874 and December 16, 1881; Military Records, National Archives.

20. Foote, 2: 309
21. *Battles and Leaders*, p. 230.
22. Edward J. Stackpole, *Chancellorsville: Lee's Greatest Battle* (Harrisburg, Pa., 1958), pp. 333–38 (hereinafter cited as Stackpole).
23. *Journal*, May 16, 1863.
24. Stackpole, p. 338; Stevens, pp. 207–8,
25. *Journal*, May 16, 1863.
26. Stevens, pp. 208–9; *O.R.*, p. 604.
27. *Journal*, May 16, 1863.
28. *O.R.*, pp. 605–6.
29. Steve̶ ̶p. 205.
30. Foote, ̶

31. *Journal*, May 1, 1863.

32. *Advertiser*, May 6, 1863.

33. *Mercury*, May 6, 1863.

34. Margaret Leech, *Reveille in Washington, 1860–1865* (New York, 1941), p. 231.

35. Sandburg, pp. 363–64.

36. Foote, 2: 315.

37. *Mercury*, May 8, 1863.

38. *Journal*, May 8, 1863.

39. *Advertiser*, May 7, 1863.

40. Ibid., May 11, 1863.

41. Letter dated May 9, 1863, from General John Martindale, Headquarters, Military District of Washington, to Major General Joseph Hooker, from Military Records of Edward Martindale, National Archives, Washington, D.C.

42. *Advertiser*, May 13, 1863.

43. Ibid., May 19, 1863.

44. *Mercury*, May 22, 1863.

45. *Advertiser*, June 1, 1863.

46. Ibid.

47. *Journal*, May 21, 1863. Lieutenant Terhune, in Bloomfield when he wrote to the *Journal*, was later court-martialed for being absent without leave but was restored to duty before the regiment returned to New Jersey. *Advertiser*, June 20, 1863.

48. *Journal*, June 2, 1863.

49. Ibid., June 3, 1863.

Company E's first lieutenant, Henry C. Terhune, compiled a war record that was either commendable or dishonorable: Lieutenant Colonel Martindale and Chaplain Morrill praised Terhune's courage during the regiment's assault on Mayre's Heights; Sergeant Major Cummings and his brother, Corporal Charles Cummings, labeled Terhune a skulker and a coward who spent his time in the rear guarding knapsacks. Regimental politics explains the antithesis. The sergeant major's unbounded admiration for Morrison, whom Terhune obviously disliked immensely, renders his denunciation of the lieutenant suspect. Government records prove, for example, that Terhune was indeed acting adjutant of the regiment for a time, a fact the sergeant major denies. Old-fashioned jealously may have been at work as well: Terhune spent an inordinate amount of time in Newark, either on sick leave or pass, a privilege no noncommissioned officer or private could hope to enjoy.

Born April 21, 1840, in New York City, Terhune was the son of James J. Terhune, a wealthy shoe manufacturer who served as clerk of Essex County from 1854 to 1859. Young Terhune graduated with honors from the Newark Wesleyan Institute, studied for three years at Bloomfield Institute, worked briefly for his father, then read law for four years in the office of Newark attorney Lewis C. Grover, counsel to two of Newark's largest insurance companies. Terhune served on Militia General Theodore Runyon's staff for a time and when Lincoln issued his call for nine-month volunteers, he began recruiting a company, expecting a captaincy. By early September Terhune had managed to enroll only twenty or so volunteers. With no time left for further effort, he and his men enlisted in Company E.

Despite his youth, Terhune was plagued with illness throughout his military career. After the Mud March, he along with thousands of others was treated in the field for diarrhea and returned to duty. On February 14, 1863, he requested a fifteen-day leave of absence to visit Newark for medical treatment. Dr. Thomas, the regimental surgeon, certified that Terhune was "suffering from general debility, the result of protracted illness, he has been under my charge for Jaundice upon recovery from which he was attacked with Bilious remittent fever, leaving him in such a condition of physical debility as to be unfit for duty." Dr. Thomas added that in his opinion, "a change of climate and mode of life is absolutely necessary to save life." Terhune was in Newark in March 1863 under the care of Dr. Hiram H. Tichenor. "He is suffering from Torper [*sic*] of the Liver," wrote Dr. Tichenor, "and general nervous disturbance consequent upon fever contracted in camp." Terhune's leave of absence was extended for an additional fifteen days upon the certificate of the doctor in charge of the U.S. General Hospital in Newark.

Terhune turned from law to banking after the war, working first as receiving teller at the Marine Bank of New York and then as a cashier for Northrup and Click, a New York banking house. In 1873 Terhune left Newark for Texas to become cashier at the First National Bank of Dennison. After a year on the frontier he returned to Newark, then in 1886 moved to Red Bank, New Jersey, to accept a position as discount clerk at the Second National Bank. Nine years later he left Second National to help organize the Navesink National Bank of Red Bank, where he served as assistant cashier until his retirement. Terhune died in Red Bank after an illness of nearly two years on August 9, 1914. Past commander of Arrowsmith Post No. 61, GAR, Terhune served for a number of years as adjutant general of the state GAR. Red Bank *Register*, August 12, 1914; Military and Pension Records, Natinal Archives.

CHAPTER 14

1. Foote, 2: 430–33; Bruce Catton, *Never Call Retreat* (New York, 1965), pp. 158–59.
2. New York *Times*, June 8, 1863.
3. Dodd, pp. 143–47.
4. *Mercury*, June 13, 1863.
5. Dodd, pp. 150–54, 160–63.
6. Pierson, *History of the Oranges* 2: 336–37.
7. Dodd, pp. 159, 154–55.
8. *Advertiser*, June 9, 1863.
9. Ibid., June 8, 1863.
10. *Mercury*, June 13, 1863.
11. *Journal*, June 10, 1863.
12. Stevens, pp. 219–20.
13. *Advertiser*, June 13, 1863.
14. New York *Times*, June 8, 1863.
15. Foster, p. 550.
16. Ibid., p. 552.
17. Stevens, p. 227. Thirty-nine of the Twenty-sixth were eventually court-martialed for insubordination at Franklin's Crossing and sentenced to the Rip Raps, a military prison near Fortress Monroe, Virginia, for three years or the duration of the war. Through the intercession of Marcus L. Ward, their sentences were modified, they were released from military prison and put to work on the fortifications around Washington, D.C. On October 12, 1863, they were ordered "sent, without delay, to Trenton, New Jersey, there to be mustered out of the service of the United States." Special Orders no. 456, paragraphs 7 and 8, N.J. Archives, Military Records, Dept. of Defense (Civil War), Box 100, Book 509, N.J. State Library; Newark *Daily Advertiser*, June 20, 1863 and July 7, 1863.
18. Basler, 6: 277.
19. Samuel Toombs, *New Jersey Troops in the Gettysburg Campaign* (Orange, N.J., 1888), pp. 85–86.
20. *Advertiser*, *Journal*, and *Mercury*, June 20, 1863.
21. *Advertiser*, June 20, 1863.
22. Ibid.
23. Ibid.
24. *Mercury*, June 20, 1863.
25. *Advertiser*, June 20, 1863.
26. *Mercury*, June 20, 1863.
27. *Advertiser*, June 22, 1863.

28. Orange *Journal*, June 27, 1863.
29. *Advertiser*, June 27, 1863.

CONCLUSION

1. *Advertiser*, April 11, 1865.
2. Ibid., April 15, 1865.
3. F. J. Urquhart, *A History of the City of Newark, New Jersey* (New York, 1913), 2: 726.
4. Ibid., pp. 727–28.
5. *Advertiser*, April 24, 1865.

Bibliography

MANUSCRIPTS

Military and Pension Records, National Archives

Muster Roll Books and Manuscripts, Twenty-sixth Regiment, New Jersey Archives, Archives and History Bureau, New Jersey State Library

Horace N. Congar Papers, New Jersey Historical Society

Thomas T. Kinney Papers, New Jersey Historical Society

NEWSPAPERS

Newark *Daily Advertiser*

Newark *Daily Journal*

Newark *Daily Mercury*

Newark *Evening News*

Newark *Sentinel of Freedom*

New-Jersey *Journal*

New York *Daily News*

New York *Evening Express*

New York *Evening Post*

New York *Times*

Orange *Journal*

Princeton *Standard*

The Somerset *Messenger*

Trenton *Daily State Gazette and Republican*

BOOKS

Andrews, J. Cutler. *The North Reports the Civil War*. University of Pittsburgh, 1955.

Atkinson, Joseph. *The History of Newark, New Jersey*. Newark, N.J., 1878.

Basler, Roy P., ed. *The Collected Works of Abraham Lincoln*. New Brunswick, N.J., 1953.

Boatner, Mark M., III. *The Civil War Dictionary*. New York, 1959.

Catton, Bruce. *Glory Road*. New York, 1952.

———. *Never Call Retreat*. New York, 1965.

———. *Terrible Swift Sword*. New York, 1963.

Cullen, Joseph. "The Battle of Fredericksburg." *American History Illustrated* 13, no. 3 (June 1978).

Cunningham, John T. *Newark*. Newark, N.J., 1966.

———. *New Jersey, America's Main Road*. New York, 1966.

———. *New Jersey: A Mirror on America*. Florham Park, N.J., 1979.

Dodd, Ira Seymour. *The Song of the Rappahannock*. New York, 1898.

Doremus Philip. *Reminiscences of Montclair, with some Account of Montclair's Part in the Civil War*. Montclair, N.J., 1908.

Dyer, Frederick H. *A Compendium of the War of the Rebellion*. Vol. 3. New York, 1959.

Early, Jubal A. *War Memoirs*. Bloomington, Ind., 1960.

Emery, Edwin, and Henry Ladd Smith. *The Press and America*. New York, 1954.

Fleming, Thomas. *New Jersey, A Bicentennial History*. New York, 1977.

Folwell, Charles H., ed. *Pierson's Newark City Directory for 1863–4*. Newark, N.J., 1863.

Foote, Shelby. *The Civil War, A Narrative*. Vols. 1 and 2. New York, 1958, 1963.

Foster, John Y. *New Jersey and the Rebellion*. Newark, N.J., 1868.

Greene, Larry A. "The Emancipation Proclamation in New Jersey and the Paranoid Style." *New Jersey History (Proceedings of the New Jersey Historical Society)* 91, no. 2 (Summer 1973).

Hatch, Carl E. "Editor David Naar of Trenton: Profile of the Anti-Negro Mind" *New Jersey History (Proceedings of the New Jersey Historical Society)* 86, no. 2 (Summer 1968).

———. "Negro Migration and New Jersey—1863." *New Jersey History (Proceedings of the New Jersey Historical Society)* 87, no. 4 (Winter 1969).

Hesseltine, William B. *Lincoln and the War Governors*. New York, 1948.

Hudson, Frederic. *Journalism in the United States from 1690 to 1872*. New York, 1873.

Johnson, Robert Underwood, and Clarence Clough Buel, eds. *Battles and Leaders of the Civil War*. Vol. 3. New York, 1888.

Knapp, Charles M. *New Jersey Politics during the Period of the Civil War and Reconstruction*. Geneva, N.Y., 1924.

Lee, Francis B. *New Jersey as a Colony and as a State*. Vol. 4. New York, 1902.

Leech, Margaret. *Reveille in Washington, 1860–1865*. New York, 1941.

Lockward, Lynn G. *A Puritan Heritage*. Privately printed, 1955.

Mathews, Joseph J. *Reporting the Wars*. Minneapolis, Minn., 1957.

Miers, Earl Schenck. *New Jersey and the Civil War*. Princeton, N.J., 1964.

Mott, Frank L. *American Journalism, A History: 1690–1960*. 3rd ed., New York, 1962.

Myers, William S., ed. *The Story of New Jersey*. New York, 1945.

Nevins, Allan, ed. *A Diary of Battle: The Personal Journals of Colonel Charles S. Wainwright. 1861–1865*. New York, 1962.

New Jersey Civil War Centennial Commission. *Proceedings, Third Annual American History Workshop*. Trenton, N.J., 1964.

———. *Proceedings, Fourth Annual American History Workshop*. Trenton, N.J., 1965.

Pierson, David L. *History of the Oranges to 1921*. Vol. 2. New York, 1922.

———. *Narratives of Newark*. Newark, N.J., 1917.

Platt, Herman K., *Charles Perrin Smith: New Jersey Political Reminiscences, 1828–1882*. New Brunswick, N.J., 1965.

Robertson, James I., Jr., ed. *The Civil War Letters of Robert McAllister*. New Brunswick, N.J., 1965.

Rogers, William Warren. "C. Chauncey Burr and The Old Guard." *Proceedings of the New Jersey Historical Society* 73, no. 2 (July 1955).

Sandburg, Carl. *Abraham Lincoln: The Prairie Years and the War Years*. New York, 1954.

Schonbach, Morris. *Radicals and Visionaries: A History of Dissent in New Jersey*. Princeton, N.J., 1964.

Shaw, William H. *History of Essex and Hudson Counties, New Jersey*. Philadelphia, 1884.

Siegel, Alan A. *Out of Our Past: A History of Irvington, New Jersey*. Irvington, N.J., 1974.

Sinclair, Donald A. *The Civil War and New Jersey*. New Brunswick, N.J., 1968.

Sparks, David S., ed. *Inside Lincoln's Army: The Diary of Marsena Rudolph Patrick, Provost Marshal General, Army of the Potomac*. New York, 1964.

Stackpole, Edward J. *Chancellorsville: Lee's Greatest Battle*. Harrisburg, Pa., 1958.

Stevens, George F. *Three Years in the Sixth Corps*. 2nd ed. New York, 1870.

Stryker, William S. *Record of Officers and Men of New Jersey, 1861–1865*. Trenton, N.J., 1876.

Tandler, Maurice. "H. N. Congar's Letters from Hong Kong." *Proceedings of the New Jersey Historical Society* 84, no. 2 (April 1966).

———. "The Political Front in Civil War New Jersey." *Proceedings of the New Jersey Historical Society* 83, no. 4 (October 1965).

Tebbel, John. *The Compact History of the American Newspaper*. New York, 1963.

The War of the Rebellion: A Compilation of the Official Records of the Union and Confederate Armies. Series I, vol. 21. Washington, D.C., 1888. Series I, vol. 25, Part I. Washington, D.C., 1889.

Toombs, Samuel. *New Jersey Troops in the Gettysburg Campaign*. Orange, N.J., 1888.

Urquhart, F. J. *A History of the City of Newark, New Jersey*. Vol. 2. New York, 1913.

Weisberger, Bernard A. *Reporters for the Union*. Boston, 1953.

Wiley, Bell Irvin. *The Life of Billy Yank*. Indianapolis, Ind., 1952.

Wright, William C., and Paul A. Stellhorn. *Directory of New Jersey Newspapers, 1765–1970*. Trenton, N.J., 1977.

Wright, William C. "New Jersey's Military Role in the Civil War Reconsidered." *New Jersey History (Proceedings of the New Jersey Historical Society)* 92, no. 4 (Winter 1974).

———. *The Secession Movement in the Middle Atlantic States*. Rutherford, N.J., 1973.

Index